INTER LUDE

Happy(ish) Ever After

Ellen Nasser

ISBN (Book): 978-1-988355-80-1
ISBN (Audiobook): 978-1-988355-81-8
ISBN (E-Book): 978-1-988355-82-5

All songs and original lyrics featured in the book are the sole property of Ellen Nasser, who has released music under the names Ellen Kolenick, Elly Thorn, and Ellen Nasser.

Publisher: The Obscura Agency
Cover design by: Rock+Bloom
Editors: Ashley Opheim, Chris Casuccio
Transcript Editor: Lorraine Millaire
Author photo: Eric Hua

INTERLUDE

Ellen Nasser

CHAPTERS

INTER LUDE

FOR JOHN,
BELLA, MILLIE,
SAM, AND WALT

CHAPTER ONE

WHAT...ARE YOU GOING TO WRITE A BOOK NOW?

May 23, 2022
7:30 a.m.

I woke up from a dream, knowing I wanted to write about my first forty years on this beautiful planet.

I started writing and immediately had to get up and go diarrhea. Oh, my constant guiding compass—my beloved nervous bowel—a true sign I'm excited about something, which is a true sign I am lit up, which is a true sign this is happening.

I am writing a book.

Deep Breath.

✦ ✦ ✦

In my dream, I was thinking about what stories I could write about. I've never written a book before. I've written newsletters to my clients, I journal daily gratitudes and prayers, I write songs, I tell our kids the odd story of when I was young, but I've never actually sat down to write a book.

This is absurd. Who do I think I am... wanting to sit down and write a book about what I've learned and experienced in my first forty years?

Deep Breath.

So, I had this dream right before I woke up at 7:30 a.m.

When my alarm goes off, I usually go straight into my twenty-minute meditation, but this holiday Monday was different. I had a quick look at my WhatsApp and my group chat, with Fishy and Eric, called 'My Darlings'. I had a message from my forever friend in Australia, Eric.

A friend of mine had his 40th, and the theme was Liza Minnelli's birthday party. They're born on the same day... so much fun and hilarious.

It's a sign—I love signs.

I meditated and made my way over to our walk-in closet, where I began lighting my three precious everlasting handcrafted candles, a present from my dear friend Diana, and began writing.

I started writing about the laughs we shared the other night with two of my three siblings and my Momma in our music room. My beautiful sister-in-law Kriti was also with us, and we talked about my recent trip to Montréal and Toronto with John, and how I was trying to connect with an old friend and how funny it was.

When we were talking about my life experiences, my sister said my story sounded like it was out of a movie. When I was in Montréal, the friends I met were saying my stories were so funny... they could listen to them all day long. My husband said, "Naw, trust me—you'd get sick of them." Which, of course, made it all the funnier.

I married a man almost twelve years older than me. I got dumped by someone I was dying to marry and fell into a deep, dark hole of despair, thinking that no one would ever want me again.

I'd never heard this quote, but John told me that "One man's junk is another man's treasure."

I grew up in a small town of about 500 people called Saltcoats, Saskatchewan. My parents built a beautiful home on the lake next to my Mom's parents. I was born a creative soul—I think we all are. I can remember my childhood creating was centered around performing, planning, gifting, entertaining, helping, connecting, singing, laughing, and loving. I can remember people telling me that I was a bright light. I remember liking that feeling; in fact, someone, somewhere told me that my name meant light—hold on, now I'm googling that.

Ellen is a girl's name of English origin, meaning "torch, shining light."

Oh Lord, even writing this I'm thinking, ugh what is my family going to think of me writing my life story? I'm so ignorant, I don't even know what the word is for life story. Is it an autobiography? Nope, looks like what I'm writing is called a memoir. Google says: "Have you been reminiscing about your life? We can help you self-publish a book about it." Ewww, is that what I'm seriously doing? Lord love me.

No, no, not at this point. At this point, I'm just writing. It's now 8:43 a.m. and I'm just writing. Someone is up now at our house—one of the kids. I can hear them play the piano. By the sounds of it, it's our 10-year-old, Millie.

Walt is up, now—I hear, "Mom! I have gweat (great) news!"

Our 4-year-old, Walt, walked into our bedroom closet with his freshly washed and dried night-night (blankie). He just got it from the dryer and came into our closet all wrapped up. It's going to be a great day.

Sam entered next. "Hi Mom, can we go to Auntie Amy's house? Did she say yes? Okay, and Walt can't come, okay? Please don't let Walt come to Auntie Amy's. I want to go. Please, no Walt."

I'm in my closet, trying to sneak in some peace and quiet, and it's clearly showtime at the Nassers. Years ago, someone once said to me, "Not my circus." I thought she was talking about me and our household. I was so offended. I thought, how dare she call our household a circus. I took it very personally. I don't know if she was being unkind or if she was just merely stating a fact. I don't know if I was being extra sensitive, postpartum, or if I felt so overwhelmed that everything seemed to hurt or offend me. The truth is, it can be a circus. It's an overwhelming state of questions, schedules, comings/goings, activities, problems, concerns, emails from extra-curricular activities, highs and lows. It's draining. She was right, it's not her circus. It's mine. It's ours.

And, with this circus comes so much more than the chaos, busyness and overwhelm. With our circus comes magic, music, mastery and life. There's so much excitement in our circus.

I like swapping out words and shifting the energy from:
I'm so nervous to—I am so excited.

I'm scared to—I am motivated.

This is draining to—I can do hard things.

I am exhausted to—I need some time to rest and recalibrate.

I'm feeling overwhelmed to—I need to get creative and
delegate.

I am swamped to—I need to hire someone to help us
with the laundry.

Okay, it's 9:01 a.m. Millie has come to take our sweet-
heart Cavapoo, Sofi, for a walk. The boys are downstairs
with Johnny, and our almost teen is sawing logs. I have
a glimpse of what it's going to look like. I am in the flow
of writing, and it feels good. For some reason, I've been
called to write a book—for some reason, I'm listening.

Weird, but not totally weird.

I am a songwriter, storyteller, expresser and connector.
I love sharing light and have always known deep down
that I'd write a book one day. I can remember going to
the movie theatre to watch *Little Women* with the ladies
in our family and was *SO* moved.

My sister turned to me and said, "What? Are you gonna
write a book now?"

I knew what my answer was, but I was too embarrassed
to say it out loud. Yes, I was going to write a book. Lord
knows, I don't know what I'm doing, but it doesn't really
matter because I just started writing, and it looks like

I'm doing it.

Hold on, let me Google when *Little Women* came to theaters—December 7, 2019. The spark was lit. Amy said it out loud. My neighbour Shannon read my January newsletter and said it was like a good novel that she couldn't put down, and that she wanted to turn the page to see what happened next. Another friend of mine emailed and said, "I kept reading your newsletter over and over—it's so good."

Another funny part is that my newsletter sat on my Mom's coffee table for six months. I'm not sure why it sat there for so long, but it was a little reminder and nudge every time I stopped by, that I thought, *Why is my newsletter out?* It's February. It's March. It's April. It's May. It's gone. Strange. We didn't talk about it or why it was there; it was just a little nudge from my angels—a reminder that the letter was enjoyed by a few people, and that I can connect with people through my writing. It was validation that even though I only went to university to study philosophy two evenings a week and then dropped out, I could write a book if I felt like it. It'll be far from perfect, but that'll be the two of us.

It's bright and early, I'm sitting in my walk-in closet, in my home in Saskatoon, Saskatchewan, shutting out my husband, four kids, music and real estate careers, for a few precious moments when I can just be me.

Me and my book—perfectly imperfect, showing up one day, one page, and one word at a time.

Here's my January newsletter:

Happy New Year, Everyone!

I decided to send you a New Year's note this year instead of a Christmas card.

It felt like a better choice for our household. December always seems to be jam-packed, over-scheduled, scattered and a bit chaotic for me. I take full responsibility for most of it.

I used to *LOVE* Christmas so much, but it seems like I enjoy it less and less, as the years go on. Maybe it's because I'm writing you this note at the beginning of January, and this morning, I literally heard the harsh, cold wind blowing the snow up against our bedroom window. It made me think that we live in a deep, dark, cold tundra. It's kinda how I've felt off and on for a few years now. I fantasized about staying in bed all day, but the nagging inner dialogue of the lunches needing to be made got me up and out of the warmth of our blankets.

Today was back to school for the kids... bittersweet.

So happy to have the house to myself again, to practice yoga in peace, sipping on tea, while allowing my incense to majestically flow without commentary on how "that one's stinky!" But, in all honesty, we could have taken another week, cuddled up in our jammies, vegging and playing with the cousins.

Don't get me wrong, we had a lovely Christmas. It took a lot to get there but, like a wedding, Christmas seems to have a very big buildup for a day that just ends up coming and going like any other.

I saw a cute thing online where a child said to his Mom, "Oh, Momma—I just *LOVE* Christmas, I'm so excited for it! YOU must just *LOVE* it, too!"

Mom hesitates and answers, "Umm, yes, it is a beautiful time of year and there's lots to be excited about. What makes you think I *LOVE* it as much as *YOU* do?"

"Well, I was thinking, finally a day where you and Dad can just sit around and let Santa do all the work!"

> *Unpacking all the boxes,*
> *CHRISTMAS, they are marked.*
> *And then, about two hours in,*
> *it looked like Christmas barfed.*
> *The four kids running round the house.*
> *I told myself I wouldn't yell...*
>
> Elly Thorn, 'Am I the Only One?'

I love Christmas decorations, music, the performances I often get to do around the season, but I notice I get thrown off my center more easily around this special time of year. I know it's the expectations we all put on ourselves and each other. I'm getting to the point in my life where I know what mine are and what I need to let go of, but it all can be quite draining. If I look at it with my "cup half-full" eyes, it can also feel empowering and freeing. I'm forty years old in August... I can feel the shift in everything.

So, I've been taking this parenting course online that is rocking my world. Nothing like a Zoom class to humble you and make you look at most things in a whole new perspective. Can I have my money back? Dr. Shefali has been amazing, but oh, lots comes up in a course like this.

John said to me, "Seriously, we're taking a parenting class?"

To which I answered, "Do you see this getting easier any time soon?"

Our kids: Bella, twelve, Millie, ten, Sam, seven and Walt, four. We both laughed, and John followed up, "Parenting: It's the only thing on the planet that you can sign up for without having to complete, at minimum, a weekend course." Needless to say, we sent the payment.

✦ ✦ ✦

We lost our Dad in June.

It's been a year of so much growth and acceptance. I've been healing through music—seems to be a blessing in my life. With very few performances in the past two years, I turned to piano lessons with Martin Janovsky, completing my Level 5 with an 86% and working on my theory, as well.

With many of us in similar boats and our mental health being so fragile, especially these past few years. I thought it would be a great exercise for my brain, as well as help heal my broken heart. In the silence of the house this afternoon, the stillness of the day, my pain rears its head. I notice it, I feel it, and I used to want to just push it away. Not anymore, I sit with it, allow it to be, let the tears flow, and slowly move on. It's necessary for me to release, recalibrate, recover, and rest—more so now than ever.

This marks two years of my brother and I working together. I've been so blessed to have Lee as a part of our team. He'll be licensed by the end of the year, and we will be able to serve our clients in even more parts of the real estate industry, in agricultural, residential and commercial. It's been so beautiful to watch my business grow over the years, and now, Lee brings so much more to the table. He reminded me that our Grandpa (Wilf) and his brother (Uncle Keith) worked many years together, owning five hardware stores along the Yellowhead Highway. Lee said he's Uncle Keith, and I'm Grandpa. I keep thinking this as our business grows and grows. I'm so honoured to work with my sibling—there's no better business partner to have.

My Broker messaged me yesterday saying, "You're number nine, out of ninety, in the office for 2021! Congrats."

What a way to close the year! I text Lee to share our news, and his family came over to drop off a birthday gift for Sam, who turned seven years old yesterday, and we popped a bottle of champagne to toast 2021.

Lee said, "To Cloud Number Nine…"

I said, "Dad would have been so proud of us." Then Lee did this whistle, that Dad always did when he wanted to cheer all of us kids on. I used to have this love/hate with it because it was kinda ear-piercing and annoying, but I would always know where he and Mom were in the audience.

What I'd give to hear it again.

Sending peace, love, and gratitude.

What a ride.

> *Buckle up, it's gonna be a bumpy ride.*
> *Shooting 'cross the dark lit sky, riding on this star tonight.*
> *If you see stardust, even if you simply catch a glimpse.*
> *Go ahead and make a wish. Make it good and hold on tight.*
> *Twinkle, little, darlin' star.*
>
> Ellen Kolenick, 'Buckle Up'

✦ ✦ ✦

Well, since I'm writing a book, I may as well introduce the stars of my story—the stars of my life, in no particular order, because if I could, I would put them all first…

SEVEN-YEAR-OLD SAM

How can I begin to tell you about our Sam Sam and describe what he's like?

Our Sami, our Sammy Whammy, our Cham Chamaroonie. What a kid, he's truly one of a kind.

Sam is the third-born, same as me. I tell him that's probably why I like him the most, but not to tell any of the other kids. He asks me all the time, "Mom, who's your favourite? I know it's me, I know I'm your favourite. Tell me. Just tell me. Seriously. Just whisper it quietly in my ear. I won't tell anyone. Seriously, I know it's me."

Born on the same day as my eldest brother, Sam is quite the Sam. He is so full of love. His biggest passions are building Lego and playing with his little brother. Walt absolutely adores Sam, even to the point where if Walt gets sick or hurt, he asks for Sam instead of John and I. It irks me a bit, but their bond is that tight.

Sam is a precious, precious boy. Always has been. From the day he was born, he literally came into the world with the biggest and brightest eyes. He was so gentle and perfect. Oh, and his eyelashes—we'd never seen such long eyelashes on a baby.

It's funny, before we had kids, I used to feel sorry for people when they only had boys. Isn't that ridiculous? I would hear someone would have a couple of boys, and I thought to myself: "Oh, that poor Mom, only boys…"

I always dreamed of having girls and thankfully got them, but boys?! I actually didn't know how a person could really love, LOVE a boy.

Now, I have my boys.

And, now I know.

> *Rock-a-bye baby, rock-a-bye boy.*
> *Rock-a-bye baby, rock-a-bye boy.*
> *Rock-a-bye baby, rock-a-bye boy.*
> *Rock-a-bye baby, you're my every joy.*
> *The moment I met you, I gave you your name.*
> *With eyes wide open, and a heart just the same.*
> *The moment I held you, my whole being knew.*
> *I'd love you to pieces, from here to the moon.*

Ellen Kolenick, 'Song for Sam'

I can't explain the love for a son. It's beyond my wildest dreams. I didn't even know; I didn't even have a clue. Just thinking of my boys right now makes my heart skip a beat and my throat tighten with tears. Who knew?

Sam, even at this age, still hasn't lost his tenderness. When I tuck him in, I say, "Jeez, I'm hungry, can I just have a little snack? Come on, just a quick bedtime treat? Please, help me out here, Sam."

Then, I'll snort around pretending to eat the side of his face and then when I get to his earlobes...

"Don't mind me, I'll just have one small lemon drop." Crunch, and then I proceed to nibble on one of his ear lobes...

"Don't mind me," as he turns his head, "I'm just dying to have a small piece of chocolate cake." Crunch, I nibble on his other earlobe.

He laughs and I laugh—sometimes he says my nibbles are too hard, which makes us laugh even more.

When Sam was in Kindergarten, he had the most beautiful teacher, Madame Devine. She looked like an angel. Warm and gentle eyes, the most beautiful smile. It was around Christmas, and when I was tucking Sam in, I could see the wheels turning in his head. And, I knew something was up; you can always tell with Sam. He finally said he built some special "ship Lego" to surprise Madame with.

I said that was super nice and that Madame will love it.

Then he started thinking and asked if he could give Madame one of my rings or necklaces for Christmas?! I hesitated because I didn't want to appear selfish, but I also didn't want to give my jewelry away to his teacher. And then I noted, I didn't even know he knew about my jewelry, so I made another mental note to hide it in a better place.

I told him that I should probably keep my own rings and necklaces, but it was indeed a very generous idea for Madame.

Then he said, "We should go shopping," which he never says.

And then, he followed up with, "And, we could get Madame two pairs of golden earrings... A necklace ... and a ring."

I laughed and I said that was a lot, so he should probably just pick one thing that he'd want to get her.

He said, "Oh, I have an idea! A CROWN!"

Someone loved his Madame.

That's Sam. Such a huge heart. That's also the way his mind thinks. I'm not sure what it's called, but it seems like he rarely misses things and builds on each creative idea, leading to the next. It's hard to explain—it's really cool to observe.

Sam's a feisty, wild, kinda spastic little guy who thinks so far beyond his years. He asks so many questions; it kinda drives us crazy. John, the girls and I often smile because he comes up with the quirkiest things. The stuff he thinks of and asks about include: Heaven, electronics, languages, Lego, architecture, engineering, snorkeling, volcanoes, lava, dinosaurs... If you give him a book, he'll finish it in a couple nights. Oh, and he loves the smell of a fresh new book. He can really focus and enjoy when he loves something and when he doesn't—let's just say John calls him "Wiggly Worm"—and that's the perfect description of him.

He's also so curious. I remember driving the kids to school and passing some sort of new power box likely used for cell phones, and he looks at it, taking it all in and says, "Look at that new power box, wonder what's inside that metal box? Hmmm, if you opened it up, what would all the wires and devices look like? What do you think it's actually used for, Mom?"

Bella looked at me and said, "I didn't even notice that thing."

Millie just smiled in the backseat.

Sam also tells the truth...

One night when he was ticked off at me for something, I said, "Night Sam, I love you."

He followed up with, "Well, I don't love you." Dramatic pause. "Actually, wish I didn't pick you as a Mom. You're actually the worst Mom ever. You're actually the most holobowl mother in the woooold."

I almost died laughing. Even telling this story cracks me up because it was a phase where he couldn't say his R's, and it was beyond funny. So, if any of you Moms out there worry that you're the worst Mom, you're actually not. Sorry, I am.

Sam is funny without even knowing it. Also, you should see his dance moves. No words on how his little body can move.

Wiggly Worm. Perhaps that's why he's my favourite.

God knows I'll keep you as long as I can.
Rock-a-bye baby, rock-a-bye boy.
Rock-a-bye baby, rock-a-bye boy.
Rock-a-bye baby.

Ellen Kolenick, 'Song for Sam'

10-YEAR-OLD MILLIE

I wrote Millie her song when she was four years old. Some of her lyrics include:

> Let's make a date, just you and me.
> I'll grab a coffee and you ice cream.
> I oughta tell you, baby, you are something.
> You spin around without a care.
> You toss your arms, and you hug the air.
> I oughta tell you, baby, you are something.

That's Millie—just picture that. A lively Earth Angel full of energy and verve. Feeling lit up, ice cream on her face and dancing along Broadway in Saskatoon...

> *Let's make a date just you and me.*
> *I'll grab a coffee and you ice cream.*
> *I ought to tell you.*
> *Baby, you are something.*
> *You spin around without a care.*
> *You toss your arms and you hug the air.*
> *I ought to tell you, baby, you are something.*
> *Walking along Broadway,*
> *the sun's beating down on me.*
> *You put your hand in my hand,*
> *there's nowhere else I'd rather be.*

> Ellen Kolenick, 'Sweet Millie'

That's our Millie. She is a mixture of carefree and deep caring. She is a combination of wild and likes her pristine bedroom and getting her homework completed. She can be a bit reckless, but is also totally and completely organized. She loves playing, dressing up, laughing and planning. Millie is always ready for action.

Born all bald and pink, Millie is the action girl of our household. She gets the gatherings happening. She plans the outings. She wants to make the day fun. Sweet

Millie loves sweets, treats, gum and snacks. She asked me to get her a plate of snacks and said she's placed her order, so if I could please deliver it, that'd be great. Constantly ready to entertain or be entertained, this is our household "Hostess with the Mostess."

> *And when you grin, it's in your eyes.*
> *Your spirit's free, but you're oh so wise.*
> *I ought to tell you, baby, you are something.*
>
> Ellen Kolenick, 'Sweet Millie'

Second child, second daughter, born Gemini, Millie wants to make people smile. She wants to make sure people have fun, and she has a deep, wise soul. She is aware of people's nuances and catches certain tones and expressions. It's funny, Millie may appear one way; however, she knows, and I know her depth.

Millie also likes to throw our house into added chaos just for fun—knocking on the table to make Sofi bark is one of her tricks, phoning her friends and arranging play dates, trying to see which parent will say yes first. She is a bit of a tease. Millie likes to poke. Millie likes to get a rise out of her parents. Millie's friends love her, her coaches love her, and she has a beautiful touch on the piano. Millie is a prankster. Last night, she asked John to peel her some oranges, and took off his hat, placed the oranges in it and put it back on his head. That's Millie. She also reminds me of my brother Lee and sister Amy.

Perhaps that's why she's my favourite.

12-YEAR-OLD BELLA

Our firstborn. What a gig for Bella, being our firstborn and eldest of four children. Bella arrived ready to go. Born Isabella, strongly recommended by her Dad and Uncle Danny, that she needed a real full name: Isabella, not just Bella.

Bella is a Bella. Not Isabella. Don't worry, she'll let you know.

I only call her Isabella when I'm calling her home from the park, or when I'm mad. Also, don't I dare sign her up for things as Isabella. She's Bella.

So strong, independent, bold and empowered, Bella knows what she wants. Bella, our Lioness, is truly grounded and powerful. Expressive, quick sense of humour, and up for an adventure. Bella is ready to enjoy and I've life to the fullest. Sensible and logical, Bella's communication is like no other twelve-year-old I know. The other day, when she and I were driving together, I snapped and I told her to put her phone away.

Silence.

Soon after, I felt badly because I was unnecessarily short with her, and I tried to repair by saying, "I'm sorry, Bella, I could have done better there. I just wanted to visit with you, and I could have said it in a different way."

She just kindly answered, "It's true, had you just said you wanted to visit and connect, I would have finished up what I was doing and put my phone away, no problem. I would have heard you."

Twelve years old.

Wise, a true ability to communicate, use her words, to heal, to evolve... and to forgive her Mom. Bella is a very determined young woman. A feminist at heart, and teaches me things just by being her authentic self.

Bella babe close your eyes.
While Momma sings you a lullaby.
People were completely right,
we'll be up most of the night.
Holding you in my arms.
Protecting you from world's harm.
People were completely right,
you're the hardest job of my life.
My Bella baby, Bella boo.

We brought Bella home to a downtown condo. John had been living there a while and then met me. After he proposed, I moved in. Now, we were a family of three. We enjoyed watching the ever-changing riverbank views. Breathtaking, really. Every season, the Saskatoon riverbank shone like a star. We loved that condo, the people, the views, the river. We have so many beautiful memories there. Including the first paella John cooked for my Mom and Dad. I can remember on that same kitchen counter, we gave Bella her first bath in this little green turtle tub. In that kitchen, late into the night, I was pacing the tile floor with our newborn, while her love song was being written in my heart and me humming into the world. I know, Bella complains to this day. "Why is my song so slow and depressing? Wish it could have been more radio-friendly."

Feel your smiles, feel your pain.
Make all the hurt go away.
People were completely right,
any battle for you, I would fight.

Ellen Kolenick, 'Bella Babe'

Bella changed who I was. Bella showed me what true love was. Like many new parents, I didn't know what to do; everything was trial and error. I felt young, I was young. Just turned twenty-seven years old, new to being a wife. I didn't know how to be a mom, and it was even more clear that I didn't even know who I was. And now, I had a baby, a child of my own to care for.

Hah...

I will always remember the beautiful morning Bella was born. Labouring all night, and her arriving bright and early. Our angel had arrived. Oh my gosh, writing this made me feel like I was filling up with milk. A letdown, aren't our bodies incredible? The memories the cells hold... I can't believe it.

I can remember my Mom, Dad and sister waiting patiently and excitedly outside our hospital room door. Mom gently poked her head in, and John was cradling his most prized possession in his arms, and immediately turned to my Mom and asked, "Do you want to hold her?" I couldn't believe it. I think my Mom was as shocked as I was.

Bella had this full, dark head of hair; she was just so beautiful. Bella was our first for everything. Perhaps that's why she's my favourite.

4-YEAR-OLD WALT

I had to meet Walt. I knew someone was waiting for me to say yes.

Some of Walt's lyrics from his song:

> *Lying in my bed, gave it up to you.*
> *No longer with my thoughts,*
> *I knew my truth… as you do.*
> *You were there, waiting just for me.*
> *To look within, not around—*
> *My heart be free… as it should be.*

We should have known when we named him Walter; Walter Wilfred Wade Nicholas Nasser, he would be just like a little old man.

> *Something in me had to come say hello.*
> *Something in me wouldn't let me say no.*
> *Something in me couldn't let you go.*
> *Something in me… had to say yes to my soul.*

Elly Thorn, 'Something in Me'

Too many names and hats can take a toll on a person. Raspy voiced, stern browed, fiery and fiercely tenacious, Walt tries his best to keep up with this action-packed household. In fact, Walt can actually hold his own and does.

Walt is a force.

I never thought our fourth child would be such a character.

Ask anyone, he really is. As my Mom says, "You place your order and you never know what you're gonna get." I find it absolutely mind-blowing that two people can create four children together and the kids all be similar, yet completely unique, in all their own ways.

More lyrics:

Came in with the wind, carried on His wings.
We both took a breath.
What hope you'd bring...
Let the choirs sing!

And then, he turned two. Walt spent his first two years calmly observing all of us, taking everything in. I have a photo of him standing beside our coffee table, staring at this beautiful ceramic angel. I couldn't figure out who was more angelic.

It seems like Walt turned two years old, and he was off to the races. Quick to yell and tantrum, he never looked back! Walt keeps us all on our toes. He also has a hilarious sense of humour and body language. Quick to shake his booty and tell someone to stop looking at him—he's quirky and a handful.

Something in me had to come say hello.
Something in me wouldn't let me say no.
Something in me couldn't let you go.

I remember being in a healing session wishing I wasn't so quick to anger, and the practitioner reminded me that there can't be two two-year-olds. Yeah, what a novel idea. Let's just say that statement resonated with me and I'll hold onto it forever.

Something in me—had to say yes to my soul.
    Elly Thorn, 'Something in Me'

You are there without me, I will be there soon.
    Ellen Kolenick, 'Twelve Thirty Four'

I always dreamed of having four kids; something in me knew I always would. Walt is named after a few different Walters and Walt Disney, one of them. Walt believes in magic and dreaming. Our Walt is connected and still mentions missing his Papa.

My Dad passed away when Walt was three years old. I'm surprised that Walt still brings him up. A few days ago, Walt said, "I still miss Papa." He was just quietly looking out the window at the sky and clouds. Walt is my dream come true. Perhaps that's why he's my favourite.

✦ ✦ ✦

It's 9:10 a.m. and I'm going to sign off now. I have two houses to evaluate. I need to get Bella up to introduce herself to kids she may babysit soon. I need to do a quick yoga stretch and start my day. Oh yes, I also need to note, the dream was that I began my book on the morning of my fortieth birthday, which is August 5th. Then I had a better thought: Maybe I'll *finish* it on that day.

This is wild. So, I'm just writing. I don't know where it's going. I'll let you know when I get there.

CHAPTER TWO
LOOKING BACK

May 25, 2022
6:26 a.m.

> *How do you look so good?*
> *I often wondered,*
> *though I knew you would.*
> *And now these butterflies*
> *they tell me I should*
> *run away.*
>
> *How do you feel the same?*
> *That great big hug*
> *and your grinning face.*
> *And after all these years*
> *my knees still gave.*
> *How do you look so good?*
>
> Ellen Kolenick, 'Looks So Good'

It's funny how you can think your life is going in a certain direction and then it does a complete 180, and you have no idea what happened.

I was in love.

I've been in love a few times, really—I love very easily, and I usually scare people off. I can remember dating a guy named, let's call him Tom, when I was younger—about twenty years old—and he said I was like a forty-year-old trapped in a twenty-year-old's body. I've always been an old soul. I never really "dated" properly, whatever "properly" was. I always dated, thinking I wanted to get married and have kids. If the boyfriend wasn't on the same track as me, then I couldn't figure out what the point was.

Don't get me wrong, I was still fun to be around when I was dating. I was just always looking for a ife partner. Dating for me was serious business, and all of my siblings were in serious relationships except me. I wanted so desperately to have an end game, possib y a happily ever after, too. I thought there was such magic around marriage and children. I wanted what my Mom and Dad shared. I admired their relationship so much that I wanted it for me, too. It wasn't perfect, they weren't perfect, but what they created together was a beautiful love story.

Now, as I reflect on this time in my life, my early twenties, I sorta wish I hadn't been so weird. After I was dumped by another guy I thought I was going to marry, I ended up back home in my parents' basement starting my entire life from scratch. I was offered another contract singing and dancing with Norwegian Cruise Lines (NCL), and my Mom encouraged me to hunker in for a bit at home to cool my jets. Also, around this time, Mom and Dad hired a painter to paint their fence, and I sat inside with my face pressed against the window, drooling and longing for someone to love.

I see you in the backyard,
the sky is cloudy and gray.
You're painting the fence,
and I'm unhappy today.
Can I help you out? I wanted to say.
But I'm so shy and nervous,
I just looked the other way.

Oh, Mr. Painter,
won't you paint a smile on me?
Mr. Painter splash the sky with blue
and the grass with green.
Hey, Mr. Painter,
take your time,
and please don't finish the fence today.
Oh, Mr. Painter,
is it wrong of me to pray for rain?

Ellen Nasser, 'Mr. Painter' [unreleased version]

I was the absolute opposite of being present and in the moment. I bet it was such a turnoff to anyone I dated, leading to the destruction of many relationships that could have potentially been something. But there's a reason I'm not with any of those people. I didn't know it, but John was waiting for me.

I'm a romantic at heart.

I don't sit around watching Hallmark movies, but to this day, I fantasize about romantic things. Like John simply touching the small of my back, or surprising me with a kiss on the cheek, bringing me flowers, a plant, a Starbucks or a cozy sweater. I tell him that's such a turn on to think of him shopping and looking for clothes or something special for me.

Speaking of shopping, I... I really can't stand shopping for myself. I'm not much of a shopper at all. I usually go into a store or mall and immediately need to find a washroom. This kind of diarrhea is completely different from the "I'm going to write a book!" diarrhea. This diarrhea is: Oh Lord, too many clothes to go through, the lights, the people, the pressure to find something, the overwhelming feeling of stores and options. Some people love shopping so much that they call it retail therapy—I, on the other hand, feel like retail could send me into therapy. My Grandpa Wilf used to get annoyed at my Mom and Grandma and their shopping around Yorkton. I can remember him saying, "I don't understand what the fuss is all about, walking around pinching clothes." I must have found those words very entertaining because it has stuck with me all these years.

> At times, we plan too much,
> often we talk too much.
> At times, we wake up wondering
> what happened.
> Our minds are spinning out of control.
> We need to stop and ask ourselves a question.
> What is this all for?
> What is this all for?
>
> Sometimes we love too much.
> Sometimes we're scared of that stuff.
> At times, we wake up wondering
> what happened.
> Our minds are spinning out of control...
>
> Ellen Kolenick, 'At Times'

I feel the creative energy flowing through me. The passion for creating... I love it. If I told John I was writing a book in the wee small hours of the morning, he would absolutely groan and roll his eyes. Most people would. This is our little secret, don't tell anyone.

One more thing, just like when I shared my January newsletter, I wanted to show you where I was at. Losing my Dad, almost a year ago, is a huge part of my story.

So, I want to let you know what he was like, by sharing this beautiful obituary our family created, mostly my Momma:

With family by his side, in the early morning hours of Sunday, June 13, 2021, our beloved husband and father, Peter Stephen Kolenick, passed away peacefully at age 69, leaving a legacy of love, humour, and integrity. Peter was born on February 2, 1952, in Cupar, Saskatchewan, to Peter Sr. and Esther Kolenick. He had two older sisters, Gayle and Janet, and a younger brother, Paul. He was accelerated in primary school and at the age of 19 gained early entrance into the College of Law. Soon after his 22nd birthday, he graduated with his Bachelor of Law Degree. It was in his first year of Law that he met the love of his life, Wanda Thorsness, a nursing student who happened to be visiting a classmate in Wakaw for the weekend. A lift back into Saskatoon, with Peter, was the beginning of their love story. He often told the tale of her "throwing the ring back in his face" and that "if she changed her mind, she'd be the one proposing." Soon thereafter, she came to her senses and proposed. Best decision of her life! On July 20, 1974, Peter and Wanda were married at the Saltcoats United Church.

Peter articled and worked at the law firm, MacDermid and Company, until January of 1977, when he accepted a position with Legal Aid in Yorkton. Peter wanted to "put down roots," and Wanda's dream was to raise a family, so as a "team," they decided to begin the next chapter of their life together in the nearby town of Saltcoats. They built a beautiful home on the lake next door to Mom and Dad Thorsness, whom Peter loved to the fullest and they, him. In 1978, Peter and Wanda welcomed the first of their four children to be born in a six-year span. Life was busy and so good.

Peter always dove heart-first into life, whether he was driving across the frozen prairie to defend a client in need; staying up too late hand-crafting a wooden locomotive for a son with an unhealthy train obsession; clearing and maintaining the annual skating rink on the lake; or spending way too much money on a bionic elbow for "Potash" the adopted family cat. He served his community well, spending seventeen years on Town Council and almost as many as a member of session for the Saltcoats United Church. He helped with the coaching of the kids' sporting activities, of which there were many.

He loved loud music, jokes, and blue rare steak. He loved physical fitness, playing tennis, shinny, crosswords, basement ping pong and Nintendo pinball. Above all, he loved his wife and children.

Peter played old boys' hockey with the Saltcoats 'Gang Green'. He was a loyal fan of the Philadelphia Flyers and the Saskatoon Blades. Even at the onset of his illness, he loved playing in the 60-plus league in Saskatoon.

Peter served nearly 20 years as a lawyer with Legal Aid. During that time, he served as President of the Yorkton-Melville Bar Association and was appointed Queen's Counsel. He also served as a Bencher and later as President of the Law Society of Saskatchewan.

He contributed immensely to the legal profession and was dedicated to his clients and the administration of justice. In July 1996, he was appointed to the Saskatchewan Provincial Court where he served for over 16 years.

For the past eight years, our world has been clouded over by Peter's declining health. As the sun set on his brilliant life, it was reflected in those clouds of grief, illuminating our lives in ways we never could have imagined. We are thankful to him for teaching us throughout his life and for the lessons we learned while losing him. We will treasure the time spent by his bedside; reminiscing, laughing, crying, playing piano, and singing softly (most of the time). It was truly a time of healing.

Peter believed in God and knew he was blessed, and with that awareness came an unwavering spirit of generosity and care. Losing Peter is a source of deep sadness for us, but as we grieve, we also feel an enormous sense of relief that his suffering is at an end. He is now at peace.

42

CHAPTER THREE

CONNECTIONS AND COMMITMENTS

May 26, 2022
6:37 a.m.

I feel like making a commitment to something is so important. Every day, I honour my daily devotion to connecting and beginning a fresh, new day on a balanced, positive note. When I open my eyes, I immediately meditate. It's the first thing I do. I'm guessing it may be the first thing I do for the rest of my life. Encouraged by my brother Lee, in October of 2018, our entire family took a meditation course over Thanksgiving weekend, and I have truly enjoyed my daily practices ever since. Apparently, Transcendental Meditation is very grounding and healing.

My takeaway from the two-day extensive is that you are given a mantra, you are to get comfortable, close your eyes, breathe, and repeat it whenever you notice your thoughts. The most challenging part for me is completing the 20 minutes and then wondering if I did okay. I still don't know if I'm doing it right. I don't know if I'm doing anything right.

I've been letting my second meditation of the day slip; the ideal practice would be to meditate for twenty minutes right when you wake up in the morning and then again, at about 3 p.m. I'm going to start to practice my second meditation before the kids come home from school. It's a great way to get aligned before the after-school rush begins.

After the kids get home from school, I often find myself in a state of fight or flight, going in so many different directions and getting more centered would definitely help. I remember hearing that Jerry Seinfeld is a strong believer in meditation. He claimed that if he would have incorporated a second afternoon meditation into his daily routine, there would have been more episodes of *Seinfeld*.

Have you ever noticed that there are people who just keep showing up in your life?

> *It's a late night and I'm awake,*
> *with a hum, the vessel makes.*
> *My feet are planted to the ground,*
> *though I can't stand still.*
>
> *I don't mind my stay*
> *but I miss you more each day.*
> *I'm learning lots about myself*
> *but some things never change.*
>
> *I miss you more each day.*
> *It's time I come back home*
> *I don't know why I roamed so far...*

I have two friends who have been in and out of my life since Grade 12. These friends of mine have intermittently shown up in my adult life. I'm convinced they're some of my angelic cheerleaders who support my inner artiste. They just seem to pop up with words of encouragement and support unknowingly in my lowest times.

Home, home, home... home, home, home...
Home, home, home...
Home...

Ellen Kolenick, 'Come Back Home'

It's almost like they've sensed when my creative spark is dimming, and I get a text or a call about my music.

When we bought our house on Collins, they, and their four kids, lived behind our back fence. We bought the house to be closer to my parents because Dad was sick. Magically, and when I needed it most, they reminded me to keep performing, taking photos of their sound system on family road trips with my songs blasting away. Videos of the kids belting out 'Am I the Only One?' or 'You Should Be You'. Getting messages like that never gets old; it just lights me up to think people are actually enjoying my creations. They also hired the band and I to sing for their backyard celebrations. This was at a time when Dad was really quite sick, and they'd request and I would decline, truly not thinking I could find my voice, and Stef would actually text me saying: "Sorry to ask you again, but I'm not taking no for an answer." My Dad was always such a huge support of my performing, so it made me wonder.

Most recently, we were out for dinner, and my friend said I should write a new song. He said he was getting so sick of listening to all of my piano songs. He wanted a new song, this time with lyrics.

✦ ✦ ✦

I went home that night and wrote 'You Let Me Go'. It's one of my best songs yet, and I sent it to them. They messaged back that evening—*What a nice gift, we didn't tell you, but it's our anniversary!*

I didn't know this in high school, but my friend is part Lebanese, so of course she and John have that in common, as well as both being entrepreneurs in their family businesses. All four of us love chatting about life, living outside the box, and of course, performing arts and music. The same friends actually encouraged us to go on a Disney Cruise. John really didn't want to go, but they insisted there weren't many holidays where someone with four kids could go on and relax, so we ended up going and had one of the most relaxing holidays of our lives. We were treated like absolute gold. Funny story, we ended up booking a second cruise and boarded the airplane, only for John to notice their parents on the flight. We ended up chatting with them, and they were actually going to meet *all* their children and families boarding the same ship we were getting on. We ended up cruising along with them and their extended family, not even knowing we had the same holiday plans!

CHAPTER FOUR
THE BEAN SPILLER

May 27, 2022
6:08 a.m.

I spilled the beans. Ahh... I couldn't continue to keep my secret any longer. I had an energy session with one of my dearest friends, Melissa, founder of sweetsoulsister. ca, and the beans were spilled.

My workday started out a bit scattered. I had a 9 a.m. house possession, and then the carpet cleaner from our team called and said he was locked out of the house he was supposed to be cleaning. Finally, I hunted down access to the house, and by this point, the carpet cleaner texted at 9:26 a.m. and said he got in, but just an FYI, "Someone is snoring in bed."

At that point, I knew my day was off to a rock n rollin' start. I got the keys, paperwork and gifts off to one set of clients, raced over to the other house to wake up my other client, and eventually made it to my 10 a.m. energy healing. I knew I needed it.

The session yesterday was beautiful. I feel amazing today. I could feel my energy so aligned and clear. It's a full
body and soul experience. When I lay down on the bed, I
fall into this deep state of relaxation. It's a state of deep
rest and recharge... It's magical and unexplainable.

> *Never mind what they say,*
> *the day the snow was fallin'—*
> *with tulips on my table.*
>
> *We'll pay no heed to what they say.*
> *'Cause no one really knows*
> *what a person really goes through.*
>
> Ellen Kolenick, 'Champagne Shoes'

Wait a minute. Why is someone coming upstairs? I hear
footsteps again. John snuck off to the gym this morning,
and I know Millie is planning on biking to school. Ahh...

A couple weeks ago, we invited Millie's soccer team
over for a swim after their tournament. In my opinion, impromptu parties are the best. Throw out the invite! Whoever can come, comes. They laughed, played,
swam, dressed up, and toured the park in costumes and
lived it up—they asked for a sleepover, I said, "Not a
chance!" We ordered a few pizzas, and it was a blast. If
I would have planned to host a twenty-five-person swim
party that Sunday afternoon, I would have had to plan
snacks, drinks, think about a bunch of different possible
scenarios, a start and end time, should I invite everyone's
parents and siblings to swim, etc. Instead, other parents
brought drinks and donuts, we ordered pizza and had
chips, and all the team *LOVED* it.

Personally, living in the flow is where it's at. Planning
kills me. Sure, there is a time and place to plan, but it
takes up too much brainpower for me. I easily get overwhelmed with plans constantly changing and trying to

please everyone and their schedules. You'll never win. I believe most things work out for the best, that's just how we roll, that's just the way it is. Whatever happens, happens. I feel tired and deflated when I start thinking too much about how something is going to happen, because it never goes as planned. There are always going to be a million reasons why not to do something. If I sat down and planned to figure out *all* the steps, to actually map out how to write a book, think, ponder, rethink, doubt, second-guess every story and thing I was going to write about, etc., I'd be dead in the water. Not a chance I would be able to do it; in fact, I'd never even begin. This way, there's no pressure. None, zero, zilch.

So, back to my bean spilling. I really wanted to keep this writing a secret because it sounds a bit crazy, but after my session, I said it out loud to Melissa. Uh oh, now this is real. I told her about my vision that I was going to start my book on my birthday, but then all signs were pointing to starting it NOW and completing it *by* my birthday. I knew there was no other time to fit this project in besides bright and early in the wee small hours of morning.

Party is over—Millie just walked into my closet and it's 6:31 a.m. She said, "What time is it? Can I meditate with you?"

Fully dressed in her bright, pink shirt and tight green camouflage pants. I said, "Get back to bed, you have another hour of sleep to get, come on."

I tried to be a bit kinder, "Go snuggle up in our bed then." She listened. Who will be next to come into the closet this morning? My money's on Walt.

When Dad passed away almost a year ago, my brother-in-law Brian wrote a funny and precious write-up about my Dad, to pass along to the legal community. His message inspired me to write one for my social media. Brain diseases can be unpredictable, and it was so new to our family that we all just took it, one day at a time.

✦ ✦ ✦

I wanna hold you close.

Saying goodbye to someone you love, little by little, is one of the hardest things I've ever done. By the end, you don't even really know how it all played out.

I wanna make your dreams come true...
Ellen Kolenick, 'Hold You Close'

You don't know how or when it got to the point of your Dad in a day chair, only eating certain things so that he wouldn't choke. When and how did that all happen? Even the details are blurry. All I know is this empty, broken feeling that sneaks up on me more often than I'd like to admit. I think I'm doing okay, and suddenly I'm not. Sometimes when I feel really broken-hearted, I feel embarrassed because I think maybe a year later, I shouldn't still be overtaken by such great pain. This is reason #2783 why I'm writing this memoir; I need to keep reminding myself that there is a much bigger picture.

Here's my post about Dad:

In the wee small hours of Sunday morning, our darling Dad peacefully passed away.

We have been grieving Dad in many ways for quite some time.

Now, having him physically gone makes my heart hurt.

I thought I'd be okay because he's not suffering anymore, but I'm not. Well, I guess I am at times, but then I have a huge wave of pain wash over me. It's hard.

There's nothing like watching a loved one slip away little by little. Throughout this last week, Mom, Amy and I witnessed some beautiful purple, pink and blue skies, as the sun was setting.

Dad was a gentle yet fiery soul, kind and generous, driven, positive, glass-half-full kinda guy. Our family was always talking about how we honestly never heard him complain about anything. He just accepted life as it came and truly taught us kids that "this too shall pass," when any roadblocks inevitably happened.

> *I wanna laugh with you all day.*
> *I wanna laugh with you all day.*
> *I wanna make your dreams come true,*
> *no matter what I do.*
> *I wanna somehow make you stay.*
>
> Ellen Kolenick, 'Hold You Close'

Dad coached our baseball teams, hockey teams on the weekends. He drove me to Churchbridge for figure skating, and he came to every show of mine that he could possibly attend.

He absolutely adored my Mom until his last breath. These past years she cared for him like you wouldn't believe—her love, commitment, and devotion to him was like no other. Mom lost her best friend.

They had such love for each other, it was beautiful... in recent years, she always took pride in giving him a good shave, washing his face, combing his hair—when we'd FaceTime, these past 14 months, she'd say, "Isn't he handsome?"

She would go visit him at the care home and breathe life into him. Letting him have his dignity.

He deteriorated greatly these past three weeks of lockdown.

He missed his beautiful bride.

Apparently, some of his last words were, "I love my wife Wanda, I love hockey, I love my kids, and I'm a Judge." That was reported by his Caregivers and made us all laugh.

That basically summed up Dad.

He really was fun, amazing and a man of integrity. And, as my brothers said, "Dad always showed up, no matter what."

He loved us kids to pieces, and we all felt like a priority. Our parents always had a way of making us feel like we really mattered.

I'm so honoured to be one of his daughters and to be a part of this journey. My heart feels so heavy. And truthfully, I'm still putting the pieces back together again and noticing it'll never be the way it was. I'm one of those people who notice things. I can also notice slight, unintentional pauses, body twitches, the way people hold their resting hands, distant glances, certain looks. I just notice these things.

> *It wasn't short of a fairy tale,*
> *with the sunshine rising on the lake.*
> *And with Grandma and Grandpa right next door to us,*
> *who could ask for anything more?*
>
> Ellen Kolenick, 'If I Become'

I'll always remember the evening Mom and Dad were leaving our house. John and I had Bella and Millie at this point, and Mom was just running something out to the vehicle. It was just Dad and I in front, and I noticed a distant look in his eyes, and I asked him if he was feeling okay. I really didn't want to hurt his feelings. He just gently smiled and said he was okay, and that was that.

Growing up, I can remember hearing my parents say, "Don't trouble trouble, till trouble troubles you."

Ahh… dear, Millie is back—6:57 a.m. I told her she might not be able to bike to school again because she got up so early. She said she must be excited.

I'm looking at my three candles that I light every morning, and one has gone out—that basically sums up my morning so far. I'm a mess. A great, big friggin' mess.

Sofie barfed carrot chunks on my bed.

Millie got up at the crack of ass.

One snuffed out candle.

Another stupid idea to write a memoir, in the wee small hours of the morning.

Why Ellen? Seriously.

Oh yes, and keep it a secret, except now Melissa knows, so that makes it real, so now I can't quit.

Faaaack.

7:28 a.m.

I just received a text from Millie's friend's mother saying Millie can come to their house at 8 a.m. to bike together. So, let me get this straight: Millie has been ready since

6:31 a.m., and the plan was to meet at 8? This is Millie to an absolute tee. She has been in and out of my closet three times, pacing the house for the past hour and a half, driving me nuts, and the plan is to meet at 8 a.m.

Deep breath, Ellen...

> *The wind in the trees blows right through me.*
> *Chills me to the bone.*
> *The light, in the distance, flickers off and on.*
> *Though nobody is home.*
> *Do you think of me? Like I think of you.*
> *Do you think of me? I know you do...*
>
> Ellen Nasser, 'Do You Think of Me' [unreleased version]

CHAPTER FIVE
EVERYBODY HAS A TURN

May 28, 2022
8:23 a.m.

Ahh... that's a nice sleep-in. I'm back to my closet sanctuary. Sam and Walt have joined me. Sam is talking about Victoria Day, which is another little nudge because, as you know, that's the day I started my writing journey. Remember what I said about there being no coincidences for me? Well, it's true. He's trying to figure out why there's a Victoria Day, and who she actually is, and exactly how many presents did she get on her birthday. That's our Sam. Very inquisitive, always curious and contemplative. Most kids are happy with just getting a day off of school, whereas Sam, almost a week later, is still trying to make sense of the situation. He's also thinking about Victoria's birthday presents because he tends to feel a little hard done by regarding his birthday present situation. Sam's birthday is January 3rd, so even though he gets separate birthday presents, he's fully aware that he only really gets presents once a year, unlike his friends who get their birthday and Christmas gifts separately. I'm certain he's thinking about that as well. He's a funny little thing.

Okay, now everybody is up. Bella is heading to swimming soon. She had a late night of playing baseball under the Nutana Park lights. She carpooled with someone, and I missed her game. When you have four kids in activities and everyone is going in all different directions, carpooling is a game-changer. I got that tip from one of John's sisters. Sometimes, I feel guilty about missing the kids' games—but I'll be honest here: I'm tired and have other interests, too. I honestly think it's okay for our kids not to have us at *every single thing* they do. Maybe that's just my coping mechanism to soothe my guilt. Instead of watching Bella's baseball tonight, I stayed at home and recharged. I played the piano, visited with my Mom, Lee, sister-in-law Kriti, and enjoyed a lemon drop martini that John recently learned to make.

If you need permission to rest, which you don't, but if you feel like you do, permission has been granted. Ellen Nasser, Queen Shit of Turd Island, has granted you permission to periodically not give a fuck. There, I said it. Permission granted.

Let's talk about alcohol. It's definitely a topic in my life. The past couple of years, I have indulged very little. Part of it was because I noticed I wanted to indulge often and a lot. When the pandemic hit, many people we knew were hanging out at home perpetually blitzed, and John and I decided to do the complete opposite. He said to me one day, "Let's do all we can to feel good and healthy throughout this." The reasons:

+ Being hungover is the worst.
+ Being hungover with four kids sucks even worse.
+ Being hungover with four kids at home during a Pandemic is the worstest.

John and I had uprooted our family from their home and neighbourhood, and rented a little semi-detached in Buena Vista, so that we could build our new house. The Pandemic hit, and we had all four kids at home, under 10 years old. John's Mom broke her hip. Sam slipped on the stairs carrying a glass bowl of snacks and sliced his neck. Ambulance came, and thankfully, it missed his main artery. We were still training our new puppy, Sofi, and of course, Dad was sick, under lockdown, and slowly passing away in the care home.

Yeah, what did they say life's five biggest stressors are?

+ Moving
+ Major illness or injury
+ Job loss
+ Death of a loved one
+ Divorce

I can't believe, that you chose me.
That you were waiting for this.
It blows my mind and it baffles me
that you still choose to be.
After all of this
and all the things we've been through.
Baby, it's still you.

Ellen Kolenick, 'Champagne Shoes'

Back to booze and why we are choosing not to indulge in it all the time. Don't get me wrong, we still indulge and enjoy it, but we don't feel the need to drink every time it's offered to us. It seems like it can turn into a nasty habit pretty damn quickly, and we don't want that. We also don't want our kids watching us drink all the time. Once in a while is fine, but I don't want them thinking I need a drink to relax, or to have fun, or whenever we host. Alcohol is totally glamorized in advertising and seems to be accepted and often encouraged almost everywhere we go. If I overdo it and drink too much, I know I'm not at my best. I'm super entertaining for the first part of the evening, typically when I have a captive audience, and then inevitably end up fighting with John or overreacting to something. It's a vicious cycle, then I end up sleeping like crap and feeling like garbage for days. If someone could have a couple of drinks, turn to water and call 'er a night—it would be perfectly fine. If I happen to choose *not* to indulge, it never fails, people want to know why. It's not the norm yet, but I think more and more people are choosing to drink less or not even at all. We really do try to keep it as a treat these days, but if I do get carried away, my Dad would always say, "Everybody has a turn." I've had many turns in my life, but I think the trick is to not have "a turn" every time you choose to indulge. John always says I'm the one person on the planet who doesn't need booze to have fun. "Why even bother drinking, Ellen?" He said that more than once. "You don't even need it. Most people drink to feel how you feel naturally."

I remember one time I went out for dinner with friends, and this old high school friend came up to our table and said she recognized my voice and laugh. She said I hadn't changed a bit. She followed up with something about "how I'd be feeling the next morning." I think she thought I was drunk, and the funny part is that I was drinking soda and lime all evening. There have been numerous times in my life where this has happened.

John just walked in wearing his SK (Saskatchewan) Made bunny hug and underwear. He just put on his new reading glasses and stared at me. He didn't say one word. I looked up and told him he looked cute. He smiled. I think we are both starting to feel our age a bit. John turned fifty-one in May, and forty is knocking at my door. Clearly, it's rocking my world.

I keep going round in circles about why I wanted to create this memoir, and why I felt the pull and had the desire to wake up and write. I grew up watching Mom journal; she journaled for years, mostly in the evening. I also love that both John's parents have written books. I haven't read Kay's yet, that's on my to-do list once my piano exam has wrapped up, but I devoured Dora's. They're both ninety-five years old and still remarkable. Not to be a Debbie Downer, but I can't imagine I'll be making it to ninety-five years old, so why not share my stories now? Plus, there's not a chance I could remember all of this.

Dora has a total of five children, the first three daughters close together, and then there was a ten-year age gap, and then she had Rosie and my hubby John when she was forty-three and forty-four years old. That alone is something to celebrate and write about. With a total of five beautiful and healthy children, they have created a wonderful and abundant life, and Dora's story is so amazing and inspiring. It was honestly like watching a TV show, I couldn't put the book down. I told her and she just smiled. The words were written straight from her heart and shared with such openness and vulnerability. It's her take on her life, which is so cool because that's all we have. It's our perspective and how we choose not only to see our lives, but how we tell our stories. I can remember years ago, at lunchtime, she was brainstorming titles for her memoir; I couldn't believe she was writing a book.

We were sitting around their kitchen table tossing book title ideas around. The smell of her delicious Lebanese food filled her yellow-painted kitchen. I can easily picture it, heck, even smell it. Nana was usually in a lovely dress she'd sewn herself, with her bright white hair and glasses. She always has a spark and interest for life, education, family and neighbours—I thought to myself, holy crap, Nana's seriously writing a book. Of course, now I know that Nana listening to her heart was also lighting a spark in mine. I would have never thought I could write a book, and now look, there's no stopping me.

When I listen to my own heart, I'm in the flow. There's no doubt about it, life feels easier, things fall into place, and the dance is quite effortless. When I overthink, my brain races to find all the answers and, with that, all the problems, too. I start to believe all the made-up stories in my head, and inevitably, my emotions get triggered, making everyday life a real struggle. Before I know it, I get thrown out of alignment, and shit starts happening. I truly believe the low vibrational energy keeps attracting more and more low vibrational energy, and before you know it, everything around me is falling apart. Or, so it seems. Coming back home and listening to your heart makes everything right again. Try it. Close your eyes.

Place both hands on your heart and breathe.

A simple trick that my sister-in-law May taught me was to breathe deeply through your nose like you're smelling a rose. Feel the expansion in your lungs while holding your breath for four counts. Then, slowly breathe out through your mouth like you're blowing out a birthday candle. Exhale as long as you can. It'll be much longer than four counts. It could be closer to eight. Repeat this three times and notice how you feel. Ask yourself, "Am I okay? Can I change anything right now? Is there a chance for me to get out into nature, get some fresh air? Maybe this situation could be a practice in surrender and acceptance?"

I just practiced intentional breathing, and my head feels clearer. My lungs feel spacious and expanded, my heart feels strong and alive, I feel like I have fresh blood pumping through my body. The benefits of one single, intentional breath is so rewarding. And guess what? We all have access to our own breath.

I've had to work on my breathing over the years. When I was studying at the Canadian College of Performing Arts (CCPA) in Victoria, British Columbia, we actually had a breath class. I thought *wwwhhhhaaaat?!*

But now, noticing my breath, or lack of breathing, is very healing. I still notice I have shallow breathing when I'm playing piano for people, especially at my RCM (Royal Conservatory of Music) concerts. It's my nerves for sure. I'm a Nervous Nellie. Even as I write this, I start to sweat and can feel my solar plexus tighten up.

Breathe, Ellen. Remember to breathe.

CHAPTER SIX
THE ENTERTAINING NASSERS

May 29, 2022
12:04 p.m.

It seems like our weekends are a little more scattered than I'd like. I was sad I couldn't make it to my niece's dance recital, but it's okay. Sometimes, something has to give. I'm curious, though, what rocks my weekends? Is it because my daily practice slides, and I sleep in? Do I stay up too late? Out of my usual rhythm? It's tricky because part of me wants to listen to my body and stay in bed, the other part of me knows that if I continued to stay on track with my daily devotional routine, seven days a week, I would be better off. Our entire household would be better off. But sometimes sleeping in feels soooooooooo good.

I heard my phone buzz at 9:06 a.m. and knew something was up. It was a minor real estate situation. Over the past decade of listing and selling houses, I have learned that most things are fixable. I've had to be coached not to totally fly off the handle at every little hiccup. I talked to my longtime friend/stager Shannon with infineorder.ca and we figured out the solution. I had to zip out to help with a little situation, and on the way home, I stopped in at the grocery store for croissants and fruit and got home to enjoy brunch with our family.

There, Sunday morning saved, it wasn't a total write-off.

Back to last night. One of John's forever friends came over and said he had never tried a lemon drop martini in all his fifty years of living. Well, hearing that lit John up like a Christmas tree. Lemon drop martinis coming right up!

✦　✦　✦

John is an amazing host. That's one of the things I love most about him: His ability to open up his home to entertain and host. He is Lebanese and comes from one the best cooks around. He loves hosting as much as I do. It's awesome because I like to bake and fuss around the house, making it a comfy space, tidying up and getting ready, setting the mood lighting, etc., and he loves cooking and serving our guests. We don't get too hung up on anything being too perfect. In fact, John often runs out to get groceries at 3 p.m. when we are hosting at 5:30 p.m. He always asks me what I want, and then he goes and buys what he wants. It's a standing joke between us. He'll say, "Do you want this or that...?" I'll say, "That," and he'll say, "Are you sure you don't want this?" It never fails. He's hoping I'll say the things he wants, and I rarely do.

Whether it's my family, his, or our friends, a good time is usually had by all. I think our kids love having people over even more than we do. One problem, though—no one likes cleaning up. I actually do most of the cleaning afterwards because he does the cooking. When John reads this, he'll roll his eyes and shake his head because he would say he does most of the cleanup, which is a total load. Johnny, if you want credit for doing most of the cleanup, write your own book!

Back to last night. Take two. John loves grocery shopping, prepping, cooking, making drinks and bossing around his sous chef—that's me. He had so much fun making lemon drops all evening. Holy, they were delicious. Like pucker your lips and glands salivating under your tongue, delicious. I can almost feel it. The last of our friends didn't leave until 1 a.m.

At one point, one of our friends' sixteen-year-old came back to pick up his parents and brought their dog and another dog they were babysitting. So, including Sofi, there were three little white dogs running around, lemon drop martinis flowing, dirty dishes, friends laughing, a four-year-old still up at 10:30 p.m., with our kids saying, "We're still hungry!" the minute all of the food was put away. Now, talk about a circus.

And guess what? We love it, well, most of the time.

> *I like coffee, tea is fine,*
> *I've got a man that I call mine, that I call mine.*
> *I like a nice cold drink*
> *in hot sunny weather,*
> *hangin' with my babe*
> *makes it that much better.*
>
> Ellen Nasser, 'Hangin' With My Babe' [unreleased version]

John grew up with his four older sisters, so there were five of them. There were four of us. I grew up with two older brothers and a younger sister. We both wanted to create something very similar to what we grew up with. And no, we're not mirroring Nana and Bumpa exactly—no more for us! Walt was our final piece—our puzzle's complete, and boy, does it feel good. We are so lucky—so fortunate. It's a roller coaster sometimes, but I wouldn't change it for anything.

Open your heart, let somebody in.
We don't know how lucky we are.
Open your heart, and let somebody in.
We don't know how lucky we are.

Free to share my voice and tell you how I feel.
We take this for granted at times.
Beauty surrounds us,
with the changing of the leaves.
Take some time for each other and believe.

Open your heart, let somebody in.
We don't know how lucky we are.
Open your heart, let somebody in.
We don't know how lucky we are.

Ellen Kolenick 'Lucky We Are'

CHAPTER SEVEN
My Most Favourite

May 30, 2022
8:30 a.m.

*T*his idea to share my music with my stories is an interesting one I'm working through. I suppose I could put my lyrics in the book and let people read them, but my vision of an audiobook makes much more sense. I kinda feel like when I start thinking about the how's I get out of the flow of creating. So here I am, seven days into writing my story and I'm curious about how it'll all play out. I think that's my self-doubt taking over because I'm not typically a huge how person. I'm more of a jump in with both feet, then maybe think about it later. We've got a lot done because we don't think too long or hard about things. My brother Danny once said, "God never gives us anything we can't handle." I totally agree with this.

We had a full weekend. Yesterday, Bella had a high-performance swim camp, and Johnny and I juggled the others. Both middles, Millie and Sam, had their first piano recital at The Bassment. They each played a song, and it made me cry. When Sam finished playing, he scurried back to our table and sat down beside me with his little hands tightly clasped together at his heart, with his fingers touching his chin, whispering, "I had stage fright."

His heart was racing; he was very matter-of-fact—he knew exactly what it was. Stage Fright. I get it sometimes, too, though nobody knows.

When Millie went up there, she played her piece, and it truly touched me. She really feels the music. Her timing, her flow, her presence—it was just beautiful. I teared up and held her hand and told her how beautifully she played, and she said in true Millie fashion, "I know, I'm your favourite." They all say that, and I insinuate that they are all indeed my favourite, but not to tell the others...

"Yes, you are 100% right—you are my favourite."

"Don't tell the others, I can't believe I'm saying this... you're my favourite...
12-year-old...
10-year-old...
7-year-old...
4-year-old..."

They get annoyed when I do that. And, I love it.

Another thing we do is that when I tell them, "Night, I love you."

They say, "I love you more."

I say, "Nope, not a chance."

They say, "Yup, there actually is..."

I say, "Nope."

They say, "Yup, there is…"

It's just a sweet little back and forth… You know, on the nights I'm not gritting my teeth and trying not to scream my head off. Yin and yang, ebb and flow, ups and downs. We are all doing the best we can with the tools we have. Bedtime routines can be dreamy, or they can be a bit of a nightmare.

I ran into a friend who said, "Putting his two boys to sleep, 6 p.m. to 9 p.m., is the longest eleven hours of his day."

Well, I would die a million times
over again, my love.
For you, over and over again.

Ellen Kolenick, 'Over Again'

I just picked up my phone and counted May 23 to August 5—seventy-four days. What's magical about this? What's so important about what I have to say? I don't have some great big message to share. Well, not overly, any-way. I am a Mom in the thick of raising children in various ages and stages, trying to make wise choices, messing up, grieving, sharing my stories, and music. That's all. In fact, this entire process has been healing and fun for me. It may resonate with others just because I'm showing up and expressing myself. It's also just a small glimpse of how I live my life, and I don't know about you, but I am always inspired by others.

So, the piano recital basically starts with the young-est student and goes on to the furthest advanced. It's amazing to watch because it demonstrates what time, experience, and a daily practice evolves into. The recital ends with my piano teacher playing an incredible piece. The master. I had no idea why I wanted to start piano lessons again. I had quit at about eleven years old and was on my RCM level three—that's what I remember, but to be honest, I don't think I actually even took the level three exam. All I know is that I wanted to take lessons again. In January 2019, I was asked to sing four of my original Christmas songs with our Saskatoon Symphony Orchestra. I thought to myself, I've got about eleven months here. I better learn how to sing properly before I get onto that big stage.

> *It's almost Christmas, the snow is all around.*
> *Joy throughout the town, except in me.*
> *It's almost Christmas, I'm feeling all alone.*
> *Tell me you're coming home, back home to me.*
>
> *I almost think that there's no use; should we just give up?*
> *I almost think that I'm confused, beyond a doubt.*
> *'Cause I can't shake those memories on the lake...*

Elly Thorn, 'Almost Christmas'

I have a natural talent for singing, a very good ear for harmony and a passion for performing. I ended up asking one of Saskatoon's top vocal coaches to train me, and she passed on me, twice, but who's counting? She then recommended an equally amazing teacher, Janice Paterson. Every week, I'd go to Janice's and train my voice. I had a year to get ready. Even though I knew I'd be playing gigs and writing songs, I knew I needed to get my performance voice into shape. I needed to hone in on my skills if I'd be singing with a symphony. I needed to focus and commit to a year of lessons. Somewhere in all of this, Bella and Millie ended up taking lessons.

They enjoyed it for a bit, but weren't super keen—by the end of it, Janice said, "Millie is a piano soul."

The minute I heard those words, *piano soul*—I knew I was a piano soul. I hadn't even heard words like that before... "a piano soul." I asked her who Millie should study with, and she said Martin would be wonderful, and the rest is history. Bella, Millie and Sam all study with Martin—Janice was right, Millie is a piano soul, and so is her Momma. I would've *NEVER* thought that would happen, not in a million years.

When I called Martin up, we arranged for me to go to his studio. I walked in and saw two huge grand pianos next to each other—I never saw such a thing. The ceiling was vaulted and there was a real fire burning in the fireplace. No joke, I thought I died and went to heaven—pianos, music, and a fire crackling and burning in a fireplace? Ahh... seriously. Every Wednesday at 2 o'clock it is truly the highlight of my week.

Something you don't know about me—yes, I've had my blood checked, had my physicals, and my health is perfectly fine... but I live my life as a frozen turd. I am cold—all the time: My hands, my feet, the tip of my nose. I'm cold. If I checked it out again, the doctor would likely just say, "You are a frozen turd, put on a sweater." Yes, I know it's sweltering out, and yes, I still want my sweater. I know I have blankets on my bed, and yes, I still want my socks, my toasty jammies, my fuzzy light pink housecoat and sometimes in the winter when I'm really cold—I've been known to add a toque, if I really want to crank up my sex appeal. Frozen turd—it's true, that's me. What's worse?

Finally, summer arrives, and I can warm up. Nope, John wants to crank up the A/C—is there no mercy? Mom and John have many similarities. They both laugh and get annoyed when I say this, but it's true. I'll say something to both of them, and they'll both come up with the same sarcastic retort, not having a clue they both said the EXACT same thing. Then, when I tell them, they both roll their eyes and laugh. Also, Mom and John keep their homes at a stupid, uncomfortably cold temperature, and both say to me, "You know, it's much easier for you to put on another layer of clothes than for me to take off a layer of skin."

They both came up with this one. No joke, they're so annoying. I'm almost forty, John's fifty-one and Mom's pushing seventy. The minute I wrote that, I wondered if John will even want to read this book? Well, I mean, I'm sure he will, but he's just so used to me and all my stories, he may find this book boring. I hope he reads it, though. What about our kids? Will our babies want to read this? If they do, when? I don't know, should I create this just for our family or share it with everyone? Oops, there goes my monkey brain again, my "barking dog" is yapping away—I think that's what Eckhart Tolle calls it.

CHAPTER EIGHT
MY PLACE IN SPACE

May 31, 2022
6:21 a.m.

I set my alarm away from my bed, so I must get up to turn it off, and I don't press snooze. I think snooze is the worst idea. Who came up with snooze anyway? It's like a form of torture to me. On what planet does anyone want to keep drifting back to sleep, only to be woken up again and again, *AND* to be the one in control of that torture? No, thank you, barf.

Ahh... When our family took the Transcendental Meditation course... what a segway... everyone, but Walt, cause he wasn't quite old enough. They said to put your feet comfortably on the ground. I actually just sit up in bed and rest my head on the headboard—I'm guessing I would get a great, big YOU FAIL stamp, but as you're starting to see, I celebrate the small wins. I'm up. I'm meditating. I'd say I'm winning.

My brother Lee reminded us of the story about a friend of Uncle Keith (my Grandpa's brother, so Great Uncle Keith, I should say). Anyway, when we went to visit Uncle Keith when he was dying in the Saltcoats care home, Lee remembered a story of Grandpa, Uncle Keith and Vic, all old hunting friends, chattin' away, saying, "You know, the good thing about getting up in the morning is that you only have to do it once." That memory made Uncle Keith smile, and I often think about it when I get up in the morning. Then, I think of people who hit snooze and have to get up over and over and over... Ahh, no, thank you.

As you know, Grandpa and Uncle Keith were brothers who worked together. They were about ten years apart in age and were very close. As I mentioned in my news-letter, they opened five hardware stores across the Prairies: Yorkton, Saltcoats, Bredenbury, Churchbridge, and Langenburg. From what I could tell, they loved working together and had a great amount of mutual respect for one another. As you know, my brother Lee and I work to-gether, too. He comes to the table with so many talents that have made my business flourish. He has his film and editing degree, he's a journeyman electrician, and truly a jack of all trades. The most special thing about my brother is his level of consciousness. He is such a calm support. There's not a chance I would have been able to keep up with real estate this past year and a half without him. Not a chance.

So, now as I'm writing, my mind goes to "should I be typing this out on my computer?" You see, my unnoticed mind tends to wander and get off track, trying to create problems that aren't real. I'm a fixer by nature though, so when my mind starts creating problems, it also cre-ates solutions. I initially thought that it is so good for me to physically write and keep doing what I'm doing. The neat part about all of this is that it's just capturing—seventy-four days.

I was dreaming last night about what I was going to call my secret book. Maybe *Seventy-Four Days until Forty*, too wordy... gosh. No wonder the editor had to axe twenty-five thousand words: *Morning Muse, Morning Writing, Morning Story, Morning Memoir, My First Forty Years, May Long Weekend Monday, Victoria's Birthday Gift, Victoria Day Idea, Making Memories, Seventy-Four Days of Real, Capturing Time, Creating Space... Victoria's Secret*—oops, that one's taken.

✦ ✦ ✦

I was born and named Ellen Kolenick almost 40 years ago.

Mom and Dad said I came out all pink and golden. Hearing that always made me feel special. I had this thought that I was a ball of light—as you remember, my name comes from light, so I think that's another reason why I feel the way I do. I generally wake up and feel good. Most days, feeling good isn't a real challenge for me. I've had a few spiritual teachers and mentors in my life, and I always used to say to them how lucky I was. Some of them disagreed with that statement. They said there are so many factors, but to just paint my life as "I'm lucky" didn't really resonate with some of them. As I learn more about life, healing, energy and the importance of making wise choices, I do suppose it all plays a factor. I do know it's not all just a matter of luck; it's a combination of so many things. I don't think it's luck that I choose to get out of bed early each morning to align myself and create a sacred space. I believe it's a combination of luck, birth order, astrological signs, how my Mom felt when she was carrying me, how I entered the world, life situations, relationships, a small part genetics. You know, you can give two people all the same opportunities and gifts, and the outcome will be completely different. There are unseen factors like passion, drive, courage, inner strength, and mental health, only to name a few. Even genetics are playing less and less of a role in a person's overall health outcome. John told me about this book he's reading called Being Mortal, and it says even the length of time which your parents live only has 3% impact on ultimately how long you live.

So, back to my morning routine. Lately, I've been enjoying my 'Priestess Aura Spray' created by Melissa. I find grounding in saying the beautiful prayer that she created with this spray. Typically, my writing had been daily gratitudes and prayers, and now it's taken a sharp detour to writing my memoir. Once I've journaled and written down everything that's in my heart, I've been listening to my piano creations while doing some morning yoga. I only stretch for about ten minutes, always starting in child's pose, gently rubbing my third eye side to side on my mat. It's so calming to me. Sofi sits cuddled up beside me and sleeps. Once I'm done a good stretch, I do ten minutes of Mandarin on Duolingo. I've been learning Mandarin for almost 160 days now. Now, that's a tough language to learn. All of this takes me to about 7:35 a.m. and then I usually start to hear pitter patters—John will have woken up the kids, or else they will have woken up on their own. I'll have a quick really hot shower, about ten minutes, then crank it absolutely FREEZING cold for about a minute. John has started with the cold shower thing, too, and it feels so good to have the shock of that cold water first thing in the morning. We didn't know this, but it's actually called *The Wim Hof Method*. Now, that book is an amazing read on healing.

Actually, now that I'm here and have the time, I'll Google the benefits. Side note, I do realize you can find *ANYTHING* online to support your newest and greatest stupidest idea... blast of cold water at the end of your shower helps... drum roll, please:

1. Muscle Recovery
2. Improved Blood Circulation
3. Stronger Immune System
4. Depression Treatment
5. Metabolic Boost

Let's just pretend I know what that last one is... ha, ha, ha, ha.

Anyways, I have just felt overall better, which is a good thing. Do you know how this all came about? It was the end of April and the boys and I were in the hot tub, and we were watching the ice chunks floating around, melting in our pool. In John's opinion, the ice wasn't melting fast enough. Oh my gosh, that's so John. He was annoyed because the pool people were supposed to come the next day, and the pool wasn't going to be ready for them. Well, I was in my swimsuit and wanted to help him out and said, "Want me to go in and throw some ice chunks outta the pool?"

He said, "Oh yeah, I'm so sure."

Oh, I took that as a challenge. Out of the hot tub I came, and went into the pool to throw huge, thick chunks of ice out. Smash, crash—I would toss them onto the concrete. It reminded me of the sound of the glaciers falling into the ocean while I was performing on the cruise ship. We would visit Glacier Bay once a week, and it was breathtaking watching the glaciers crash into the depths of the water. John captured my nonsense on video to send to our family because it looked so ridiculous. Personally, it felt extremely exhilarating. John's caption ideas were: "Pool's ready!" or "How's this for an icebreaker?"

I watched the clip, it made me laugh, and posted it on my

social media. Before I knew it, people were messaging me telling me about the health benefits of "cold plunging," and then another colleague phoned and said she loves cold plunging and the entire Nordic Spa experience is unreal. She said in her opinion, one of the best ones in the country was in Winnipeg, Manitoba and that John and I should try it out sometime. Hilarious, as usual, I just happened to be going to Winnipeg for Bella's swim competition in two weeks. What are the chances? I'd say pretty good. Coincidence? Mhm, mhm... uh, uh... saying something is a coincidence over and over erases all the magic. Anyway, that takes me to about 7:50 a.m. I'm thinking of titles again: *Almost Forty, First Forty, Forty Stories, Goodbye Thirties, Slowly Forty, Turning Forty, Starting at Forty, In it at Forty, This is Forty, Seventy-Four Days Until Forty, Sneaking Up on Forty, The First Forty, Finding Forty*... That's like, ahh... that almost feels like ahh... oh yeah, finding me... yeah, *Remembering Forty, There Goes Forty, Here Comes Forty*, there... these are getting quite dramatic... *There Goes Forty, Here Comes Forty, Fast Forward to Forty*. I don't know why those voices came, but they did.

Oh, and as I'm telling you about my routine, I may as well tell you about my space—my most special space: My Closet Sanctuary. What does my closet sanctuary look like, you ask? Some of you may wonder, some of you may not care in the least... in any event, if you're still here with me, let the tour begin. What's your closet look like? I'll show you mine if you show me yours.

As I've mentioned, it's a cozy, intimate space. When you walk through our ensuite, you reach our closet. Our closet shelving is wood. As a realtor, you'd think I'd know what kind of wood it actually is, but I don't. I'm guessing it's a maple or a walnut. It's got a grainy look to it. In fact, when we first took possession of our house, I didn't really like the look of the dark, grainy wood, but it's grown on me.

We have two beautiful lights dripping in sparkly crystals hanging from the ceiling. Looking up at them makes me wish they repeated somewhere else in our house because they're that beautiful. They're actually *too* beautiful for our closet. Right when you walk into our closet, smack in the middle, the big, dark grainy cabinet has two doors on them with four drawers below. Those drawers belong to John—it works as his armoire. The second one is absolutely stuffed with fifty-plus of John's precious T-shirts that he prides himself on still having. He tells me about where he got this one, where he got that one, the year, the situation, who his friends were in that exact moment of time. I actually had a hissy fit not too long ago, and plunked all his prized T-shirts onto our closet sanctuary floor and asked him to please go through them. The drawer actually couldn't physically close. He insisted it was the way the T-shirts were stuffed in the drawer. Of course, John, it has nothing to do with the fact that there's fifty-plus of them. Reluctantly, he went through them. He thought he did really well—he parted with four... four. I repeat... four. Four that were so worn that you not only couldn't donate them, you could actually see right through them. They were so old, they were as soft as a baby's bum. In his defense, his T-shirts do get worn. The kids often wear one of his T-shirts to bed, the girls more often than the boys. Actually, one night, all four of them went to bed with one of his T-shirts on. I'll admit it, it was pretty sweet.

Back to the closet, when you first walk in and look to the right, there is a section for my dresses and long gowns. I have quite a few gowns from my performing days. As I look at them, I'm kicking myself because when we lived in our Collins House, we had no room for my gowns in our closet there, so I stashed them in one of the kids' closets. When we moved to our rental, I decided I didn't need all of them and sent them to Community Living. Ahh, I miss my puffy, mauve-coloured princess dress. Just sayin'.

Stuff.

The collecting of stuff is completely overwhelming. When I go to homes where the owners have lived forty to sixty-five years, you can't believe the amount of stuff people collect. They don't mean to; it's just the accumulation as the years go by. By the time people need to declutter and go through their things, I can see the sheer horror on their faces. The thought of it is so overwhelming for them.

You know what they say about moving? Three moves are as good as a fire.

Back to our closet.

To the left of the cabinets are four open shelves with two on the top, two on the bottom. I can hang my shirts, sweaters, scarves—anything I want. Right in front of me, I've been sitting on my yoga mat staring at hanging pants, a few skirts and some cardigans.

The bottom shelf has my two journals tucked in the corner, my Aura Spray, two pens and my candles.

I learned a little secret from my stylish friend Colleen; no matter how big or how small your closet is, keep it totally organized and decluttered. Doing so will bring clarity to your life.

She recommends one item in—one item out. When you buy an item and bring it home, always take a few items out and give them to somebody who needs them. Also, get rid of any and all plastic and wire hangers—they look terrible.

Go to Costco, treat yourself to those lovely black, velvety hangers and hang all of your items so that they are facing the same direction, and you can colour coordinate if you wish. Consider this the organizing your closet part of my story. Go ahead, try it. I dare you.

Don't worry. At first, I thought this was silly, too, but when babysitter Camille seconded the motion, I was convinced. I love it now because you can actually see everything in the closet, and it feels good when my personal items are in order, especially when, at times, my real life feels completely opposite.

Behind me are all of John's jeans, other pants, dress shirts, ties, suits and a few jerseys.

And this concludes our tour.

CHAPTER NINE
BLESSED

June 1, 2022
8:54 a.m.

Yesterday was a very busy day. We listed two lovely properties around the million-dollar mark, and my phone was off the hook busy, even at that price range. It's currently a very hot market here in Saskatoon. I went to bed with two accepted offers, but I have to admit, I feel exhausted. Whenever the market is hot like this, it's really challenging for the buyers and the buyer's agents. Properties hit the market, and then everyone is in a scramble to view it. The stakes feel high.

Just had a chat with Lee. He reminded me that we are so blessed to have a thriving business and helped me notice the positives. We were saying that our real estate business is growing, and it's wonderful because we don't even have to do much advertising anymore. We are getting to the point where it's repeat clients and referrals as well as word of mouth. It's wonderful. We still have the ability to work with our own schedules; help manage our families when they need us most and earn money. I find I love it most of the time, but I also feel overwhelmed by it. There is a lot of juggling involved—right now we are dealing with buyers, sellers, new builds, possessions, multiple offers, and I admit it, I'm feeling my anxiety. I don't talk a whole lot about it because I really do a lot of self-care to manage it, and I know it's stupid, but I feel a bit of shame that I do the work and still feel crappy sometimes.

When Lee called, I had a big cry. It helped me process some of my pain.

I also turned to my piano compositions, which helps soothe my soul. I'm hoping I can get my ten compositions out into the world by the fall. Sometimes I set goals that are pretty tricky to attain, but if I didn't set them, I don't think I'd complete them. Well, I'm going to stop writing now because I feel like I'm pushing a cart uphill. My breathing is shallow, and I'm noticing my headache a bit, my plate is obviously too full. I'm feeling unsupported. I'm almost forty, and I feel like I need my Mom and Dad again, and all I want is how it used to be. They were together, strong and healthy, always ensuring me that everything would be okay.

I think of my Dad sitting alone in his chair at the care home, and it breaks my heart. Those were tough, tough times, watching him slip away. There wasn't a thing any of us could do about it. Such a strong, handsome, intelligent, funny, driven guy... and it all ended up like that. I think that's why I have such a different outlook on life. When you watch someone you love die, everything changes. I'm not even close to who I was five years ago, three years ago, a year ago, six months ago. People do change. Everything changes. It's the only sure thing in life.

I still feel silly writing this memoir. Maybe I've added a

bunch of unnecessary stress to my life by doing it, but I want our kids to have something to read and to enjoy one day. No doubt, I'll want to read this, too, when I'm older and relive it a bit. The kids will say, "Neat, this is what Mom was like right before she turned forty." I won't be the same person when I'm fifty, or sixty, so it'll be fun to reflect and catch these days, seventy-four to be precise.

Today, my beautiful Momma turns seventy. We are pretty much thirty years apart. I often wonder what she was like when she was turning forty. We do have videos, but they're tricky to watch now because they're VHS, and the machines are starting to become obsolete. Again, change... see there's no escaping it. Okay, I'm going to go celebrate my Momma. Bye for now.

CHAPTER TEN
SENDING A FOX

June 2, 2022
6:28 a.m.

Yesterday started out a bit rough. I'm finding the transactions with accepted offers to be added pressure. In this market, it's not unusual to have accepted backup offers. It's double the paperwork, negotiating, headaches—double of everything, except the pay. You have to be very careful not to sell the same house twice, so being diligent in the wording on the contracts is a must. When you think about it, at this current moment in time, any agent can be dealing with forty-plus people at any given time, whether it's listings, buyers, new builds, possession, custom builds, referrals in other cities. Then, of course, there's the additional weight of dealing with the other agents, our conveyance officers, our own employees, people who put up the signs, home inspectors, mortgage specialists, bankers, house cleaners, carpet cleaners, extended family members out of the country, having an opinion on selling their parents' house as well.

I can remember being busy like this a few years into real estate, and I also remember that was one of the most challenging times of my life. There was no balance. Bella and Millie would have been 5 and 3 years old. I was run ragged, and John and I were fighting and arguing. We were both exhausted and couldn't keep up. I can remember my hands trembling and running to back-to-back open houses, meeting so many people, delivering postcards and attending weekly coaching classes to try and build my new business. I was drinking a fair amount, more than I would like to admit, just trying to escape, relax, cope, which of course was doing the complete opposite. So, needless to say, I don't look back on those days as a very peaceful time in my life. Even writing this makes my stomach ache. It was more of a volatile time for me personally. We had young kids, my new business, and I was totally consumed in the ego of it all. Looking back, I feel like that was the route I had to go at first to get my footing, get settled into the industry, and learn from my mistakes. I figured out pretty quickly that if I wanted longevity, I had to make some different choices. It's a wonderful industry, but if you get totally addicted to it, everything important in your life will fall apart.

After ten years in the business, now, I also feel like I have more personal boundaries, I'm asking the right questions, and I get to work and choose the people I connect with.

I often start adventures and about halfway through, maybe two weeks in—I think, what was I thinking? The reason I have to keep writing is because of the signs. My angels don't just wave quiet little signs in the air, for me, they literally take a frying pan, wind up and smack me in the face. For example, the evening before my Mom's birthday, I picked up Walt after school. It was only Walty and I in the car, and he asked me if we could go to

Gramma's house. He doesn't always ask for this, so I phoned Momma to see if it would be okay if she had a little visitor for a bit? She said yes, so I dropped him off. After I left, apparently, Walt started having a conversation about Papa. Out of nowhere, Walt said something like, "I wish I heard Papa's voice."

So, here I am in the middle of writing this secret memoir, and of course, been wondering about how I can add my music and my voice, you know, so that our kids can always have a keepsake of our lives. Then Mom calls and tells me what Walt said about Papa's voice. Lordy... I know right away—frying pan, in my face. *This* has to be an audiobook, got it!

Later that evening, my Mom called and said something else happened. She has this basket by the blue chair in the corner of the living room. Over the years, she has collected her greeting cards there, and when Walt was over, he had been playing with the cards.

Mom said, "I can't believe it! Dad gave me a birthday card."

Mom was about to call 'er a night, and there was one card left on the living room floor. She went over, picked it up, looked at it, and on the front it said,

> To My Wife:
>
> Seeing you smile is about my favourite thing in the world. I hope this year is full of surprises and good times for us that will bring that light to your eyes that just makes my heart miss a beat.

When she opened it up, it said, in his handwriting:

When she called and told me, we both cried. I know Dad is with us, there is no doubt. Mom hadn't been feeling him near as much as she'd like, so that card was a massive sign.

Here's another good one. Mom and her sister, Myrna, affectionately known as "Moomoo", were talking about Dad one day after he passed away. Mom was talking about how she notices this mourning dove showing up in her life, and she knows it's a sign that Dad is near. The dove appeared the morning of Mom and Dad's anniversary in July, a month or so after Dad had passed away in June. She always knows when her mourning dove is near. Even though Mom doesn't remember having this conversation, she told Moomoo, "If my dove shows up on my birthday, then I'll really know Peter is with us."

Fast forward months later, Moomoo was here in Saskatoon to celebrate Momma's seventieth birthday. Moomoo was doing her morning prayers and gratitudes and asked in her heart for Peter to be with Wanda on her special day. The moment she said that, she heard the distant cooing of, you guessed it, Mom's mourning dove. Moomoo rushed upstairs to tell Momma, and they both saw the dove was sitting in her backyard. And, there he sat, I bet the dove was saying: "Happy Birthday, Toots"— that's what Dad used to call her.

Another sign, then that same morning, Gigi wasn't feeling too well, and Moomoo took her into the Mediclinic to get a prescription. When they went to leave, the vehicle wouldn't start. Moomoo had just travelled from Calgary to Saskatoon in their lovely Acura with no problems whatsoever, then suddenly, the dash of their vehicle was flashing, and it wouldn't start. Then, we went to meet for lunch at a wonderful Greek Restaurant called Mano's, and on the way, Amy saw a rabbit. We all had a beautiful lunch, talking about how Dad is always showing up in the most magical ways, especially on Mom's birthday. We even had a nice visit with the owner, Manoli, who came to check on us and to remind us to order more because John was paying the bill—that made us all laugh. We talked about life and the loss of his first wife, and he just reminded us to make the most of every single day. It was so nice to connect with him. After we ate our delicious food, I made my way home, practiced some piano and then went to a home inspection. Guess who ran across the street on my way to Stonebridge—and that's the area where Dad's care home was located... that's right, you guessed it, Peter Rabbit... too funny. After that, I went to pick up some ice cream treats and a "Happy 70th" birthday log from Dairy Queen for Mom's big weekend, and the total came to exactly $70 dollars—when does that actually ever happen? We went over to Mom's, took them their treats, Millie jumped out of the shower and ran over to Grandma's in her pj's, and brought Sofi puppy to meet us. As we were reflecting on the entire day, talking about Mom's birthday, all the magic, Dad, family, work—just enjoying each other's company, I was leaving, and wanted to turn on the light at the front door nook. That's where Dad's ashes are. They're in a beautiful marble heart, he's in half, and Mom will be in the other side. Side note: The grandkids all argue about who's going to get Grandma's and Papa's ashes at their house when they grow up.

Anyway, I went to turn on the light right before we left and nothing, it wouldn't turn on. Can you believe it? All the stuff that was happening on that day. It was another sign. I couldn't believe it all. Then when we went to leave, as we walked out the front door, we saw there was a fox running across the street. I had never seen a fox in the city like that. The kids started to run towards it, thinking it was a dog to say hello to. He kinda looked like he was lurking. So, I instinctively yelled at them to come back and get into the car, all the while scaring the crap outta them. Millie said she almost jumped a mile. A fox in the city, on Mom's birthday.

When we got home, we immediately looked up to see what a fox sighting meant spiritually and found this: *Cleverness, Independence, Playfulness, Mischievousness, Beauty, Protection,* and *Good Luck.*

Oh, my gosh. I'm looking back at yesterday's entry at 8:54 a.m., and I wrote that my Dad was: *Strong, Handsome, Intelligent, Funny, Driven.* Look at the set of words again. I said, my Dad was strong. The fox was a sign of *protection.* I said my dad was *handsome.* The fox was a sign of *beauty.* I said my Dad was *intelligent.* The fox was a sign of *cleverness.* I said my Dad was *funny.* The fox was a sign of *playfulness.* I said my Dad was *driven.* It said the fox was a sign of *independence.* I was missing two adjectives on how I would describe my Dad the day before: *Mischievous* and *good luck.* I'd like to think our mischievous dad sent my Mom a fox on her birthday to bring her good luck. Isn't that crazy?

John just walked in and said, "You're journaling this whole time?" Then he peeked over my shoulder and started laughing because he just read that sentence... he followed up with, "Ooooh, are you telling your journal on me?" Can you imagine if he actually knew what I was up to. Back to the fox, I seriously had to put down my pen for a moment and look at that again. Oh my God, how do I tell my Mom about this fox adventure without telling her I'm writing a memoir? Ugh. Maybe I can just sit with it or merely just mention I've been journaling. No, I can't tell Mom. I can't tell anyone. My heart is racing; you can't make this magic up. I'm not even kidding you; I told you already, I lack imagination. This is just the truth. Those are the facts. Honestly, the more magic I see, the more there actually is.

Okay, I'm going to buy a Surface or something today so that I can start typing my entries. My hand is getting so tired, and I have two writing bumps on my finger. This is just a little secret for now, but all this magic has to be shared. I would be doing a disservice not sharing all these wonderful stories of love, hope and faith. Dad, I love that you're with us, and I am so grateful you're giving me the courage to share my heart with whomever needs it most.

P.S. I just picked up my angel card as I was getting ready for the day. Walked over in my bra and jeans to my stack of cards on our dresser and simply said, "Dad, please be with me today in the one card I pick."

You'll never guess.

Magic—It says, "Magic has a way of touching the heart and drawing power from the soul."

I'm not even kidding. I couldn't make this all up even if I tried.

I told you, it's unbelievable, but anyone who knows me— knows it's believable. I'm just now writing some of my experiences down because there's no chance I could ever remember all of this magic.

Okay, I'm off to surprise Walt's teachers with a coffee.

Ripple effect.

CHAPTER ELEVEN
I AM WRITING A BOOK!

June 3, 2022
6:32 a.m.

Well, the magic burst, or so I thought.

Mom messaged me, bright and early, and said, "Well, we thought the fox last night didn't look real heclthy." Ahh…

Here I am writing my story and my magical takes on our fox sighting and everything it represented, holding on so tightly to all hope I felt. My heart sank. I went over to Mom's, and she, Gigi, Moomoo and I were sitting around the kitchen table talking about Dad and all of the magic from her birthday. It really was unbelievably stacked with magic. I was feeling emotional about everything, especially with Dad's one-year anniversary right around the corner. I told them about my journaling and what I wrote about Dad on Mom's actual birthday, the adjectives I wrote about him, the magic of it all. Talked about the day, the signs from Mother Nature, the vehicle not starting, the dollar amount from DQ, the light not working where Dad's ashes were, the thing I found online that completely aligned with what I wrote about Dad, the day before and then out of nowhere Auntie Moomoo said, "You should write a book!"

Mic drop.

Two things about me that you're learning: We've already determined that I have very little to no imagination, and the second thing is that I'm a crappy liar. That's just the truth. I actually didn't know that people just lied. I honestly trusted most things people told me—you can even ask John. I didn't grow up with many experiences of people not telling me the truth, so in my later years, when I experienced untruths, I was surprised by it.

Right after Moomoo said that, my Mom chimed in, "Oh yeah, what... in *all* of her spare time."

I couldn't *not* respond and blurted out, "I *am* writing a book!"

And Mom said, wait for it, "What about?"

Are.you.kidding.me, Mom?

"About this. About life. About this moment in time. About the magic." Crying, I said, "About healing!"

I told them how I devoured Nana's book, laughing and enjoying every page. I wanted to do the same for our children. I wanted to share my little secrets and my journey. So, my secret book now has three more people who know about it. I really wasn't planning to tell a soul. I told mi-ladies that I knew the nudge came to me for a reason and I've been getting validations EVERYWHERE, so many, that I couldn't deny it. We laughed and cried—two of my favourite things to do with people I love the most. Then Auntie Moomoo said, "Well, maybe my friend Carla will be able to help point you in the next direction when you're done."

I had totally forgotten that one of Moomoo's best friends is Author C.J. Carmichael. Well, I guess there's a reason I spilled the beans, again. There's a reason for every-thing. I had told them about my idea of creating an au-diobook and weaving my songs and music throughout it, basically sharing my life in words and song. My Auntie Myrna said, "Well, you sure are entertaining."

I think my Momma worries that I want to do too much, but all I do is listen to my heart. I just want to tap into things that light me up. I want to surround myself with people who I feel good around. It's really not that com-plicated. I didn't want to tell a soul about this—and now a few souls know. What I thought was a bad thing this morning—Mom texting about the sad looking fox—end-ed up being a really wonderful thing because of my con-versation with Mom, Moomoo and Gigi. Who knew?

Side note: I looked at C.J.'s Instagram, and guess what I saw. It was a picture of her smiling and holding up someone else's book called *Flirting with 50*. I took it as a sign, wouldn't you?

Okay, another thought. I want to be as efficient as possible with my time. After I told the ladies about my morning writings, Moomoo also said I should really think about getting a small tablet and a comfortable place to type. Ahh... Maybe I will, we'll see. I'd miss my yoga mat, and the last thing I want to do is turn this into a job. I'll think about it, though, because writing this in my journal and then transcribing it onto a computer will be a huge amount of work. This may have been a divine bean spill-ing and end up saving me hours of work. On the other hand, though, this is why I don't want to tell many more people about what I'm up to because, like John says, people are like belly buttons. No, no, that's not it. Opinions are like belly buttons, everybody has one, right?

People's opinions usually come from a good place, but they can also come from so many other different places. Their opinions are often formed by their own life experiences, their perceptions of reality, their own personal childhood traumas, their fears, their religion, their education, workplace, family values, the media, social media, their peers and friends, parents, etc. The list can go on and on. Again, that's why one of my strongest messages is—remember, we must listen to our own hearts and be true to ourselves. No one knows you like you know yourself. Be sure not to be reckless and abandon yourself; if you follow this way of being, everything will just magically fall into place.

> *Finally, you're home now, time to take a break.*
> *Throw a couple logs on and start a fire by the lake.*
> *Suddenly it's peaceful, baby, you can breathe...*
> *Well, I have a thought, you should be you, and I will be me.*
>
> *No matter how your day was, no matter how the time flies...*
> *You never seem to be far, always crossin' my mind.*
> *Sitting by the fire, staring at the skyline.*
> *Get over here, you're my only one, baby you're mine.*
>
> *The sun is setting, now the moon is bright.*
> *The stars aligning, tuck the kids in tight.*
> *When I look into your eyes, baby all I see.*
> *Pour us some wine, you should be you and I will be me.*
>
> *No matter how your day was, no matter how the time flies...*
> *You never seem to be far, always crossin' my mind.*
> *Sitting by the fire, staring at the skyline.*
> *Get over here, you're my only one, baby, you're mine.*
>
> Elly Thorn, 'You Should Be You'

CHAPTER TWELVE
A BUMP iN THE RoAD

June 4, 2022
11:58 a.m.

Well, that was a crap morning. Slept in, had a quick little chat with John as he was so excited to run off to pick up our coffees and then have our family watch Millie play soccer in the park behind our house. Out of nowhere, I had competing offers on a condo that I had listed a while back. So odd how sometimes it doesn't sell, doesn't sell—and then two buyers want it at the exact same time. Anyway, as I was talking to one of those agents, John called. John called again. I didn't answer. Then he sent a simple text: "Call me."

Ahh... oh, that's unusual.

I called him back and he said, "I've been in an accident." I asked if he was okay and if anyone else was hurt? And, he said he was okay and no one was hurt. Hallelujah. Now, what happened? So, John was driving and fussing with his phone trying to connect his music to Apple Play.

And, it was saying on the dashboard that it was connected but only playing through his phone. He looked
down to fiddle around with it and in a split second, he
hit a boulevard and a sign at a crosswalk. Distracted
driving is the worst.

So, that was my morning. It's now afternoon, and we
are all going to head to the mall to pick out new outfits for our family photos for Mom's backyard birthday
celebration, in a few hours. Oh, and to top it off, Mom's
stomach has been off all day. Millie's mad about John
missing her soccer game. She got a shutout because
she was playing keeper. I'm feeling anxious and tired, no
meditation, my Mercedes is smashed and the front two
tires blown, and now, we have to go shopping. I'll find
myself a dark salted caramel and decaf coffee, have the
family photos and guess what? I'll post them on Instagram to celebrate a milestone birthday with smiles, fun,
and togetherness, and people will have no idea what our
morning was really like. That's why I want to share my
stories and my life, because I know what's behind the
picture holds far more substance. I'm finding more and
more that the real beauty is found in the journey, the
messes and everything else in between.

> *I think it's harder, as I grow up, as I show up.*
> *I'm thinking too often, creating nonsense.*
> *Time to notice my mind.*
> *In this world I am living, caught in the web of doing.*
> *And the choices I'm making—*
> *'cause I think I've got time.*
> *I think I've got time...*
> *I think I've got time...*
>
> *Maybe I'm different, might be a misfit.*
> *Maybe I don't care.*
> *I feel the pulsing, watch people walking—going nowhere.*
> *In this world, I am living, caught in the web of doing.*
> *And the choices I'm making—'cause I think I've got time.*

I think I've got time... I think I've got time...
>Ellen Nasser, 'I Think I've Got Time' [unreleased version]

97

CHAPTER THIRTEEN

OF ALL THE SONGS IN THE WORLD

June 5, 2022
7:58 a.m.

I think it's safe to say the kids have had a wonderful weekend of family, soccer, cousins, Grandma's birthday, and this morning Bella's swim banquet. John is grabbing us a Starbucks and said he'll try again. He said yesterday was obviously a flop. I got curious and I asked John what song was he trying to listen to. Pause. He answered quietly, "I... I don't know." Pause... Crickets... then he mumbled, *"The Greatest Showman!"*

Of all the songs in the world, I wouldn't have pictured John driving around Saturday morning, by himself, listening to 'Come Alive' from *The Greatest Showman*. I'm still laughing. I can just picture him driving along, trying to crank his tunes and pumping his fist to this awesome soundtrack. Years ago, a lovely owner at Modo Yoga recommended that I listen to this soundtrack. It's so awesome!

Back to the distracted driving, my sister-in-law Kriti said if we all just take that extra moment to set up our music, navigation and connect our device, we would all be better off. She's 100% right. If a message is that important, ask your co-pilot to check it and read it out loud, but let's be real—nothing is that important. Your phone can wait. I'm saying this as much to myself as to anyone else; the phones are getting to be a filthy habit.

> *Now imagine, if you woke up, and everything had changed.*
> *Now imagine, if you woke up—could you remain the same?*
> *Now imagine, won't you imagine—could you stand the pain?*
>
> Ellen Kolenick, 'Imagine If You Woke Up'

Our friend and neighbour Shannon saw John's accident and phoned to check in. She said she was just telling her teenaged kids that it only takes a split second of not paying attention, and you could ruin the rest of your life or even someone else's. You know, we all need to disconnect and reconnect. I remind our kids and myself, phones should never take the priority of a real-life interaction, but they do. I'm as guilty as anyone. They're becoming a real addiction.

Millie just walked in fully decked out in her soccer gear saying, "Why is Sofi in such a great mood these days?" Petting her belly and gritting her teeth.

I answered, "Just because she loves life so much."

Millie said, "I think she especially loves summer."

I think we all do. That was an exceptionally long winter. My spirit always lifts with the weather. Yes, I love the change in the four seasons, but I'm really getting over the extremes and length of it. I'm actually getting tired of extremes in general. I used to live my life so up and down. I still feel the ups and downs, but I am more aware of it. I'm also noticing that I can let go of many things now because I know I can't control them. I know my cranial sacral sessions and energy healings over the years have added greatly to the balancing of my nervous system. I can remember when a spiritual coach of mine, Tara Preston, she introduced the idea of a morning power hour, and I thought, "Is she for real?" Who has time for that? It's funny, now I'm hooked, and it's often the most beautiful parts of my day. All a person has to do is go to bed an hour sooner and get up an hour earlier. The benefits in every aspect of your life will be undeniable. It'll probably suck for the first week or two, but it's so worth it.

John and I went on this twenty-eight-day clean-eating cleanse about nine years ago, and one of the things we had to let go of was coffee.

John said, "Nuh-uh." He would join me, but he needed to have his two cups of coffee a day. I told him not to do it then because I really wanted to do it right. We cleaned our system of sugar, gluten, dairy, popcorn, corn and caffeine. We never felt better, and neither one of us ever went back to caffeinated coffee. Even though John only drank two cups of coffee a day, he said he often craved it, felt a bit shaky, was sweaty and irritable. Now, he sleeps so much better, and his sweats are nonexistent. It's crazy to think that made such a big shift in our lives. Now we've added green tea, it's even better. Our morning beverage is two cups of green tea, and then often a decaf at work. I'll also treat myself a couple times a week to a chai half-sweet latte with coconut milk.

Okay, John just walked in and surprised me with a tea and had to make fun of me and said, "Oh Journal, John just walked in and is disturbing me again." He's such an ass. He honestly has no idea that I'm writing my memoir. He'd say that I'm crazy. Well, he's definitely got the first two letters right—I am "C....R..."

I'm creative.

I can remember driving somewhere with John's Dad, and it was just he and I. Now that I'm reminiscing, I think it might have been the time where music Professor Dean and I (mostly Dean) made a song of one of Kay's poems and performed it with a choir. I'm guessing we were driving to one of those meetings together. Anyway, I can remember Kay saying something along the line of "never stop creating, when you stop creating, you'll die."

Lee stopped by our music room and just poked his head in and said, "I wonder how many new pathways your brain is creating while playing that music."

Wow, music is medicine.

My goodness, what magical words to say to someone.

Of course, that's the reason I choose to take piano lessons, learn Mandarin, brush my teeth with the opposite hand, let the kids skip school sometimes, cross my legs with the other leg on top. That's why I make all of these personal choices, for my health, my brain and my journey. And, to have a brother who walks by, listens to me play, stops and says words like those is only more validation that I want to keep surrounding myself with people who fuel my inner fire. I don't want my fire to go out, when it does—it's tough to get it going again.

CHAPTER FOURTEEN
SPENDING TIME WITH DAD

June 7, 2022
6:09 a.m.

*T*his morning is the track and field city finals for Bella and Millie. Bella made it for shot put, and Millie made it for long jump. I'm not sure if they're that excited... Bella more so than Millie only because Bella is more competitive in nature. Millie came home after school one day and said, "Funny thing happened at school today, we had track and field and I was so fast and beating lots of people. I had to go to the bathroom and was holding it and holding it, and I finally got a chance to go. When I came back, they had run the finals and I had missed them."

Ahh... I naturally said, "Millie, are you kidding me?"

I felt annoyed, and mad, and frustrated—like really, come on... how could anyone not notice Millie was in the washroom and just continue the race? I noticed my ego, my disappointment, my inability to roll with what is. Millie, at the other end of the kitchen island, obviously noticing all of this in me, too, smiled and just said, "Mom, it's not like it's the Olympics or something."

Just like that, it was over. I took a step back and noticed it was *MY* pain, *MY* ego and *MY* disappointment. Millie honestly found it kinda entertaining, and after John and I talked about it, we found the humour in it, too. It's not all about me. So, fast forward to this morning, I just looked out the window and saw some blue peeking through the clouds. I'll zip Walt over to his school a bit earlier today and get Sam on the bus. And, I told the girls, John and I will see them compete later this morning. I thank God and Creator that they are strong, healthy, and open-hearted young women—we've already won. Track and field is just a bonus.

Having our first child, Bella, was such a shock to my system, I couldn't believe how challenging it was to be a new Mom. I expected it would be easy, and it wasn't. People don't really talk about it; it just seems to be something women go through. Some new Moms flourish, and many of us don't. I look back at photos and think I looked like I was doing okay, but I really wasn't. When Bella was 13 months old, we got pregnant with Millie. We were so excited and surprised. We certainly wanted to have two children, but we weren't particularly thriving in those first months of parenthood. When Millie was born, she was a ball of gold and pink—born at 3:33 in the morning, the same time as my beautiful sister. Millie loves animals, especially her Sofi, but I know she'd love a big dog. I told her big dogs mean big poops. Mil's a live wire in our house and sometimes drives me crazy—and then when she's not around, everyone in our household comments on how quiet it is and asks where Millie is. Millie loves running around the neighbourhood with friends and asking us to make plans with other families.

One day, I came up with this idea to take the girls out

separately so that they could have some one-on-one time. I thought it would be good for everyone. So, I took Millie to Broadway to get a treat and have a walk. She was four. I was concerned that I hadn't come up with her song yet, who would have ever guessed that this was going to be the moment. I was writing the words on a napkin, the music was playing in the streets, she had ice cream on her face and Millie's song was falling from heaven into my heart and into our date.

She says to John and I sometimes, "Don't worry, I'll be living with you until I'm thirty years old."

We say, "Don't worry, Millie, you can live with us for as long as you wish." That goes for all of them.

✦ ✦ ✦

We are nearing on the first anniversary of my Dad passing away. I had to tell Diana yesterday. I was feeling on a verge of a breakdown and had to tell her why I have been distant lately. With Momma's birthday coinciding with the busiest real estate week of our lives, and of course, our few family ups and downs, I was absolutely drained. I'm also finding my Level Six piano exam to be stressful. I had my lesson yesterday, still struggling with finding the C# (Sharp) Minor Melodic Scale, C# (Sharp) Minor Harmonic Scale, and also the B Minor Melodic/Harmonic Scales. In theory, I know what they are, but you know when you kinda know something and it hasn't quite sunk in yet? That's where I'm at. Martin has taught me many valuable lessons. He honestly says, if you don't put time and effort into practicing your piano, you will not get the results. Simple as that. And, if you don't take the time to learn something, you won't know it.

I can remember starting lessons with him in 2019, and while I could play chords well enough to write a song, my fingers couldn't even play a C major scale. I remember he said, "Of course, there's an element of talent, but most of all, if you have the drive to do something and show up every day and do it, you will get good at it." He has been such a gift in my life. Piano has been such a gift in my life. To play and sing, to heal and write. Cry and release. And, all whenever I want. This piano is mine, in our home, and I am able to create space to get into my beautiful music room one hour a day. No one can take that away from me. I can't blame anyone if I can't get there; it's mine. Martin's funny, too—I think I'm drawn to funny people. I love not taking life too seriously.

I know, I know—I was blabbing about being so drained and what about shifting my language from I'm drained to I'm motivated. You know why I haven't? Sometimes a person has to sit with their crap and feel crappy. I am totally convinced. I am all for shifting and moving into a new, higher vibrational energy any chance I can get, but there are times when the best thing to do is just sit with it all. When I'm feeling sad and victimized, I know the stories that want to come and float through my mind. When I feel like this, I think about, you know, the handful of guys who dumped me, a comment that stung, that was said by someone I love, I think about Dad passing away, I watch the stories turn into more. And the more, and the more... I sit with them, it shapes my morning, and my afternoon and my days, sometimes my week. I make up stories of what I could have done, what I could have said, what they should have done, what they should have said. I wrote this song after Dad passed away—almost a year ago. I was feeling heartbroken, and I actually didn't even intend to write it about Dad. It was a combination of a few things going on in my life.

Last night, Mom came along to keep me company to show a townhouse. We just cruised in Dad's car. It's hard to believe that John crashed my car. There were no rentals covered by insurance, so he asked Mom if we could just borrow Dad's car until mine was fixed. I don't think I had ever driven Dad's birthday car in my life, and now, I'll be driving it for a few weeks. Dad's always there when I need him most. I just can't believe it's been a year since he's been gone. The way it unfolded was magical and yet unexplainable. It was actually a year ago when he stopped eating and just started to slip away. He had been choking a lot when he ate, so Mom guessed he aspirated at some point, causing the pneumonia. His disease had slowed everything down. All of our family members got to be there with him to say their goodbyes.

Mom had him all snuggled up in his bed, wrapped up in his special blankets with all of our faces and photos on them. He looked so peaceful and so content. The nurses were making sure Dad was comfortable. He was peacefully laying in his bed, no doubt listening to all the comings and goings, our laughter, singing and joking coming from his living room and outside his window. The nursing staff were so full of love and cared for "The Judge" so much. At one point, they let us bring the piano in from the dining room, and we played, and sang, laughed and cried.

Honestly, we had so much fun at his bedside as he was slipping away. What a gift.

The nurses couldn't believe he kept holding on. Dad was so comfy laying there, enjoying the reunion, communion and togetherness with all of us who loved him more than anything—you know, *HIS* circus.

Finally, on the Saturday, John decided he was going to make a big steak dinner and feed and host our family.

That's the way John shows his love. He joked that the smell of Dad's favourite meal from our house to the care home would wisp him away. Dad was still with us, though. By now, it was day five with no food or drink for Dad. Mom phoned around 3 p.m., and it sounded like he was going to pass away. I lit a candle and said goodbye for what felt like the 100th time, then I called Momma, and he still hadn't passed away.

What the heck? We couldn't believe it. He just kept holding on.

She called a couple of hours later and told us that he was still with us. Mom and Amy were at the care home, and Mom thought if I wanted to come, maybe I should come sooner than later. I actually didn't really feel the need to be there when he passed away. In fact, I really didn't think I was going to be. Mom and Amy spent a couple of nights at the care home, and so did Danny. We were all just tag-teaming around the clock. I was okay with not being there in the actual moment. Time kept passing by, and I decided I should go back. Thinking that Mom and Amy would be hungry, I stopped at Pressed Sandwiches, and got sandwiches in Stonebridge, dawdled a bit, decided to order some smoothies as well. Paid for it and left. Then I decided to pick up some coffees, so I drove through the drive-through, ordering our drinks, fully believing Dad would have passed away by the time I got there. Just writing this is making my body shake a little. You know what, I think I do have some more work to do. I'm still processing all of this. I know it's been a year, but it's still only been a year.

Part of why I've been called to write this is likely because it will be part of my healing journey. When I told Diana that I was writing this book—this memoir, she said journaling is one of the best ways to work through traumas and heartaches.

I got to the care home with all my treats in hand and walked up to Dad's window, and was certain he had died. Mom said, "No" (she shook her head), and said, "He's still with us." When you're saying goodbye to someone with a disease, it's the worst (although I don't think there's a good way to say goodbye to anyone you love so dearly). But you are basically saying goodbye to them one small step at a time. In our case, it was almost eight years of farewells.

Goodbye to Dad's work, to his retirement, to his ability to problem solve, to his logic, to his friendships, to his normal day to day, to his hockey team, to his driving, to his independence, to his rationale, goodbye to my parents as a team and as a couple, goodbye to our family as we knew it. I was sick and tired of saying goodbye. But here I was, back at the care home, saying goodbye (again).

Remembering this all makes my eyes fill with tears. Great big, heavy tears. Lips quivering, tears. It's hard, and it's been a massive heartache for all of us. By this point, Mom and Amy looked absolutely bagged, and we talked about what our next course of action would be. Lee came to discuss the plan, and we played piano and sang. Amy and Lee were singing hilarious harmonies, pretending they were singing in our Saltcoats United Church choir. We were watching that epic figure skating fart video and laughing until we cried.

Have you seen it?

I claim, I don't find farts funny—I really don't. Some people love farts, and then there's the rest of us. I don't really like farts. I don't find them funny; I think they're gross. And, saying this makes John laugh even harder because he said, "It's almost like I'm offended by farts." And, I know it's not rational, I know it's a natural part of life, but I really don't find farts that funny. I don't really like the big production of them. I... however... this video is outrageous. When you're sad, do yourself a favour and Google: Riverdance Figure Skating Fart Video. Turn it up, like WAY up. And sync it to your TV—you'll thank me later.

Anyways, we were watching it in Dad's living room, absolutely SPLITTING our guts. Like, once us Kolenick kids start laughing, it's game over for everyone. Wiping the tears from our eyes, the three of us then decided to mute a reality TV show and each of us improvised what the actors were saying—just typing this made me laugh out loud again.

It was *HYSTERICALLY* funny.

It's no wonder Dad didn't want to leave us quite yet. It was like we were all sitting in the family room at home and Dad was laying on his bed in their bedroom with his legs crossed at his ankles and his hands folded on his chest watching his favourite hockey and listening to us kids howl in the other room. Honestly, it felt like I was back at home, like we were all back home where we belonged. By midnight, none of us knew what to do.

Amy and Mom needed sleep, Lee was yawning, and I said, "I would rather stay there tonight than stay the next night, which was Sunday, because of school and lunches the next day." In all honesty, I never really wanted to stay the night—but thought I should at least get one sleepover in. Everyone decided that would work, and I wanted to make sure everyone was okay with my plan.

"I'm going to stay, but I'm just going to sleep on the couch, and I want to make sure that everyone is okay with that? I'm not going to sit up with Dad all night."

I asked Mom, "What should I expect? What could happen?"

I was so scared; I could feel my jaw start to tremble a bit. I don't even know why.

Mom asked me what I was afraid of.

And, I said I didn't know, maybe that Dad would jump up and scare me.

Can you believe it, a thirty-eight-year-old mother of four, scared that her dying Dad was going to jump up and scare her? I had no idea what was going to happen. I was in WAY over my head, and I was scared. And in my defense, Dad always liked to scare us kids. It reminds me of a story, one time when we were little. We were having a sleepover in our family room with our neigh-bours, and we were all getting tucked in for the night, and we heard a ratta tap tap on the window. And, all of us looked at each other and were like: "What the heck was that?"

Then again, tick-tick-tick-tick-tick-tick-tick at the window.

This time we all ran over to the window, looked into the dark, and there was nothing...

We heard it again, tick-tick-tick-tick-tick-tick-tick-tick-tick-tick-tick-tick. This time at another window. We ran to try to look into the pitch-dark night, and there was nothing. We ran to another window and all of us looked out, and then we saw a flashlight under my Dad's chin, and did the biggest "uuhhhh ha ha ha ha ha ha ha" he had ever done. I think we all almost filled our pants.

Anyway, I blame him for me feeling so scared that night. Just joking, but really, I do...

Mom said I have nothing to be afraid of, and Amy re-minded me that if Dad happens to pass away, to remember that I'm not actually leaving him when I leave, his soul is coming with me and that we will be leaving together. It's just his body that I'll be leaving behind. I found such comfort in her words. I asked Mom what will happen, and she said no one really knows, however I may start to notice a change in his breathing. Mom kissed him goodnight and said, "You have a good sleep and I will, too... I love you Peeps."

She was so exhausted; everyone was. Not only exhausted from the long six days, exhausted from the long eight years of caregiving and saying goodbye.

So, I went to lay down on the couch and said it exactly how I said it when I was a child, "Night, Dad, love you—see you in the morning." I honestly had a flashback to being upstairs at our house in Saltcoats. Later, I found out, on their way home, Mom and Amy saw two white bunnies out and about at 1 a.m.

One thing I'll always remember Mom saying to Dad, throughout those few days, was "Who needs any other friends, when you have the best friend in the world?"

CHAPTER FIFTEEN
I GOT DUMPED

June 9, 2022
6:11 a.m.

There are no coincidences, as Jann Arden said in her concert last night, "Good things come from bad things." What a concert! I bought the tickets a couple of months ago to celebrate Mom's birthday week—John has a sister that believes in a week-long celebration, so naturally, I got on board with this idea years and years ago. It's called Birthday Week. I love it! Jann Arden was excellent. I threw it out there to all our women relatives, and Auntie Cheryl and Mom joined me. Jann's interesting... she said she was turned down by every record label in the country, and then they all said no a second time. She's funny, and no doubt it's probably true.

At the show, I ran into two beautiful sisters whose Mom used to sing with my Momma in the choir. I think about them often because their Momma was so vibrant, and they had such a close family like ours. Anyway, their beautiful Momma passed away May 1, 2021, and then our Dad passed away June 13, 2021. They asked if we were planning anything for Dad, for his one-year, but we aren't. I told them I'd been a mess this past week and that somehow, I ended up in his Audi. I have felt his presence every time I sit in his car. I was at TCU (Teachers Credit Union Place), visiting with these two beautiful sisters about life, and loss, and all the in-betweens, watching Jann Arden.

Even though I'm an entertainer like Jann, I don't go to many shows, but I've seen her probably three times. She's real, a bit of a mess, and that's why I like her. I can relate. Honestly, she looked like she was nursing a bad knee or back, or else uncomfortable shoes, and she was just up there doing her thing. Her show was a bit darker than I thought it would be—I was actually going to go for a pick-me-up, but her show was just a reflection of the past two years and the overall state of the collective. It takes me back to the night John and I met at The Granary, the end of August 2006.

I got dumped big-time.

I got dumped hard.

Like heartbroken. Dumped. Is there any other word for it? I think you get the point.

I don't know if there's an easy way to dump someone. It just sucks to lose someone you loved so much, and finding out they don't feel the same. I took it hard. So hard. I remember coming back home to Saskatoon, beyond devastated. I remember the pain being so bad it made my Grandpa tear up. Unrequited love can make the deepest wound. When I love someone, I seem to love them forever. The funny part is, I've loved many people, too. I am a LOVER. It's true. I've always known that. When I first met John, I said, "I'm a great, big heart with two arms and two legs,"—remind me to tell you about that story later.

> *I never knew what a kiss could bring.*
> *Now that you're gone, I regret everything.*
> *So, fly off to your ivory tower.*
> *Inch by inch, hour by hour,*
> *I'll get over you, like you got over me.*
> *Writing songs in the den,*
> *underneath the roof of my parents again.*
> *When I think about our sad goodbye.*
> *You said you loved me.*
> *And then I said that I loved you.*
> *And you mentioned how you'd miss me.*
> *God only knows why I'd miss you, too.*
> *I didn't like you at the start,*
> *I feel the same way as we part.*

> Ellen Kolenick, 'Story of Us'

Summer of 2006, my childhood neighbour Keleah phoned our house and said, "Hi Ellen, I'm putting on this event in Swift Current and we really need some entertainment. Is there any chance you could come to Swift and sing a couple of sets?" It was a request sent from heaven. It gave me a distraction, the music started to heal me, it lit me up to find a band, and off we went to Speedy Creek. Keleah knew I was a performing artist and had just finished studying two years at the Canadian College of Performing Arts and a singing contract with Norwegian Cruise Lines, but she didn't know finding a band was completely out of my wheelhouse.

I could get up on any stage and perform anywhere, anytime, but I most *certainly* didn't have my own show. Not yet at least.

Needless to say, I got a band together and I've been creating music ever since.

I remember playing this song at the pub on Broadway, probably 11 p.m. one Friday, only me and my guitar. I don't know what made me think it was a good idea to share this song, especially in the vulnerable state I was in.

Why do I miss you?
More than I'm willing to admit to...

I don't think I could actually make it fully through the song. There was someone from my high school there, and after my set she came up to me and said something along the line of, "That was a nice song, but I sure hope I don't feel as much pain as that. You sounded so sad."

Why say the things that you do...
yet leaving me is what you chose.
Why does my heart ache?
Come back home, for heaven's sake.
Can't you see it's a big mistake, that we both have made.

Who are you? I used to know you well.
Who are you? I knew you inside out.
Did you change, or was it me? Let's fix what's meant to be...

Ellen Kolenick, 'Miss You'

I was so sad.

The thing with me is that when I feel joy, everyone seems to feel joy around me. I guess that happens when I feel the other stuff, too. I guess I can't have one without the other.

Like Jann Arden said last night—good things come from bad things.

If I wouldn't have gotten dumped, I wouldn't have had these stories.

If I wouldn't have gotten dumped, I wouldn't have created all this beautiful music.

If I wouldn't have gotten dumped, I wouldn't have found John.

If I wouldn't have gotten dumped, I wouldn't have our four angels.

If I wouldn't have gotten dumped, I wouldn't have had all this healing.

If I wouldn't have gotten dumped, I wouldn't have created this magical life.

And if I wouldn't have gotten dumped, I wouldn't have been back in Saskatoon.

Yesterday, I spent most of the morning crying. I talked to one of my dearest friends from Whitehorse, the Fishiest Fish around, and she was a mess, just like me. She laughed and she said she was sorry to say this, but she took great comfort knowing I was falling apart, too, because she always thinks I'm a superwoman. I told her that I always thought she was a superwoman, but I think we need to take it easy on ourselves. John popped into my sanctuary and gave me a kiss goodbye. He's off for a guys' weekend that had been planned for a while, now. He said, "Take it easy on yourself this weekend."

Kind of a dumb thing to say, as I have to juggle Millie's friend's birthday party, Sam's soccer tournament, real estate, two adult birthday gatherings, piano practicing and a partridge in a pear tree. Sometimes we need to hear that from loved ones. Take it easy, drink lots of water, sip on a tea, lay on the couch, watch TV, get a weighted blanket, meditate, read, do nothing. Rest. The dishes can wait a day. Mental health, communication, and recharge are so important. I heard this once: "Listen to your body whisper, so that it doesn't have to scream."

Listen, breathe, welcome the peace in, the stillness. Sit with it.

Oh, I forgot to tell you, fast forward to after school, and the three kids literally come home yelling, laughing, pushing, and shoving each other, walking into the house. The Nasser eagles have landed. Millie came to the couch and said that she's had a really strange day.

Now, another kid asked her if she had a crush on him because he has one on Mil and it's a *really* big crush. Millie was just laughing and telling me about it... Bella standing at the front door, listening to the conversation, and I could see her taking off her backpack, slowly shaking her head and finally saying, "No offence Millie, but I don't get it."

I'm dying laughing. I reminded both girls what Mom told me growing up. Choosing your life partner is the biggest, most important decision of your life. Whether you like it or not, often your partner can make or break the rest of your life. Take your time, there's no rush.

> *Speak to me, speak to me.*
> *I am listening, I am listening.*
> *Speak to me.*
>
> Ellen Nasser, 'Speak to Me' [unreleased version]

And, most importantly, no pressure. Also, another little tidbit—just because someone has a crush on you, you don't have to feel badly for not having the same feelings back. Be picky, there are so many wonderful people in the world to choose from. Listen to your heart and make a wise decision. And, if your relationship doesn't happen to work out, know that there's never, ever any shame in that. That's just life.

As you know, while I'm creating and expressing myself, I've been working closely with my dear friend's Aura Spray called Priestess. Again, no coincidence in all of this. Before I begin my writing, I read Melissa's beautiful Devotional Prayer:

Dear Priestess,

I invoke your innate gift of Authenticity. Shine through me, honourable Priestess, with honest values of heart, with yearned desires of soul, with genuine expressions of spirit. Usher me closer, to my faithful natural essence, unfolding wider, revealing truer, emerging fuller. Have me advance inward, willing, intentionally, lovingly. Activate deep rememberings, of divine connection, of sacred presence, of holy light. May I actuate from the very core of my beautiful, boundless being. Thank you, Bless You, Love You.

How can I love? How can I love?
I am listening, I am listening.
Speak to me.

Ellen Nasser, 'Speak to Me' [unreleased version]

CHAPTER SIXTEEN
GETTING ON WITH IT

June 10, 2022
6:12 a.m.

I've leveled up my closet sanctuary by putting my laptop up on a cushioned step stool—my back is killing me. All of my information processing typing class recommendations are coming back to me. Lift your wrists, don't look at the keyboard. How am I doing, you ask? You don't need to ask. What about the part about sitting in your closet on your purple yoga mat, crossed-legged with a freshly groomed puppy sitting in your lap? They forgot to mention those things.

I'm listening to one of my piano songs. A local musician is currently putting some strings behind one of them. It's sounding good, but I'm wondering if I should just keep them as raw piano songs. I've been considering having my piano teacher, Martin, play all of my piano pieces for my *Stillness* album instead of me. He is so unbelievably gifted on the piano. If he recorded them, the feeling would be delivered so much more clearly because he is so articulate. I'm a bit messy and amateurish. What about my producer, Bart McKay? Maybe he could play the songs for the recordings? I'm surrounded by the most talented people; it's crazy. Maybe I'll ask Bart and ask him to simply add keys to my playing. I know I'm still learning the piano, and it's not as good as I hoped, but maybe that's where the beauty is right now. I'm sitting here listening to my composition, *Surrender*, and I'm moved. Guess that's all that matters.

This song is so tender and vulnerable. The repetition of the high note reminds me of the heartache that won't go away.

We have a relative, a distant relative, that I see ever so often. We were talking about the pain, as she has also experienced deep pain in her life. I asked her if you ever get over it, and her answer has stuck with me forever: "You don't get over it, you just get on with it."

She's 100% right. I will carry the pain of losing Dad forever.

That was the night that John's relative and I really connected. We were standing on the stairs at Persephone Theatre. After our conversation about pain and how we process it, she left paying me the sweetest compliment I have ever heard in all my life. She said she was trying to think of a word to describe me. My unkind, inner dialogue was thinking of words like: Oh... loud, annoying, a bit obnoxious, over the top, a bit aggressive, blabby, jealous. That evening, leaning up against the railing, the word finally came to her. "Luminous."

She called me luminous.

It's funny what we hold onto. A lot of things happen in my life every day, with many words tossed in my direction. I've been blessed to experience many compliments over my lifetime, but this was a new word for me. Wow, did it ever feel good. "Luminous," I asked her what it meant. I seriously didn't know. I do know that it touched my heart, and that I had a special feeling. Luminous, it still touches my heart.

Luminous

Adjective: *Giving off light, bright or shining: The luminous dial on his watch. A luminous glow, figurative: Her eyes were luminous with joy.*

Wow. I'll take that compliment. What a beautiful word. "Luminous." It reminds me of the candle in *Beauty and the Beast*—what was his name? Lumière? Anyways, he was a tender and sweet animated character. I'd like to wake up each day and make a choice to be more luminous.

I don't know how to love you.
Like I'm supposed to, like I used to.
I don't know, how I'm supposed to hold you.
Haven't got the slightest clue.
When it's really not you.
What's easier?
Losing someone one day?
Or one day at a time?
What's easier?
Losing you, or losing my mind.
Goodbye, old friend—please forgive while I cry.
Wasn't ready to say bye, old friend.
How selfish am I?
Goodbye, my love—not ready for this show.
But I must let you know my love.
My world, you will hold.
My world, you will hold.
My world, you will hold.
I must surrender, and let go.

Ellen Nasser, 'Surrender' [unreleased version]

Sam needed me to sign a permission form, and we were

talking about his upcoming field trip. And, I asked him if he'd like me to come, and he actually lit up like a Christmas tree. So, field trip is booked.

Ahh... then, out of nowhere, I get a text from Bella, "Hey Mom, concert for band is today at 11:00 a.m., if you want to come, no pressure though. Love you."

I had to be at Meewasin by 11:30 a.m. As usual, I didn't spend much time trying to figure out how I was going to make it all happen. I got to the school at 11 a.m. and watched Sam get onto his bus, zipped into the school in time to hear Bella play her three band songs (had to ask my teacher friend what instrument Bella played). Not a personal win for me. As I asked the question, I remembered—TRUMPET! TRUMPET! TRUMPET! Bella plays the trumpet. That was John's instrument; he was apparently the first chair and a fine trumpeter. To this day, I hear trumpet sounds from him all the time, but no sign of an instrument, anywhere.

And, no, I don't like fart jokes.

It was super sweet to see all Sam's classmates running around. Free spirits, loving life and thriving in the outdoors, surrounded by their friends. They were climbing, and jumping, and spinning, and falling. I had five little boys I had to chaperone, and I felt like a bag of nerves. I can take our four kids to the park and not really miss a beat, but watching someone else's kids in a great, big sea of kids it was a little nerve-racking for me. I seriously couldn't keep track of them all! Where on Earth could they be? I abruptly left a conversation I was having, trying to remain calm, but I couldn't find them anywhere. It was such a small area... what the heck?

Eventually, I found Sam, and he helped me find the rest of them. The sun had come out, and then, without me knowing, all five of them changed into their swim clothes, for the spray park. Took their hats off, and they honestly looked like five different kids. Anyway, we ate our lunches. I calmed down. We walked, and played, and enjoyed the sun and fresh air, and then it was our time for the train ride, merry-go-round and Ferris wheel. I think I enjoyed it as much as they did.

✦ ✦ ✦

When do I feel my best?

It usually involves creating, family time, alone time, being in Mother Nature, being near the water, feeling the wind in my hair, moving my body, performing, breathing, laughing, biking, no technology, getting a treat, singing, meditating, studio time—I'm pretty much a little kid at heart. My inner child is often asking for attention, gentleness, connection—we must listen closely so that we can thrive as adults. I want to have more creativity, more fun. I want to enjoy this life. I want to enjoy everything it has to offer.

I get my cards read by a friend of mine, Jessica Elfar. Her Instagram is @StarBabeOracle, and she once told me that souls were lined up, waiting and wanting to be part of what we're experiencing here and now on earth. We are in a shift. There's so much change happening in all aspects of our lives; we are in a time of experiencing many firsts. We are in an ever-changing, awakening time. It's messy, overwhelming, and it's beautiful, all at the same time. Sure, it's going to be bumpy at times, but that's the joy of being here. Being one of the chosen few who get to experience this Earthbound life, getting to live here, and now. We aren't here to live in pain and suffering; we're here to experience it, learn from it, heal, and rise up. We are here to enjoy the ride and accept that it's going to be bumpy. So, buckle up.

You don't need permission to enjoy your life or to choose happiness. You also don't have to feel guilty for celebrating feeling good when you do feel good. You also don't have to look to other people to dictate what you should be feeling. If you feel like you do need permission, then allow me to give it to you. Again, permission granted.

It seems like we've been in such a heavy, energetic rut that now feeling good feels a bit foreign to us. Is it just me, or do many people seem to be dipping their toes in the water of feeling good, but get pulled in by the undertow of shame and guilt for wanting to feel a lightness and joy again?

Ahh... It's 7:22 a.m.—I told Bella I'd wake her up at 7:15 a.m., she wants to have time to straighten her hair. John is still away; he'll be away till Sunday. Of course, I woke up to a text from him saying, "I'm missing all the action."

He loves *his* circus so much.

> *Hello up there, can't you give the world a break?*
> *And, let it rest for heaven's sake—*
> *make it still for just one night.*
>
> *Man in the moon, you make way for the rising sun.*
> *Trying to figure what's to come,*
> *every morning, noon and night...*
>
> *Twinkle, little, darling star.*
> *I wonder who I am, but never wondered who you are.*
> *Way above the world so high.*
> *I wish I may, I wish I might.*
> *Make it good and hold on tight.*
>
> Ellen Kolenick, 'Buckle Up'

CHAPTER SEVENTEEN
LEARN NEW THINGS, FORGET OLD THINGS

June 11, 2022
7:32 a.m.

Yesterday, babysitter Camille asked me to play some of my piano songs for her wedding in a couple of weeks. To say I am honoured is an absolute understatement. I'm very nervous just thinking about it, but I can easily play three to four of my own compositions before mass. I need to diarrhea just thinking about it—not even kidding. Now, I'm up to four times in my book. Who writes a memoir and talks about diarrhea four times? I guess I do. Do you know why? 'Cause I'm the boss.

This is my little secret, and I'm really starting to enjoy this morning writing. I'm the boss and author of my stories and my life, and guess what? I can write whatever I want. And, guess what again? So can you.

Do you follow Dr. Amen at all? He's a doctor in the USA

that teaches the importance of brain health and the choices he and his wife make every day to help heal and create their beautiful existence. As usual, he just kinda fell into my life, and I find him intelligent and worth listening to. I follow him on Instagram. He talks about ANTs in one of his clips—Automatic Negative Thoughts. He has these stuffies all around his office to remind him to be aware of his angry thoughts. I think it's amazing that we can change the health of our brain by making different choices, just by noticing the patterns we're in. Notice, shift, and watch your life change. Simple, yes, but not easy.

Yesterday, I was talking to my tutor about the benefits of learning a new language, especially a complex language like Mandarin. It is so good for my brain health. I was feeling a bit down yesterday because I would like to be better than where I am at this point with the language. See, again, impatience. Ego. The story of my life.

I've been studying for almost five months (wǔgè yuè), and I know I'm coming along, so why do I want to have a pity party for myself? I often get hung up on the end game, the finish line, but as usual, I know that isn't the real goal. It's all in the journey. That's where the magic is.

After five months of daily engagement, I can basically say, "Hello! My name is Ellen Nasser. I have four children. I have two daughters and two sons. This is Bella, Millie, Sam, Walt. I love my husband. Today, I ate spicy noodles and I drank lots of water. I like tea and rice. Today, the date is June 11. I love my dog. This is my dog. 1, 2, 3, 4, 5, 6, 7, 8, 9, 10..."

10 (shí)
Shí + 1 (shíyī) is 11
Shí + 2 (shíèr) is 12
Shí + 3 (shísān) is 13
Shí + 4 (shísì) is 14

So, you see what they do, they basically say yī, èr, sān, sì, wǔ, so there's 1, 2, 3, 4, 5, and then there's liù, qī, bā, jiǔ, shí, so you're counting to ten. And it's so awesome because they take the 10 and then they start again with yī, so they say shíyī is eleven. Shíèr is twelve, like it makes sense. I don't know. I'm really loving it! Just to finish, I would say, "Wǒ shì Ellen. Nǐhǎo! Nǐhǎo ma?" Um... I would also say, "Wǒ xǐhuān chá, I like tea." I would say, "Wǒ ài wǒde lǎogōng, I love my husband." And, yes, if you're wondering if my husband's impressed, yes, he is. I have four children, Umm... I think it's like this, "Wǒ yǒu yī, èr, sān, sìgè háizi." I know, like I'm not kidding. If I can learn Mandarin, let this be your reminder that you can do anything. I'm not even kidding. It's cool!

My brain hurts just thinking about it. My lips have never made these shapes, my mouth has never said these words, and my vocal cords have never created these five tones. Some people would say that Mandarin only has four tones; there's actually a fifth, it's a neutral. I can only imagine how all this 'newness' is lighting up my brain. I'm uncomfortable, which means I'm learning, which means I'm evolving and growing, which means I'm healing my brain and making healthier choices, which means I feel good, which means I then feel guided to share my love and light with whomever crosses my path. My tutor, Zoe, and I were touching on the topic yesterday in my lesson. She also believes in healing from the inside out. It's magical, it really is. And because I watched my Dad take his last breath and I saw him slip away for years, life is different for me now.

Have you ever been in a relationship that was more off than on? The back and forth of fighting, and kissing, and making up. I suppose that's either young love or just the love between two certain people.

Ellen Kolenick, 'Bittersweet'

John and I have had lengthy conversations about how two people can bring out the best or worst in each other. I sometimes think back to the past relationships I was in, and I feel embarrassed of my behaviour, wish I could have done things differently. As John reminds me, it's really something a person must let go of because we aren't the same people, and some personalities are like oil and water—they don't belong together. And to top it all off, all those experiences led me to John, where I belong.

The main problem with this past tumultuous relationship was that I loved him. I don't really know if loving someone can be a *problem*, but I suppose it was. It was rocky, with many ups and downs, but I still think back fondly to those days. He was such a good guy. So, when I came back from performing, I saw him, and this song literally fell from my heart.

How do you look so good?
I often wondered, though I knew you would.
And now these butterflies, they tell me I should...
Run away.

How do you feel the same?
That great big hug and your grinning face.
And after all these years, my knees still gave.
How do you look so good?

Fresh outta high school, holding hands.
I was your lady, you were my man.
You loved me too much if there's such a thing—
turned on my heel, hit the road just runnin'.
Stopped in my tracks, I turned on a dime.
Wasn't gonna lose you, I knew that you were mine.
You always took me back through all your tears.
And now I stand here after all these years...

    Ellen Kolenick, 'Looks So Good'

I can picture where I was, who I was with, his shirt, his hair. We got back together again for a nanosecond, but I was still a mess from my prior breakup. He knew, and I knew. I was a mess, and we broke up... yet again.

This time, he dumped me, and this time it was forever.

CHAPTER EIGHTEEN
PiNK FLAMiNGO

June 12, 2022
8:19 a.m.

Sunday morning, and I'm missing my hubby. Last night, I went to two birthday parties celebrating our friends, alone. Jann Arden's concert keeps coming back to my mind. Like I said, I'm a fan of Jann Arden's, but it's not like I know her every song. I've never even watched her TV show, and it's not like I'm some sorta goofy fan girl for her, but this live performance was different. It really resonated with where I'm at in my life.

Sure, I get excitable. I am excitable. I... I remember this story. Umm... it was Amy's birthday party, and she was a little girl, and opening up her presents, and I'm running around so excited, "Thanks, Uncle Robert!" And, it wasn't even my birthday. I am excitable and I am an expresser. I even get excited about delicious food. John and the kids tell me to stop it, because I seriously don't even notice. John's Mom, who we call Nana, told me once that she thought I was being funny with my moaning and groaning over her home-cooked meals, but I wasn't. When my Dad used to love something, my Mom made, he'd say, "What a flavour burst!"

When Dad passed away, I saw something on Jessica Elfar's Instagram that said, "Go ahead and ask your angels and the universe for whatever you wish." She shared a story about asking for white elephants to show up in her life to give her signs, and so I thought... Hmmm... I'd try it too, and I thought, "Dear God, please give me a sign that everything is going to be okay. Please help support our family with this pain of losing Dad." I know it's dumb, but I thought I'd challenge God and give him a *really tricky* one. So, I added, "And, please send me some pink flamingos, just so I know you're listening."

Well, Millie's Birthday is on June 15, and my brother and sister-in-law came from Calgary to be with our Dad, and they gave Millie an early birthday gift. By that point, I had totally forgotten about my prayer. Millie opened the gift, and there were sunglasses. They were white with little specs on them, and Millie said, "Ahh, look what's on them, a bunch of cute little..." Looking closer, she said, "Pink flamingos!"

The minute she said pink flamingos, I remembered my prayer. Are you kidding me? I thought, nope, they were there plain as day, white with pink flamingos. Wow. I didn't say anything because it was a bit crazy. And then my brother Lee and his wife they came by, and they brought a gift for Millie. Millie opened up her gift, and it was a sweet, stuffed... You guessed it, pink flamingo. I'm not even kidding!

We all will come and go.
When the train ride ends, we'll never know.
Think of me now and again.
You're everything I am.

*You are exactly what I hoped for and wished for
all the time.*

Ellen Kolenick, 'Twelve Thirty-Four'

I have *NO* idea why I asked for pink flamingos as a sign—nobody even necessarily likes pink flamingos in our household, and here they were in front of our eyes.

After I started thinking this was kinda surreal, I had to tell them. I said it was a sign that Dad and God were with us, that all was going to be okay. And then, within the next couple of days, I was making Millie's bed, and I kicked something under her bed, and I looked down, and it was a great big sequined pink flamingo—and I gasped. That's three, God and Dad. The reason I'm re-membering this story is because at one of the birthday parties last night, I got a text from Diana asking me where I got my sequinned stuffies for the kids, because her daughter wanted one for her kindergarten graduation gift. I went to bed remembering Dad's pink flamingos. Of course, I had to share it.

After I shared my magical pink flamingo story with our family, Bella, John, and Millie said that they wanted to play that game, too. And, so, we all laughed, and they said no, really, they wanted to think of something to see if our angels, God and Papa, were listening. And, Bella said, "Okay, I'm going to pick something in my head and we will see what happens!"

That was that, and we just kept sitting around visiting and enjoying the togetherness. Then I got a message from my Mom with a picture saying, "Look at the stun-ning flowers!"

We looked at the photo, and Bella yelled, "Oh my gosh, I asked for my sign to be red roses!" The photo was a massive display of deep, crimson magenta red roses.

We couldn't believe it! Then Millie said out loud, "Well then, I want tulips!" And, we thought that was funny because she was just playing off of, you know, Bella's flower request. And, it was sweet, though, and we chuckled. And, John said, "Two lips? You want two lips? Okay, here you go, here's your two lips!" and chased towards her in the dining room with puckered lips, saying, "Here's your two lips, Millie!"

Fast forward twenty minutes, the doorbell rang, and a box was delivered. Millie excitedly opened it and yelled, "Mom, I got my two lips!"

"No, Millie, those flowers aren't tulips, they're actually called mums." And, it was this beautiful bouquet of white mums, and greens and creams—a very soft and delicate bouquet in a grey, clay pot.

She and John turned it around and told me to actually look. And, I looked at the front of the vase. It was a face with two lips... two lips. The grey, clay pot had an artistic face with ears, nose and two lips protruding from the pot. I almost died.

All we ever have to do is ask and then notice... however it shows up. Ask for whatever you want. We are always supported and loved, just like we support and love one another. That's what it's all about. Yesterday, Kriti and I were talking about life and what we would buy if we came into a huge amount of money. I said I probably wouldn't change much; except I would travel more. She said travelling isn't a huge turn-on for her because of all the packing and unpacking, so we decided if we travelled somewhere we would stay for a significant amount of time to make it worth all the hassle... Kriti said she'd like to *buy* more time.

We talked about what would happen to our lives. She

said she wouldn't quickly retire—she'd still work for a while longer. And, I agreed. But eventually, she'd retire and keep enjoying her family. She said she would start cooking from scratch and really learn how to cook. She said she'd shop for food and would take the time to smell it as she picked out the best produce. The imagery of this brought a smile to my face.

I love music, but I often drive in silence. I love my family time and dreaming, but I'm also scared my family will roll their eyes at "my latest." I am driven and have passion, but also feel like I need to be *doing stuff* in order to be worthy. I'm spontaneous and love seeing what the day will bring. But this past weekend, with John away, I feel down and lower energy, hoping this day will be done.

I am fearful of the unknown and what the future will bring, yet I love surprises. I love being outside, I love being outrageous, and I love being inside and going within. I love entertaining, and I love quiet time. I love to feel sad and create sad music, although sometimes my wallowing gets me into funks. I love writing, and some mornings I don't want to write this memoir. I love my husband, and sometimes I have moments of wanting to be alone. I love people and am liked by many, but I'm sure there are many people who don't like me. We all ebb and flow with everything in our lives. It's all perfectly natural, and it's essential to know you're never alone. Sometimes, I feel lonely, but I know I'm not alone.

> *So beautiful.*
> *Beautiful, right now.*
> *Beautiful, right now.*
>
> *Calm the world, no, calm myself.*
> *Starts within and nowhere else.*
> *Calm the world, no, calm myself.*
> *Starts within and nowhere else.*

We are all connected
We all hold... hold the secret.
We are all so beautiful.
Beautiful, right now. Beautiful, right now.

Subconscious and the conscious
Divine light throughout our souls.
We are all so beautiful.
Beautiful, right now. Beautiful, right now.

Calm the world, no, calm myself.
Starts within and nowhere else.
Calm the world, no, calm myself.
Starts within and nowhere else.

Ellen Nasser, 'Beautiful Right Now' [unreleased version]

I wanna hold you close.
I wanna hold you close.

Same day .... 10:27 p.m.

I wanna make your dreams come true,

This is the night Dad died—

no matter what I do...

—Exactly one year ago.

I swear that I won't let you go.

Tonight is a full moon, and I'm having problems unwinding. John is home now, so that gives me a sense of peace. Right in this moment, a year ago, we were in Dad's care home, holding sacred space for him. We were all so tired. My brother Danny had spent a full day and night earlier in the week. And, Lee spent most of the year prior caregiving with Mom in my parents' home, trying to keep Dad out of a care home, but here we were nonetheless...

I wanna make your dreams come true, no matter what I do.

In the care home.

I wanna tell you, you're my only one.
Ellen Kolenick, 'Hold You Close'

We were all so exhausted, and Lee and Amy and I were hanging out.

Who knows how much longer Dad could hold on—everything was completely unpredictable.

"Have sweet dreams, my love, and I will, too."

Mom gently kissed him on his forehead, had another cry and left.

This time forever.

I said, "Night," to Mom and Amy and Lee, playing all the things in my head that our family had said to each other throughout the many days of Dad slowly dying.

"Remember, whoever is with Dad when he passes away, you're only leaving his body... his spirit will come with you when you leave, and then he'll be with you forever," Amy reminded us. Amy was his little peanut.

The strangest thing is that as I'm sharing this story and making note of the time as I write every single entry. I remember now, the night Dad died, I did the same thing. I really felt like I had to keep track of everything. I felt a big responsibility to our family to make sure that they knew I looked after Dad the best I could. I didn't have a clue what I was doing, but I just comforted him. That night, it was Nurse Mabel, me and Dad—without Mabel's support, I wouldn't have had the courage to stay next to him. Mabel made her rounds, and I asked, "Mabel, do I have to stay?"

"You can do whatever you wish, whatever makes you feel the most comfortable."

"How long do you think this will go on?"

"No one really knows, it could be hours or a day... there's just no knowing."

She was so amazing and just let me come to whatever decision I wanted. There was no judgment, no insinuation of what she thought I *should* do. Thank you, Mabel, thank you for being so amazing.

I noted when the shifts in his breathing happened, what I said, what I felt, what I experienced, how he responded and seemed. I felt like I was going into labour. It really felt like a birth to me. I felt cold, and shaky, and scared, alone, and so, so sad. When the sadness is that massive, I don't even think that's the word... more like broken. I didn't know what to do or how to say goodbye to him. I didn't know how to comfort him. I didn't know how to comfort me. I felt sorry for myself because I sucked at this. I didn't know what I was doing. I felt so sad and so broken. I needed someone. I sobbed and I sang. I sang and I sobbed. It was a sound that I never heard come from me before.

At one point, a man came in. Maybe just another nurse popping his head in to see if we were okay, which we weren't. I don't know what words I was singing; I don't know what the tune was. The guilt of not wanting to be there. The honour of being there. The constant struggle of not knowing what to do and just trying to keep my head above the water. I wanted to be strong for Dad, but I also felt like I still needed him. My whole life, I was used to my Dad being strong for me. And, now it was my turn; I had to be strong for him. I had to be strong for the both of us.

I wrote 'Holy Light'. It's an accumulation of everything that has happened, including Mom and Dad, sibling relationships, trying to navigate through these muddy waters, my relationship with John, and, of course, all the while having four very young children. Our journey has been so rich in depth, and pain, and suffering, but also in connection and healing. I was so blessed to be one of his daughters.

CHAPTER NINETEEN
ONE YEAR

June 13, 2022
7:00 a.m.

He's been gone a full year. I can't even type these words without crying. I miss him so much, and I can't make sense of it all. That is why I can either choose to have the utmost faith or give up and have no faith at all.

I choose to live with so much faith because I trust there is a much bigger picture that I can only imagine. I don't think we can comprehend the vastness of it all, the master plan.

It's so hard to believe a year has passed. I think about Dad most days, I really do. We all talk about him a lot and share photos and our funny memories. Sometimes when I have extra space in my day, I get a thought that I should pop over to see Dad at the care home. He'd be at his window in his room or at his special place in the dining room with his table mate Gerhardt, where they would be sitting and enjoying the sunshine.

But then I remember he's not there. He's gone.

He's been showing up a lot lately in the mourning doves, the bunnies, the butterflies, dragonflies, the sky, the electronics, our hearts. He's making sure we know he's with us.

My Dad was a beautiful soul. He loved my Mom the most, then all of us kids and then Mom's parents, Grandma and Grandpa, next. He loved the life he and Mom created together. He was so proud of it, yet humble. All the emails that circulated as Mom, and my siblings, and I were trying to come up with the right words to describe our journey with Dad were interesting.

Dad and I had a special bond that seemed to grow as he slipped away with his illness. I was the first to notice something with Dad, maybe Mom did sooner, but didn't want to admit it. I noticed, and Dad knew I noticed, and he said to me, "That day you looked deep into my soul."

I wrote he and Mom a few letters because I seem to communicate best that way. I'm hoping Mom can find some, and I'll put one in here, maybe, we'll see.

I have to change topics. I don't really know what to write about because I'm noticing it's very easy to just write about my life and our children, because they're all mine. But when I write about Dad, I must be limited a bit because I share him with three other siblings. I'm not as private as they are, I feel like it's my duty to share and express—that's where the healing is for me, in connecting. I have to remember that everyone's healing journeys are very different, and every one of them must be honoured.

My heart goes back to Saltcoats, days on the lake where we would rip around the neighbourhood and play with Cookie and Shmurtis, and of course with Shevon and

Trent. The neighbour boys would come over and play twenty-one on our driveway. I would LOVE having people to our house... just like four other wild kids I know.

Our family would go to Edmonton every summer to visit our beloved lifelong friends, who also had four kids our age. All together, we would be called the "Dirty Dozen"—and we kids would have an absolute blast together. We also had another set of family friends in Calgary, who we also loved, and I can remember going to Calaway Park, walking to a corner store for a 7-Up Slurpee, trying to be as cool as possible in these big cities. I can remember when our Calgary family friends reno'd their house one summer; I was in awe. I had never thought such a thing was possible. That could have been the beginning of my real estate passion, especially for before-and-afters. I also remember the Momma Maureen and her daughter, Dancin' Jenn, taking tap dancing and practicing in their furnace room on the concrete floor, thinking this kind of living was from another planet. Remember, I was a Salt-coats girl. When I was a kid, the Kolenicks had to drive twenty minutes to Yorkton, *uphill both ways*, to get our Slurpee.

CHAPTER TWENTY
SiSTERS

June 14, 2022
6:10 a.m.

We had a family meeting last night about the logistics of travelling to Summerland this summer. We're going to holiday with my brother Lee's family and possibly Mom. We aren't sure whether we should fly or drive. Having a vehicle when we get there is essential. So, we'll see how it unfolds.

Tomorrow is Millie's 11th birthday—she said last year's birthday wasn't the greatest. Well, I'm sure it wasn't the biggest thrill because Papa had just passed away. Anyways, Bella said, "We must do better for Millie this year," so she got a little bit extra.

Yesterday morning, Bella and I went to the walk-in clinic to check on Bella's knee. She landed on the concrete doing cartwheels about five weeks ago and has been complaining about it ever since. Then, the other night, she was tiptoeing in the Circle K store getting a Slurpee after her ball game and slipped on the wet floor. Ugh. Needless to say, we went to check it out, and almost four hours later, they told us that they think it's okay. There could be a bone chip, but it's not too likely. After we're done at the clinic, Bella wanted to shop for Millie. She asked me, "Mom, am I a bad big sister?"

"Why?"

She said because she hadn't shopped for Millie's birthday gift yet, and her birthday is tomorrow. I told her she'd only be considered a bad sister if it was actually Millie's special day and there was still no present. So, off we went to the stores, and Bella spent the rest of the afternoon wrapping Millie's gifts and hiding them. We'll give her a treasure hunt to find them. You know, Millie, she just loves parties and togetherness. Remember, she's our party girl. I said she could have five Grade Five girls from her class for a swim and movie this Friday—she's been downright giddy. Oh, the joy she gets—it's contagious and we all admit it; lights up our household.

I saw a post last night that said, "Don't tell people everything." Hmmm… I hoped that wasn't a sign for me. When I'm in a positive frame of mind, I see all the signs pointing me into the direction of *sharingness*—when I'm low, I can twist them to signs that don't support me, and question my every move. It's also been rainy here, which adds to my wishy-washy behaviour. John says, "The farmers need it." My goal is to end up back on the West Coast, one day, but I do admit, I don't think I could live in the Vancouver grey. Victoria isn't nearly as grey; it's kinda like a little secret. You know, just like this book.

When I used to live in Victoria, Mom would call and she'd say she noticed on the weather channel what a grey and rainy day it was, and I would literally be walking to the Canadian College of Performing Arts in the sunshine. Seriously, we would get a sprinkle or rain shower, but then it would immediately clear up, so quickly the weatherperson couldn't even keep up. Victoria weather is lovely; they just don't let anyone else know.

> *Twelve twenty in the morning,*
> *and I don't know where you are.*
> *The rain is falling from the sky,*
> *making puddles on the ground.*
> *When the night falls, everything seems different to me.*
> *My heart lies in someone else's hands.*
> *Two o'clock, my confidant stained my teeth.*
> *Suburban Motel is jumping off the page,*
> *time to get some sleep.*
> *When the night falls, everything seems different to me.*
> *Let this downpour set me free tonight.*
> *Four thirty in the morning,*
> *Your call rings through the night...*

Listening to this song takes me back to the middle of the night in my Mom and Dad's den, where it was written. I can remember being so down and so lost. I didn't have a clue what my plan was. I'd been studying two years at college and then performing with Norwegian Cruise Lines for six months, not having a clue what was next.

As I'm listening to this, I feel like I'd like to re-record most of these songs, but then on the other hand, I think there's such beauty in it. Even the crafting of the songs, the writing, the year it was recorded. I noticed my congested, plugged nose. And, I can remember being pregnant with Bella when I completed this album; I guess *everything* was so plugged.

> *I'm so scared and angry all at once.*
> *I hear your voice, and I'm glad you're alright.*
> *When the night falls, everything seems different to me.*
> *My heart lies in someone else's hands...*
>
> Ellen Kolenick, 'Downpour'

CHAPTER TWENTY-ONE
THE BREAKFAST CLUB

June 15, 2022
6:10 a.m.

Before I finished my morning meditation, I could hear little footsteps in the hallway. Mille is up and excited—it's her birthday. It's hard to believe she's eleven years old. Wow. Of course, I'm a little annoyed that she's up so early because I always want the kids to feel well-rested. I'm a firm believer that everyone feels better when they have a good night's rest. Millie actually went to bed last night about 8:30 p.m., so she'll be doing pretty good.

Last night, our neighbours came over to listen to the songs I'm going to play at babysitter Camille's wedding. The setlist will be:

+ Unknown
+ Be Free
+ Sacred Sunrise
+ Ellen in the Movies

The songs she chose flow beautifully from one another. I hope it goes well. I told John that I'm quite nervous, but mostly *so honoured.*

Regarding our Summerland holiday this summer, Kriti and Lee's family have decided to drive, and we have decided to join them. John really wants to have a vehicle there, and I really don't want to travel without him. The whole point of having a family vacation is to be together.

Millie just walked into my closet sanctuary, saying, "It's my birthday, can I have a soak in your tub?" The sun is pouring in our bathroom, and she is so excited. I'm going to ask her if she wants me to drive her to school this morning and take her classroom some donuts.

Writing is a struggle for me this morning. John now has walked into the bathroom and wished Millie happy birthday. When everyone gets up at 6 a.m., I admit, I'm annoyed.

I know what's weighing heavy. I wish I had a best friend. I see lots of people with their best friends, and I think my whole life, I really wanted a best friend. I think we have to be our own best friends before we can be anyone else's

✦ ✦ ✦

Have you ever seen a childhood photo of me? John said that I look like that redhead from the movie *The Breakfast Club.* Hmmm... most people assume he's talking about Molly Ringwald, unfortunately, he's talking about the other redhead, Anthony Michael Hall.

Mom said I was precious. Mom also permed my hair

all the time. I can remember getting a Tony perm box for my birthday. I can also remember getting my hair permed the night before school pictures. Mom denies it, but it's totally true. My point is that I looked very annoying, and I probably was very annoying.

Do you ever notice your thoughts? Are you quick to judge? Are they kind observations? Do you give people the benefit of the doubt? Are you gentle on yourself and others? I'm not, but I'm starting to notice.

You can't shift something you don't notice. There have been some big game-changers for me in my life. Monumental times of change and growth. In 2018, John and I attended an Eckhart Tolle retreat in Lake Louise. It was about five days, and we took our neighbour Jess and her boyfriend to watch our kids while we were in and out of the sessions. Jess and let's call him Clayton, moved up the street from us so that they could have a bit of separation from the overwhelming Nasser Crew. Well, we stayed at the Chateau Lake Louise. We would arrange a time that they would come over in the morning, to help us get the day started. The kids had a blast, ripping around the hotel, eating out, going to the other hotel to swim, going for drives—what an incredible recharge for us, both personally and as a couple. It was one of the most beautiful trips, and there was so much healing that happened. We also gained so many tools.

Millie just came in again and asked if I was done journaling and if she can open up one present. She said she asked Dad downstairs and he said, "I don't know where they are. Did you check under the tree?" That about sums it up—Millie's birthday feels like Christmas morning around here. Okay, she's been patient enough.

So, I'm just waiting, patiently waiting.
I know I said it's over, but still waiting for you.

It's funny, on a morning like this, now I could write and write and write. Was I ever eleven years old? Oh yes, yes, I was... and Mom permed my hair incessantly, and I looked exactly like Anthony Michael Hall, and my take-away from this journal entry is that I didn't have a best friend.

CHAPTER TWENTY-TWO
BiRTHDAYS

June 16, 2022
8:18 a.m.

Does anyone else find their children's birthdays to be 100% exhausting? We didn't even really do that much, but for some reason, I find them challenging because I want to make them special without going over the top. Also, I wanna buy them things, but at the same time, I don't want more plastic crap in our house or to waste a bunch of money.

It was a wonderful day. I went to Millie's classroom and cranked up her song, and brought her classmates donuts. Millie's face was bright red and (laughingly) told me to leave. After the kids said "Thank you!" as I left. She was extra embarrassed when I wanted to answer in Mandarin—"Bú kèqi, Bú kèqi—you're welcome." So, I said, "Guys say, xièxiè nǐ, xièxiè nǐ (Thank you!), and then I'll say, Bú kèqi, Bú kèqi." Millie's like… Ugh! I love having fun with our kids. They drive me nuts, and I yell like a madwoman sometimes, but overall, we all have so much fun together.

For Millie's birthday supper, we had an impromptu gathering with two of her soccer buddies. John made a yummy dinner of chicken, ribs, fries and broccoli. Mil was up early to cruise around on her new hoverboard. I slept in. I didn't see the kids off this morning; John had it covered. He got up early and went to a sprint camp and loved it. I'm sitting upstairs in my closet, my ThinkPad right in front of me, on a cushioned stool, Sofi to the right of me. I have sprayed my Priestess Aura Spray and have said my prayers. I lit a candle this morning for a friend of ours who I just found out has cancer. I'm writing, and I'm loving the peace and quiet. Walt just came in and begged to blow my three candles out. I said, "No." He looked sad, and then I said, "Okay." I know, I know this is the problem—I don't say no and mean it. I say no, and then they beg, and ask again, and again, and then I think about it, and I think, Ellen, is this really that big of an ask? Is it necessary for me to have my candles going the entire time I write? I say, "No again," he begs, then I say, "Yes." Here we go—Parenting 101—one of the reasons our kids don't listen sometimes is because I don't say no and stick to it. Also, John reminded me the other day that our kids' hearing is amazing—they just have problems listening.

Oh, I forgot to mention yesterday morning, after I was writing about Eckhart Tolle, Mom mentioned that she was out on a walk listening to *The Power of Now*, on her audiobook. Just hearing his voice centers me. Anyway, she hadn't mentioned Eckhart in ages. And then, when I talked to Lee, he said, "That's so funny because he was tuning into Eckhart's teachings again as well." I feel a deep yearning for another workshop.

Life is good, but I know I am so easily pulled from alignment. I can so easily fall into unconsciousness. Even writing this, I pause... I breathe, and I notice. I put my hands on my heart and take a long, deep, intentional breath through my nose. Hold it for four seconds and blow the air out of my mouth, like I'm blowing out my birthday candles. I'm always making a wish, and bringing awareness, and feeling my heartbeat. Feeling the calmness and alignment within. Feeling the depth from that one breath. Feeling the clarity, the grounding, the reset. All from one simple breath.

You've got time; all you have to do is practice it. It starts with one deep breath. Meditation is one, deep, long, intentional breath over and over. Your brain will thank you, your spirit will thank you, your body will thank you, your kids will thank you, your spouse will thank you, the collective will thank you. You will thank you. Try it. If you're embarrassed and at work, go have a break in the washroom. Sit on the toilet and try it. You have to start somewhere. I have heard of people who set an alarm on the hour to remind them to take one deep breath. Can you imagine what the long-term benefits from that one extra breath would be... bringing that oxygen to your brain? Eckhart suggests we could do this right before we put our vehicles into gear; he recommends this one small daily practice throughout the day. Sit in your vehicle, take one deep breath, and then put it into drive.... Oh! Or, maybe reverse! Ha! Ha! Ha! I didn't... Ha! Ha! Ha! Oh, drive... reverse... wherever you're going, just... take mental note of what gear you put it in, so... Ha! Ha! Ha! Stop! Ha! Ha! I actually startled myself, because I thought, what if someone's in the garage... Ha! Ha! Ha! You know what I mean... You know what I mean... and have fun. Life is fun!

CHAPTER TWENTY-THREE
COMMiTMENTS

June 17, 2022
6:17 a.m.

John and I barked at each other a bit last night because of a difference of opinion regarding making a commitment and sticking to it. He wants the kids to go to their commitments no matter what the day brings. I'm on the fence about that. I know making a commitment is very important, and I'm all for showing up. But, I'm also more for listening to your body and honouring rest. I remember talking to another parent, and they said they will allow their kids to do pretty much any activity, as long as the kid is happily doing it. The Dad said the minute it turns into the parent dragging them out the front door, kicking and screaming because they don't want to go, they're done. Simple as that, they're done. I thought it was kind of a neat philosophy, but I also believe people need breaks, kids especially. Their brains are growing and developing at such a rapid pace, if the kids want to stay at home, veg and build Lego, I say so be it. As usual, I can see both sides.

I had an energy healing with Melissa yesterday. I never know what to expect when I go there. I just show up with an open heart and allow the energy to flow and do its thing. I trust Melissa, and I also trust my body and intuition. Melissa and I were talking yesterday, and as she reminded me, there are consequences for all the choices we make. I know that making wise choices makes me feel good. And then, I want to share it with the world.

✦ ✦ ✦

When I express and connect, I want to share and help others—I can feel myself evolving and transforming. It's nothing short of magic. It's living with intention. That's where I want to spend my time, being with people whose souls I gravitate to; they're my kind of people. And, that's the way of life I want to commit to living. Oh, funny... "commitment," that damn word again. I guess because it's me who has commitment issues! That's probably why real estate is a perfect fit for me. I only have to *commit* to people for about six months at a time. As I continue to grow, I'm finding which environments I thrive in. I was telling Lee the beauty of real estate is that I still get to be creative and go above and beyond for my clients, all the while meeting new people, all the time. I'm also so grateful for my job.

I finally have the courage to let go of my names. I was born Ellen Kolenick, created my stage name, Elly Thorn, my Mom's maiden name was Thorsness, so I created my stage name from that. Now, I'm almost forty years old, our baby chapter is closed, my stage name chapter is closed, and I am being creative and selling houses under one name, Ellen Nasser. When John and I got married, there was a fleeting moment that I thought I would keep my own last name, but I quickly decided that I wanted the same last name as our future children.

I'm happy to have our entire family unit with the same name. Ahh... Sometimes I look back and feel a bit embarrassed that I changed my name to Elly Thorn, but I remind myself—I'm an artist. Even with my performing arts, I was moderately talented in many parts of it. Musical theatre, stage productions, on Norwegian Cruise Line and Saskatchewan Express, TV, and most recently piano; now writing. I have an undeniable drive to create; you couldn't force someone to sit down and write a book or create like this, it's actually in me. It's who I am. I'm scared about many things; I have plenty of fears. But it seems to me my passion for creating wins most of the time. I'd rather be in the ring taking risks, even if it means being judged by spectators in the stands. I keep getting these nudges that I am supposed to be doing this or trying that. I get nudges that I am supposed to be showing up authentically and real, no matter what, and you know what? The more I do it, the more I want to do it.

Bella said she did her "concours d'art oratoire" [French public speaking] presentation at school about sexism in sports. She followed up yesterday on our family bike ride, "So, if you had a family of daughters and they all got married and took their husbands' names, could your family name be gone?"

I said, "Yes, that would be correct." Born a feminist, she thought, "Hmmm... Why can't the guys start taking the women's names?" I didn't have an answer. It's true, though, why not? Does this happen in other parts of the world?

Oh Gooooooooogle? Yooooooohoooooooo...

This is interesting... look what I found:

Custom dictates that women keep their surnames in many Spanish-speaking countries, including Spain and

Huh… You know, everything is constantly changing. The fact alone that Bella and I are having this conversation, collectively, we are all evolving; the world is awakening, things are revealing themselves, life is unfolding before our eyes, and we can either accept it all and roll with it, or we can live in fear and try to outrun it. I know for my own mental health, I must surrender.

CHAPTER TWENTY-FOUR
EVOLUTION

June 18, 2022
9:27 a.m.

Yesterday was party day for Millie. Note to self, hosting a birthday party for five little girls 4:30 p.m. to 10:30 p.m. is too long. It was full of laughter, and swimming, watching bloopers, her one friend brought her a cake. And Johnny ordered pizza, and they played hide and seek, listened to blasting music and by the end, begged for a sleepover. I can't stand sleepovers, so that was a hard no. I'm okay with the odd cousin sleepover, but lots of friends and nobody sleeping; it's the worst idea on the planet! One of John's sisters calls them "crab overs." Where no one sleeps and everyone, parents included, just end up feeling crabby the next day.

Anyways, Millie just popped into my closet and thanked me so much for her birthday party. She said it's still her birthday weekend because Auntie Kriti wants to take her shopping for an outfit.

I'm looking at all of my music that is organically falling into my stories, and I'm wondering how am I gonna pull this all together. I feel a bit overwhelmed by it, but it'll be so nice to have all of my creations, in one place, under the same umbrella.

John is out right now picking us up our weekend Starbucks. I actually laugh at our evolution of Starbucks' orders. When I started selling houses, I would order a Venti caramel macchiato. Not only was it full of caffeine, but it was also dripping in gooey, delicious caramel sugar, and to top it off, I was drinking soooo many calories. How many, you ask? 350 calories. Holy crap! Then I changed my order to half decaf/half regular because I was starting to shake from all the caffeine and real estate transactions. Not even kidding. Stress and caffeine—they don't mix well.

Then, I started ordering a Grande instead of a Venti.

Then, I cut it to half-sweet because it was all too sugary.

Then, sugar-free and half-sweet.

Then, I changed my order altogether to sugar-free vanilla latte.

Then, sugar-free vanilla latte with almond milk.

Then, sugar-free vanilla latte with coconut milk.

Then, a friend of mine just told me about the sugar-free vanilla latte with oat milk... Woo! Giddy up!

Then, Chai tea latte half-sweet.

Then, Chai tea latte half-sweet with coconut milk.

Everything has changed. I know you probably don't think this is a big shift, me sitting here in my closet Saturday morning talking about my privileged Starbucks order, but it is. It's fascinating to me because I can see the change and shifts in me over the course of a decade. I'm noticing right here and right now how I feel, how I'm evolving, and noticing what works for me and what doesn't work for me. Simply reflecting on my first forty years, living on this planet.

CHAPTER TWENTY-FIVE
NEW YORK SPARKS

June 19, 2022
9:53 a.m.

Today is Father's Day, and I got the best sleep-in… that's right, Father's Day, not Mother's Day, and I'm the one who got to sleep in. John came into our room this morning and said, "Oh, you're up? Do you know how much hell I'd get if I slept in like this on Mother's Day?"

Yeah, he's probably right.

Our relatives from outta town decided to stay over another night. They treated us to Wok Box last night, and the kids had fun together. Nothing better than cousin love. These are the cousins who we will travel with to Connecticut this summer. John has a relative that we visit there, and the kids go to a sailing camp. This year, Sam will get to go, and it'll be his first year. I'm a bit nervous, but mostly excited for him. While they're there, John, Walt and I are going to hang out in New York for a few days. I'm hoping to turn forty years old there. I'll also hopefully get to visit my friend from New Jersey.

Sam, driving home from swimming lessons, "Mom, who made the lights?" That's a good question, I'm not sure. "No, like who actually made the lights... like the street lights on the road?" Well, I suppose someone who specializes in lights, like an electrical engineer, or someone like that... I don't... I don't really know. Well, since a person made the lights and then God made that person, so technically, God made the lights, right!?

My New Jersey friend, Deb. I met Deb when we were holidaying in the Bahamas, over twelve years ago. Bella was just a little nine-month-old crawling around the hotel lobby floor, and I remember sipping a glass of white wine and pounding the free bowl of nuts and bolts. I remember feeling so overwhelmed with life being a new mother. The most important job of my life was also the most challenging and exhausting. To make matters worse, John's lovely Uncle passed away right before we left, and we found out as we boarded the plane. Also, we found out my Great-Auntie Jean passed away. So, I had my hormones and my many emotions swirling around me, and I felt no real control over any of them. I think that glass of wine in the lobby was a time where I could just escape from it all, let Bella safely roam around, watch people oooo and awe over her, and feel like maybe I could unwind a bit.

Vacationing with young children—no one ever tells you how draining it is. Anyone else out there need a vacation from your vacation? Yes please. A 100 times yes, every single time.

Back to my friend Deb. Deb was married to Big Joe, and they had Little Joe, who was around the same age as Bella. I love meeting people when we go away on holidays. It's so nice getting to know other people from around the world. John and I love seeing what other people do for a living and hearing about how they live their lives. We're inspired by others and always like to get little tips and ideas. We like looking at real estate and daydreaming. And... and, I actually have a few holiday friends that I keep in touch with. My favourites are Deb and Jackie. Deb is a true light. She is a kind, and loving, sensitive being. When we met, we didn't know it at the time, we probably did on a deeper level. But years later, we would support each other as both of our Dads slipped away from brain diseases. We are more like pen pals, really, but even the word *pen pals* seems more surface-like. There's a real connection between the two of us. She's also another one of my cheerleaders. Her support of my love of music has always stayed close to my heart; she would even play it for her Dad. I actually ended up getting to meet her Dad when John and I went to visit them in New Jersey, about six years ago. I got to meet the staff at his care home, and then I got to sing a couple of a cappella songs for the residents.

> *I used to think that you would always be here,*
> *but I also know that life can be unfair.*
> *I used to think that it would last forever.*
> *When I reach for you, no one is there.*
> *I used to be a fan of change,*
> *but now that just is not the case.*
> *Wishing it was yesterday*
> *I hate the thought of going on this way.*
> *I can't take this anymore.*
> *Take me with you, I am yours.*
> *I love you.*
>
> Ellen Kolenick, 'Used to Think'

Deb's Dad passed away about two months ago. To be honest, when I met him, I didn't think he could possibly keep going much longer at that point, which was over six years ago. Deb was his only child and his constant companion. Even while raising her two young children, Deb was always by his side. They had little Joe and their daughter Juliette, both having some health complications of their own—but somehow Deb continued to show up for her Dad while raising her young family. As an only child, Deb's steadfast love and support was such an inspiration to me. I wanted to be that for my Dad. When Deb sent me a copy of the words she wrote about her father, when he finally passed away, I thought she should write a book.

I wrote this song ('El Dorado') in New York City. It was the first of my piano compositions; it was the beginning of a big change for me. On this trip, I chose not to drink any alcohol, and I really took in the city, the musicals, culture, the excitement. I... I didn't want to spend any time hungover or wondering if I dreamt this or that. I wanted to be fully present while watching my first Broadway musicals, which were *Come From Away* and *Hamilton*. New York lit me up.

This trip was a long time coming. I went back to the building where we were staying, and there was this baby grand piano there. I stayed up late playing. Even typing this, I can feel the New York City energy. I loved it; I felt so alive. El Dorado was the name of the building we were staying at. And, El Dorado is the name of this song. I felt incredible. Babysitter Camille was at home watching our babies, and life was amazing. Absolutely amazing... except my Dad was so sick. Right before we left, he took a turn for the worse.

CHAPTER TWENTY-SIX
DONUT QUEEN

June 20, 2022
6:08 a.m.

I sat down this morning feeling a little groggier than usual. John and I shared a bottle of white wine last night. Walt got up and needed a quick warm-up. Umm... I didn't even look at the clock, and John just came into my closet sanctuary and said, "Walt got up about 2 a.m., got up again at 5:45 a.m., anyways, I'm out; I'm heading to the gym." I'm really trying to commit to the gym again because I'm convinced, although I dread it, it's so good for me.

There's no more school for Walt—he's officially on summer holidays. Sam has a stuffy nose, and so I may let them both stay home together. We'll see. Back to the gym topic, John got me going quite regularly about a year and a half ago. He said it was important for me to get some core strength and a change of scenery. I didn't know it at the time, but it was a double blessing because I would often go to the gym and then, on the way home stop in at the care home, where my Dad lived, and bring him his favourite maple cream donuts. Some days I got to go in, but by the end, because of COVID, I was just leaving his treats at the front for the staff to take in to him.

Dad would be sitting at his regular spot in the dining room. I'd drive up and visit with him, and watch him eat his donut. Sometimes I'd sing to him and to whomever else was around, other times we'd just hang out and I'd watch him scarf down his donut and call him an "oinker," and he'd burst out with a laugh. I'd yell through the glass, "Dad, you're such an oinker!" And, he just laughed!

Closer to the end of his life, the staff would help him eat his donut. It was all so gradual, I don't even recall the end of the one phase leading into the next. I do remember he called me the Donut Queen. I loved when he called me that.

I've heard people say that if you don't have time to exercise and meditate, then you're too busy. Yeah, it's... it's a saying: If you're too busy to exercise and meditate, then you're too busy.

I have our babysitter coming at 9:15 a.m. so I can sneak off to the gym, but I feel like I'm slow as molasses this morning. Funny, my sister-in-law, who studies and teaches Feldenkrais, just sent me an article that talks about the art and the benefits of slow. She sent it to me regarding my music and upcoming piano exam. Today, I will practice playing all my pieces and scales slowly. Since I'm tired already, maybe a shade hungover, maybe that won't be a big stretch.

The other day, I was driving with Bella, and when driving past this certain street, she told me that it reminded her of this guy in her class, that knew the lyrics to the song

'If I Had a Million Dollars' by Barenaked Ladies. She said the lyrics were "I'd buy you a llama," and she didn't believe him. So, they had this back and forth about the song, and he ended up finding the lyrics and proving he was right. Out of nowhere, the song came on the radio, and Bella's mind was blown. She couldn't believe she was just thinking of this friend and the conversation they had, and then the song came on the radio. It was so sweet to watch her mind be so blown like that. I love stuff like that. In the meantime, on the radio, they just said the jackpot was $55 million, and I had a weird feeling like I could win the lottery.

CHAPTER TWENTY-SEVEN
DOWNPOUR

June 21, 2022
6:06 a.m.

The downpour yesterday afternoon was like noth-ing I'd ever seen or experienced in a very long time. At about 2 p.m., the sky burst, and the rain poured so hard from the clouds it looked like it was bouncing off the pavement, coming up from the ground.

> *You came in like the rain,*
> *felt so refreshed, I forgot about the pain.*
> *But now you're gone,*
> *and the sun is here to stay.*
> *Can't believe we're through,*
> *in the blink of an eye,*
> *the clouds began to move.*
> *And now you're gone.*
> *And I have myself to blame.*
> *I want the rain.*
> *Give me the rain...*
>
> Ellen Nasser, 'Stay Rain' [unreleased version]

Since Walt is home now, he took this as an opportunity to grab an umbrella and run outside. He was so sweet. Out in the front yard, nothing but grey and wet with Walt running around in his bare feet with a bright rainbow umbrella. He's so refreshing. Then, before I knew it, our wild child ran upstairs, put on his trunks, then started running around the backyard laughing, and enjoying, and squealing. He's got this high-pitched scream that you can't even believe. It's... it's an absolute shriek. He did this full lap around the concrete and the exterior of our pool, and he just ran and ran, as fast as he could. It was so amazing to see him so full of life. He was fearless.

Do you remember Lieutenant Dan in *Forrest Gump* when he was having it out with God? It was one of the most memorable parts of the movie for me. Someone not being able to forgive God for their lot in life. Needing to blame someone for their pain. Lieutenant Dan was an example of not being able to forgive. He was so angry with God, he blamed Him for everything. Until he didn't... he finally had it out with God in that storm, while he swam in the ocean. And, after all was said and done, Lieutenant Dan found peace.

There was this laughter and release of energy between Walt and Mother Nature. I don't know how to explain it.

> *Perhaps it's just a dream, perhaps it's just a dream.*
> *Why, it's no surprise that I didn't want to leave.*
> *But now I'm gone, and the sun is in the sky.*
> *Oh I want the rain, I need the rain,*
> *and I don't know why.*
> *I want the rain (want the rain).*
> *I need the rain (need the rain).*
> *And I don't know why.*
> *And I don't know why.*

Ellen Nasser, 'Stay Rain' [unreleased version]

It was over as fast as it began. A gentle reminder to me to keep showing up and enjoying life, no matter what cards we're handed. And remember, a lot of those early years for Walt was during the pandemic. So yeah, I'm... I'm sure it... it affected him as it affected all of us.

I ran into an old acquaintance walking downtown, who I hadn't seen in a while. As we were catching up, she mentioned she had been fighting cancer. I noticed her hair growing back and felt deep compassion for what she was going through.

Shortly thereafter, gratitude poured into my heart for the abundance that I have in my life. As we finished up our visit, she looked at me and simply said, "Keep enjoying your life."

As simple as that... keep enjoying your life.

Some of these thoughts that I make up in my head are... are just like: "Oh, Ellen, always paying too much attention to work, and hobbies, and creating." Or, "Oh, Ellen, never really feeling content with... with what she has—always looking for more."

These thoughts would paralyze me if I listened to them, so I have to allow them to pass on by. This is what I'm learning over and over again: My emotions and thoughts in my head aren't necessarily true. We can notice them and allow them to pass on by. Like Eckhart Tolle says, "Michael Singer says, 'We are this constant blue sky and the emotions and thoughts are just simply those—they're clouds passing by, in a constant blue sky.'" You know my brother once said, "You don't have to let your emotions drag you around like a cart and a horse." We do actually have control of our thoughts. Well, we have control of how we respond. It's as simple as taking a step back and asking yourself... Is it true? In this case, I know they're not. Not even close. I live a unique life. And, guess what... we all do.

I'm very interested in other people's lives, what they had for breakfast, how many siblings they have, what are some of their heartaches, and what are their ways of coping and healing. I am fascinated with people.

Recently, I have figured out there are two types of people:

1. People who want to go to the self-checkout line, fight with the technology, weighing their groceries and trying to pack their own eggs.

2. There's the other people who want to stand in the grocery line, visit with people ahead of them, and have a connection with the checkout person.

On most days, I am the second person, hands down. For the most part, I love people. I feel energized by people, I love helping people, and connecting with them. And, I hope that whoever crosses my path feels a little bit better than when the conversation started. I know sometimes I'm not at my best, but like everyone else, I'm a constant work in progress. A real work of art, or is it a piece of work? Depends on who you ask. Anyways, we all are, and we must remember to take it easy on ourselves and on others.

Writing something like this does take a certain amount of courage. I pulled that card yesterday, courage, and I wondered why. As I'm writing this, I know it takes courage to wake up each morning and sit down and write with my open heart. I'm moving the energy; I'm quieting my chirping mind that's telling me this is stupid and I have no business writing my story. It takes courage to sit and feel that and let it go. Keep enjoying your life!

I'm ready, I can feel it in my feet.
I'm ready, I can feel it in my heartbeat.
Don't you know when it snows down below,
the flowers still are growin'.
Don't you know when it all falls apart,
there's a deeper knowin'.
Every time I say goodbye, I want you to stay.
With thoughts in my mind, if I wanted it this way.
Try to get some sleep, but it's just no use.
Tossin' all night long, only thinkin' 'bout you.
At times we barely made it; everything was a fight.
Wake up, cryin' in the middle of the night.
You break my heart, and be on your way.
And feel lost again, promise this time you'll stay.
I'm ready, I can feel it in my feet.
I'm ready, I can feel it in my heartbeat.
Don't you know, when the thunder rolls,
there's blue behind it.
Don't you know, when the darkness comes,
there's light within it.
Every time we try again, it's good for a while.
We both really try. I remember how to smile.
We laugh and we joke, just like it used to be.
Two of us together, why can't you see?
I'm ready, I can feel it in my feet.
I'm ready, I can feel it in my heartbeat.

Ellen Nasser, 'Feel It in My Feet' [unreleased version]

Yesterday, one of my dearest friends, who I refer to as Michelle the Fishiest Fisher around—from Whitehorse—called me to let me know that one of the songs that I'm working on inspired her for next season's dance recital. We met at the Canadian College of Performing Arts in 2004, and she is such a beautiful, exquisite dancer. Both of us were chosen from Across-Canada audition to perform in a few productions on the West Coast, and then, of course, to attend the college after a full summer of performing. We met there, didn't spend too much time together at the College the first year, but seemed to bond the second—we have stayed connected ever since.

Of course, we also have our dear Eric, now from Australia, in our little group chat as well, the one called 'My Darlings', which reminded me of my dream that ignited this creation. We are always a text or video message away. And, I laugh because Eric and Fisher were doing yoga and living a moderately clean lifestyle, way back at college. I can remember telling my niece Aidan about this awesome band I just heard of, and she giggled because she loved them too, but they were on their final tour—One Direction. I heard about One Direction as they were wrapping it up.

I can remember when I was performing on the cruise ship, everyone was talking about who their Hollywood crush was, and you could pick only one person. So, the cast we were all visiting and putting on our makeup and getting ready. And... Okay, the Hollywood crush story. I heard everybody sharing theirs, but in all honesty, I didn't even know many of the names that they had shared. I'm ignorant that way. John still can't believe I never know who... You know this celebrity or this celebrity is. He just said the other day something about someone called Elon Musk. I couldn't make this up, and I said to him, "What is that?" He asked if I was serious. John, I was dead serious. I'd never heard those words in my life.

Anyway, I was twenty-three years old and backstage waiting for my turn. I was so excited, I couldn't wait to share my Hollywood crush with the cast. Okay, Brook, Sham, Janine... Ahem, throat cleared, Ellen, I'm ready. Okay, my turn any moment now.

"Ellen, who's your Hollywood crush?"

"Tom Hanks."

Whaaaaaaaat? My cast was like, "Tom Hanks? Ellen, are you for real?!"

Someone followed up with, "What, Ellen, are you 40?!"

I was shocked, no one else named him as *their* crush. Were *THEY* for real? Whatever. I can remember telling John that story, and he laughed, saying something like, "Ellen, don't tell people that, it makes me look bad— they'll question your taste." Oh, come on, Tom Hanks is a hunk. You all know it! Maybe not in *Forrest Gump*, but he's still hunky. He is hunky! Like, even reading this out loud, Tom Hanks is hunky. Isn't he?

Back to Fisher—where was I? Right, I sent my new website for her and Eric to check out. So now, Diana has it set up so it says, *Real Estate and Music*. I love the clarity of the website. Lordy, is there going to be a new tab now? Writer? Nope, not a chance! Real Estate, Music, that'll be it. Ahh, Real Estate Artist—I... Whatever... No, Real Estate... Oh, maybe... actually... maybe Artist, I kinda like that.

Anyway, Fisher sent a text and said, "Ellen, this is my most favourite picture of you." And, she took a snap. And, the funny part is that when I phone John, he has favourited it in his phone, too. And, it's his favourite picture of me, too. He has it saved in his phone, and it appears every time I call him. It's from one of the most magical nights of my life, singing four of my original Christmas songs with the Saskatoon Symphony Orchestra. I can remember I got another little nudge from Professor Dean McNeil, and he asked me if I was going to have an album to sell the night I performed, and I thought, "How am I gonna do that?" Easy, create a Christmas album.

I told John that it was on my list of things to do before the show, and he's like, "You can't release a Christmas album, Ellen, only famous people do that."

I miss you more and more each day.
I miss you more at Christmas than on any other day.

That's the ticket, whenever John tells me I can't do something, guess what, I do it! I swear, after sixteen years, he does it just to poke me, I think.

And then, on that note, he just walked in with my green tea in my favourite 'ME + YOU' mug. Handing me my mug of tea, he's debating what to do this morning. To finish his shower with a minute of freezing cold, or not to because he feels a bit sniffly. I voted yes because I swear it boosts your immune system—I think he's voting no. He's so funny. Apparently, we're funny. People say it all the time. When we got together, and John asked my parents if he could propose to me, Mom basically said that us two getting together saved two other people. No one else would have been able to put up with me; John is a handful in his own way, too. We're a good balance, most of the time. We've had such a beautiful love story that everything after forty years for me is a bonus. I could die tomorrow feeling like the luckiest person on the planet. No one would have to feel sorry for me or our family. We all understand that life is fleeting and it could be over or change in the blink of an eye. We have faith. That's why I'm choosing to enjoy my life, and that's why I'm choosing to write.

CHAPTER TWENTY-EIGHT
SECRETS

June 22, 2022
6:48 a.m.

Last night, Bella and Millie had soccer practice, and then we all snuck off to Beppi's on 10th Street for gelato. I saw a post of a lemon curd gelato earlier in the day, and we had to go. I was telling my neighbour about it, and she texted and said to be sure to take puppy Sofi. I wondered why, and she said they give the pets a mini vanilla gelato in a cone. Are you kidding me? We took a little video of Sofi licking her ice cream; it was the sweetest thing in the world. I asked Bella to make the video a post for my Instagram, and she… she took the little ice cream song, and Sofi licking it. And, it was the sweetest thing ever.

Right after I gave birth to Walt, I had this idea where I would interview random women everywhere I went and ask them their one secret. I felt like if we all shared our little secrets more often, the world would be a better place. I called it *One Woman, One Minute, One Secret.*

They would just share a little tidbit that could make parenting easier, self-love easier, making lunches easier, life easier. I stopped collecting the tidbits, but I think I may start up again.

I'm not even kidding, who knew that Beppi's served little ice cream cones to pets? That's a little secret I'd like to shout from the rooftops because it's the sweetest thing ever, and lights people up. In fact, if you've ever listed and sold a house, you know how the showing requests may happen in the blink of an eye. Well, I coach my clients to have their properties "show home" ready; ready throughout the process, and remind them that a house on the market is not a comfortable house you live in. It doesn't matter if it's a $169,000 or a three-million-dollar listing. The property needs to be decluttered and pristine. So, I called and let her know, you know, I apologize, there's a last-minute showing request, and she said no problem and shared her secret.

"What is it?" I asked.

She had a few plastic laundry baskets and did a 10-minute tidy, throwing everything in the baskets and drives off with them in the back of her vehicle. Is that not the most brilliant thing you've heard? Seriously, throw dirty dishes in, pens, papers, books, anything lying around. Take it one step further, I thought each kid could have a basket to quickly tidy up their bedrooms, too. Honestly, this one has stuck with me for a long time. It's so smart and cuts the anxiety of showing your house in half.

Another *One Woman, One Minute, One Secret* that I got from a friend, honestly, blew my mind—I've been doing it for years now. You know how everyone wants to add more greens to their morning smoothies? I had no idea, but if you buy fresh organic spinach in one of those long, plastic containers and put it directly into the freezer, each leaf of spinach crystallizes, and you can just simply reach in and grab handfuls of spinach and put them into your smoothies every morning. Seriously! Incredible! I always thought frozen spinach were those like chunks of ice blocks, and I thought, what kind of brain surgery this is to put into my smoothie in the morning? No, you just place the plastic container into the freezer. You won't believe it. Anyways...

My Smoothie Recipe:

    2 bananas
    2 cups of frozen mixed berries
    2 tablespoons of ground flax
    2 cups of frozen spinach
    5 pitted dates
    water
    ice

I love it! It's great. And, for vitamins, I do:

    4 Vitamin D. because I think we need more Vitamin D,
    and then...
    B Complex (and some)
    Zinc (and some)
    Magnesium and Potassium, and, then I have...
    Omega 3 Oil, which is so good for your brain, and your
    nails, and your hair, all those good things

And then, for quite some time, I have done basically a hot shower, for the first 5 to 7 minutes. And then I crank it to freezing, and breathe, and gasp, and realign, and then I do it for about 1 minute to two. Hmmm... Two is being really generous. I do it a minute until I cry... No, I'm joking. I do over a minute. And, Ahh... I get out and barely need a towel because the warm air is so soothing. It's incredible and exhilarating.

And then John and I replaced our morning coffee with green tea. I know, it sounds barfy, but it's amazing once you get into it. The green tea hydrates, calms and grounds us. And, if you asked John 10 years ago if someone would ever be able to take away his two cups of caffeinated coffee in the morning, he would have said, "Not a chance." He admitted he was tired of feeling shaky, sweaty, and having a headache if he missed his coffee. We still enjoy decaf on the weekends; that's us living it up. I know. It's been a major morning shift, but there's no question about it, it's changed our lives in many ways.

Okay, on another note—speaking of secrets, another friend of mine said the greatest thing that she does for her household every Sunday is to fill a huge Tupperware container with fresh cut-up veggies. It's a perfect way to sneak more veggies into her family's lives, and the kids inevitably snack on them throughout the week. Added bonus, it's easy for people to just grab them while packing the lunches. This beautiful friend of mine also tries to make a big pot of soup or stew on a Sunday evening, just to have for people to grab a quick bowl throughout the week. You know, it's so inspiring.

I have another—I have a friend that walks downtown with a pocket of $5 to $10 Tim Horton's cards and gives them to anyone who is asking for change—that way they can find a Tim's and grab a coffee, tea, sandwich, a cup of soup, or a donut—whatever they need to fuel their bodies. I think it's a brilliant idea. And, so generous... generous on so many different levels.

Another secret—someone told me that they have an ice tray of freshly squeezed lemon juice in the freezer for easy access to fresh lemon. She said she can easily put the cubes in a jug of water, salad dressings, or when she is cooking. And, that way, she doesn't have to fuss with getting lemon, cutting it and juicing it every single time. Okay, and another—my other friend says she drinks a huge glass of water the minute she wakes up. She said it's a game-changer. I can remember my Dad having a big glass of water right before he headed out to work. It totally makes sense; our bodies are so dehydrated from a big night's sleep; it needs hydration to get into the flow of a new day.

So, all of these secrets gave me the neatest idea of creating a series of books: That's next... you ready for it...

One Woman, One Minute, One Secret – for The Mom
One Woman, One Minute, One Secret – for The Artist
One Woman, One Minute, One Secret – for The Athlete
One Woman, One Minute, One Secret – for The 40-Year-Old
One Woman, One Minute, One Secret – for The Entrepreneur
One Woman, One Minute, One Secret – for The Real Estate Agent
One Woman, One Minute, One Secret – for The Mechanic
One Woman, One Minute, One Secret – for The Lover

Wouldn't it be so amazing to travel the world and collect all these little secrets, and compile them into clips and then create little books for people to give each other? Yes, please. Who wants to help me get this project off the ground? Okay, no, not yet, hold on to your horses... I'll finish *this* project first.

It's funny because most people I talked to didn't think they had a secret to share. They didn't think that they knew something that would make someone else's life easier or better; they didn't think they had anything to share, but as we talked, you know they were right... They didn't have one; they had five to ten, and we just visited for about, you know, ten minutes. I remember a young gal in the airport said every morning, she gets up and makes her fiancé eggs. I can remember it, I can remember where I was standing, I can remember the conversation, and she said, "It makes him feel good and cared for, and she felt amazing doing something nice for him each and every single day." That's the kind of energy I love to live my life in. I believe that energy exudes health, it exudes connection—and, when we are doing these acts of kindness to each other and light each other up, we're changing the world, One Woman, One Minute, One Secret, at a time.

Another neat secret, I'm sorry, I just have one more, was from a friend who wanted to keep her love life exciting. Are you ready for this? She occasionally would text her husband using a made-up name and tell him where to meet her. She'd dress up totally different from anything she'd typically wear. They'd meet for coffee or dinner, maybe even a nice hotel room. They'd just have fun with each other, bring a lightness, play and goofiness to their relationship. They had a couple of rules: They weren't allowed to argue, and they weren't allowed to talk about the kids, the scheduling, or the in-laws.

You showed me love when I needed it most.
I needed someone who I didn't know.
You brought me in, and you made me your own.
You didn't even know me; you didn't even know me.
You watched every step, as you stood by my side.
Felt weak and sad, before I arrived.
Kissing the moon and the sun in the sky.
You didn't even know me; you didn't even know me.

I don't say a word, but I feel you must know.
Lately that I have been travelling down long, lonely roads...
Not sure what's to come.
Though there's one thing I know.
You didn't even know me; you didn't even know me.
So, come with me now, it's here I will stay.
Through all the twists and turns and changes along the way.
And starting right now, there's no time to waste.
You didn't even know me; you didn't even know me.
I don't say a word, but I feel you must know.
Lately that I have been travelling down long, lonely roads...
Not sure what's to come.

Though there's one thing I know.
You didn't even know me; you didn't even know me.
Not sure what's to come, in your arms I am home.
You didn't even know me. I didn't even know you.

Elly Thorn, 'You Didn't Even Know Me'

CHAPTER TWENTY-NINE
PiANO

June 23, 2022
6:09 a.m.

I'm on the countdown to my piano exam. I can feel my nerves. I was telling the kids if we were at a music concert and someone asked me to get up on stage and sing with them, I'd be up there, no problem. I'd still be nervous, but mostly excited.

This piano thing is rocking my world. It feels like so much work and pressure to me. When I'm playing my own compositions, I'm considerably more grounded, but this RCM stuff, this Royal Conservatory of Music. Holy, is it challenging! I had my piano lesson yesterday and had to breathe... so deeply. Just writing about it makes my breath stuck.

July 9th is the big day! I'll start with my technical part, which is the adjudicator picking any scales and having me play them. I can't believe that I know what someone is talking about when they ask me to play an arpeggio of the dominant 7th chord of the G major scale with my left hand, the tonic chords of the Db [flat] minor melodic scale with my right hand, the solid chord of the diminished 7th chord of the E major scale with your right hand. Oh, yeah! I know it, and I just said it, and I just visualized it! Crazy!

That alone is a win. I can't do it all the time, but I do understand what they're asking, and I've learned a lot in a short amount of time.

You know, as I'm writing this down, I have to stick to it. I will practice ten minutes of note rush every day until my exam. My biggest challenge is reading notes. I know I have to change my attitude, but I can't stand sight-reading. Martin explains that most pianists have their array of talents. Some are amazing sight readers, they can sit down and read and play anything put in front of them, some are beautiful composers who can create music without knowing the theory behind it, some are amazing teachers who can light up and share their gift and passion with others, nobody is great at everything—that's just the way it is. So, when someone says they're a musician, there is a huge scale of what musician means and where that musician lands on the chart. Not every guitar player can play in the studio. Some players are amazing on stage at live performances, while others... they're incredible, cuddled up in a small booth with dim lighting at Bart McKay Productions. All I know is that I had the nudge to start playing piano. My nudge was to study, focus, learn how to read music, and create piano compositions. I always listen to my nudges, even though they don't really make sense, all the time. The truth is, nothing ever really makes sense. You can't calculate every step of your life; it's impossible. We must trust.

I was watching Walt at gymnastics last night, and I looked at all these young kids, and thought to myself:

Wow, they all wanted to be here on Earth. I wonder what their lives are going to teach them. What will be in store for each and every one of them? I wonder what their stories will be? And, I wonder how they'll adapt and learn as they go? And how they'll all affect each other and one another. We just have no idea what will happen in our lives.

Even thinking about Dad, his story, Mom's story, their story, our story. I wouldn't change it. And, I know it's pointless to let my mind whimsically think about things like that. It doesn't matter what I could or would have changed.

I miss him so much. Our family isn't the same, and it never will be, but I must accept it.

I met a nice Mom at gymnastics last night, and she said she didn't like change at all. If I'm being totally honest with myself, maybe I don't really like it either. Change can be challenging. But change also brings a wealth of growth and maturity.

I have learned so much and I've had to lean into so much of my life and relationships because of this journey. I do have a deep knowing that that's why we're here. I do trust that all will be well.

CHAPTER THIRTY
HERE COMES THE BRIDE

June 24, 2022
6:09 a.m.

We had another absolute downpour yesterday. But the weather was perfect for Camille's backyard bridal brunch; our girls ended up finishing their exams early, so I picked them up and we all went. It was so much fun. Babysitter Camille's sister, Arielle, planned some games, which were super sweet. She put everyone in teams, gave each team a roll of toilet paper, got them to pick their bride and then create a toilet paper wedding dress and then get them to model down a catwalk. It was such a neat idea and a great icebreaker.

Next, we had to name about fifteen love songs, name and artist. It was tough because she would only play a little bit of the song—most songs were totally recognizable, but I couldn't believe how many artists I didn't know, not to mention the actual titles of the songs. Too funny, Arielle played a Michael Bublé song, and I got so excited thinking about John's and my wedding day.

For some reason, I can't think of our wedding song. I'd better check out a list of Michael's songs because it's going to drive me crazy. Anyway, as we were lined up to fill our plates with fresh salads, and crêpes, and fruits, and all kinds of meats, and cheese, dates and spreads, one of their relatives said to me, "Hmmm... Be sure to check your wedding video—then you'll remember your wedding song."

And, I told her it was a touchy subject. She laughed and said, "Why?" Well, that was one of our first fights as husband and wife. Yeah. Let me tell you about our wedding first.

Of course, like all of my stories, they're my experiences through my rose-coloured glasses. But our wedding was perfect. John said he started getting my ring designed after we were dating for about six months. And, I can't believe it, but he said he just knew. From the moment we met, we felt the magic. I had been dumped many times to this day, I still can't believe he wanted me... and so quickly. He knew. He said he drove around with the ring in the console of his truck for quite some time. He had Mom and Dad's permission, and was waiting for the perfect moment. We were spending lots of time together, but I wouldn't move in with him because I had done that before in my life, and it didn't end the way I hoped. We were at his condo, and we woke up one Saturday morning, and walked down to the riverbank, and before I knew it, at Riverlanding—remember this was fifteen years ago—there was only a walk path, no development, he was down on one knee proposing to me. I couldn't believe my eyes.

I still can't believe it.

After my heart was broken, I really didn't think I could love again, and most of all, I didn't think anyone would want to marry me. I was twenty-four years old, and looking back now, I know I was young, but I felt like my love life was doomed. Isn't it funny thinking back and remembering those feelings? All my siblings had found their special people, and I felt like the black sheep. Anyway, we weren't sure where to get married. We took a road trip to British Columbia and looked at a few lodges and lakes, but at the end of the day, we thought we better get married at home because it would be easier for his parents and my grandparents not to travel. We got married at the Faculty Club at the University. It was so beautiful. And, John asked if his eighty-year-old Mom could sew my wedding dress, and I said, "Yes."

So then, John's sister, Mom and my Mom went to pick out the softest silk. The pattern was simple, straight-lined and elegant—I was beyond thrilled. Everyone was making a fuss over me. I had a fiancé, and I was going to be a bride and a wife. Ahh... even just reading that... one of my dreams was coming true. We asked Dad to officiate our wedding. I walked down the aisle towards the stone fireplace at the Faculty Club, where Dad and John were waiting for me. I can remember John's Dad saying, "Oh, wow!" out loud as I walked down the aisle, and it made me laugh and relax. It actually made everyone else relax a little bit, too. There was a string quartet to the left of us, I'm just picturing it all right now, and my sister and John's best man were up there waiting. It was a heavenly August evening.

I surprised John with this song. I played it on guitar.

When I look at you,
I see forever in your smile.
And I, I would walk for miles and miles,
until I'm yours,
until I'm yours.
When I hear your laugh,
it makes me feel complete.

My heart, it skips a beat,
so glad I'm yours,
so glad I'm yours.

If there's anything that you want.
If there's anything that you need.
I am yours forevermore,
to put it perfectly.
If there's anything I can say.
If there's anything I can do.
I'll be right here by your side.
This I promise you.

When you're feeling blue,
and it's tough to see the end...
Remember, I am right here by your side.
I'm your lover and your friend.

If there's anything that you want.
If there's anything that you need.
I am yours forevermore,
to put it perfectly.
And, if there's anything I can say.
If there's anything I can do.
I'll be right here by your side.
This I promise you.

I always dreamed of loving someone like you.
I swear that I'll look after you.
It wasn't easy getting here.
I'm so happy I came home, home to you.

If there's anything that you want.
If there's anything that you need.
I am yours forevermore,
to put it perfectly.
And, if there's anything I can say.
If there's anything I can do.
I'll be right here by your side.
This I promise, promise you.

Ellen Kolenick, 'Dear John'

Straight from my heart, though, I could barely get through it. To this day, every single word is true. Almost fifteen years later.

It's true, just listening to this song makes my heart happy. It's crazy, we inspire each other and work well together. Overall, we are such good friends, and I know I've said it lots in my entries, but on top of everything, I love his sense of humour. We seem to bring out the best in each other, and I think that's the main thing for us. We want to keep doing the work and committing to each other on this journey together as long as it lasts. We honour our time together and take it one day at a time.

There have been times in the past fifteen years where we've needed counselling, space, personal healing time and workshops—but we keep choosing each other, over and over again, and I'm so grateful. If there's a time when we don't, that's okay, too. John said, "If we call 'er quits, he'd tell everyone it was okay because we had a pretty good run." And, he always jokes to me, he's almost done his life sentence, and the funny part is, we have had a pretty good run. We have done and created so much together. Our babies are our biggest joy, and I would never change a single thing.

So, after the wedding, we called our videographer and wanted to, you know, settle up and watch the wedding video. And, ahh... we don't know what happened. The tape got lost, or record wasn't hit. We don't know what happened. He doesn't know what happened. Can you believe it? We were all sick about it. All three of us, and it was just like ahh... can you imagine how he felt? How we felt? Ahh... my goodness, and we didn't end up hiring a photographer either, but thankfully, one of John's sisters took photos all night long. And, I am forever grateful for her doing that. I have this photo album that I just cherish and we look at it all the time.

CHAPTER THIRTY-ONE
CAMiLLE'S BiG DAY

June 25, 2022
10:22 a.m.

So, yesterday morning was a bit of a blur, but our whole family was dressed and ready and got to Camille and Zak's wedding by 1:30 p.m. We did it! Barely, but we did it!

I had nothing to wear, so I texted Aritzia Ashley to see if she could put some outfits together for me. I told her I was going to be playing piano at a wedding at 2 p.m., and didn't have much time. I zipped right over to the mall, and she had six outfits waiting for me. She was absolutely amazing. Remember, I'm a terrible shopper; it gives me nervous bowel. So much to choose from, how does a person know what to put together? Oh yeah, on the way to the till, Ashley had just happened to ask, "Oh, whose wedding?" And, I just happened to say, "I don't know if you'd know her, but it's Camille and she's getting married today." And then, Ashley was SO excited because she used to work with Camille's sister Arielle, who also knows Arielle's Mom. Anyways, we were just laughing at, like, what are the chances.

In the meantime, Babysitter Brooklynn took the boys for haircuts, John picked up subs and the girls from school and like clockwork, we all arrived back at home by 12:20 p.m. I walked in the door, and John had all four kids at the island eating. We said goodbye and a great big thank you to Brooklynn, and then started getting ready.

I took out my magical findings, and Bella ended up wearing one of my outfits. She said she didn't really like it, and said, in the future, she wants to do her own shopping. As I said, Bella is very clear on what she wants in her life. So, I said she can, but to please wear this outfit *just* for today.

Speaking of dresses, Camille's dress was absolutely stunning on her. She was such a stunning bride; she was literally glowing. That's one of Camille's most admirable characteristics: Her ability to just focus in and get the job done. Her sister Arielle said in her speech that she isn't very easily shaken—no kidding, she's been able to handle the Nasser household for this long, but really—it's quite amazing to see someone handle life with such clarity and grace, especially at such a young age. Back to the dress, I can't even explain what the dress was like because it wouldn't even do it justice. It fit her like an absolute glove, with embroidered lace puffy sleeves and straight across the chest. Her hair was in this elegant low bun with a veil coming from it, her makeup was absolutely on point. I told Zak that she has been such a monumental part of our lives these past eight years. We have been through so much with her; she's helped our family out so much in so many different ways. And then I broke into tears. The ceremony was lovely; the kids behaved so well. Although we did have to bribe them.

I played my piano pieces, and they were lovely. I had to improvise a little bit because we were a little behind, but I think it was fine. People were just settling in and enjoying. It was a really nice experience for me and such an honour to be asked to share my music.

Watching Camille and Zak's slideshow was precious. They were such adorable little kids, and you can see how fast time passes. Some of the photos of Camille's high school graduation honestly seemed like yesterday. I can remember seeing those pictures, and it really doesn't feel like it was that long ago, so again, there's just that lingering feeling that we need to celebrate today, and now.

We need adventure and to explore more of this life. Heck, let the kids stay up late and let 'em dance till midnight; that's what we did.

CHAPTER THIRTY-TWO
FORTY DAYS TO FORTY

June 26, 2022
9:21 a.m.

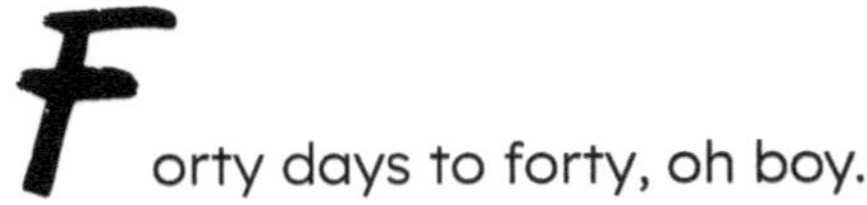

orty days to forty, oh boy.

Yesterday we spent most of the day at our neighbour's house. They invited all the guests at the wedding over for lunch. Some people make hosting look so easy. That's Joanne. She's the Queen Bee of their home and, as John says, "A true homemaker."

So, after John and I barked at each other yesterday morning, after I was on cloud nine talking about the wedding, Camille and love, just like that, John and I had it out the next morning. When John and I fight, we both usually storm around the house and inevitably end up doing dishes, or folding laundry, and... and barking at each other. Basically, trying to figure out who's the biggest victim.

So, the funniest thing happened. After our argument, which coincidentally was John being upset with the house, you know, looking like it exploded. And, we started tidying up, and you know, barking and blahhh... that was the morning. And, as we left to go next door, we stopped and we gave each other a hug, and gently patted each other on the back. And, as we were doing it, we both started laughing cause it was like hugging a stranger. Like, we barely touched each other, but we both wanted to pat each other on the back, because neither one of us really wanted to hug, but then we both didn't want to be fighting, so then we moved on with our day.

In the meantime, when we were over at the neighbours, one of the neighbours' brothers said, "You know, I... I was just thinking I'd like a quick tour of your house." He said, you know, he follows me on Facebook, and since John and I are both in real estate, he'd like to have a little check out of the house. John turned to me and smiled. This is what I'm saying about our lives—everything is always working for the greater good. Even when we can't see the blue sky through the clouds, there is always a master plan. How hilarious is it that we just spent the morning cleaning the house, and someone wants to pop over and look?

No, I don't really think it's earth-shattering that John and I had a fight, cleaned up the house and then ended up taking about fifteen people through our house—but there's definitely some magic there. Is there not?

In my first forty years, there's been pain and suffering for sure; our family's been through a lot these past ten years, but the bounty of blessings far outweighs the pain and suffering. And now I get to journey through this life knowing my Dad is with me. He's a strong spirit; he makes it known to all of us. So now, I have this inner peace and a deep knowing that everything will be okay, no matter what happens. I have the freedom to live in the moment, laugh until my stomach hurts, and I get to experience the array of emotions. I can find the strength. I can revisit conversations with our children, where I screwed up, where I wasn't my best, I can apologize, I can rework it, we can repair, we can grow together. I remind them that I, too, am learning along with them. I ask them for grace and forgiveness when I suck as a Mom. And you know what, even saying that I suck as a Mom. No, I maybe don't make the wisest choice that I could have made, and... and, as I say, how we just keep evolving together.

Nobody's guaranteed tomorrow. All the money, all the health, and all the praying doesn't guarantee you tomorrow.

I'm not saying live with reckless abandon, but I'm saying celebrate, celebrate each day. Live and make as many wise decisions and choices that you can. Drink it all in.

And I... I want to keep living this life and co-creating with God and the Universe. Together, we can create the life of our dreams. I feel lit up when I adventure, and I... I share. I want to light other people up just by living honestly. I won't be everyone's cup of tea, and in my first forty, I felt like I really wanted everyone to like me. I can tell in my next forty, it doesn't really matter. I have no control if my authenticity is driving someone else nuts; it's beyond my control, and there's not a chance in the world that I want to keep changing who I am to put everyone else at ease. I won't abandon myself.

My most sound advice is to surround yourself with people who bring out the best in you. Keep showing up with your own self-healing and continue reflecting and evolving. And, of course, living each day with love.

CHAPTER THIRTY-THREE
BE KIND

June 27, 2022
6:34 a.m.

I had a bit of a sleep-in, and it was nice. What a big weekend of celebrating! John's friend is in the city, and he's visiting from Finland, and we had a good catch-up yesterday. He's a very even-keeled, moderately tempered kinda guy. We talked about life and how it inevitably unfolds as it may without our control, and how important it is to protect our body, mind, and soul.

I'd forgotten this, but his Mom's obituary was in the newspaper, if you can imagine, the same day as my Dad's—again, what are the chances of that? John's best man, from our wedding, his Mom passed away around the same time as my Dad, and here we are talking about loss and the journey of losing a parent, almost exactly a year later. We also brushed on how everyone will experience loss differently, and how it can also show up and trigger a possible health crisis. He mentioned, he and John were previously talking about writing daily gratitudes, and he said essentially, a person is writing a prayer.

He grew up attending Church and said he prayed a fair amount as a child. As he got older, he just fell out of the habit of it. He mentioned that he'd been considering getting back into the practice of prayer. Then, very simply, he stated, "Well, there's no harm in it."

For some reason, that made me laugh because it's as simple and true as that. What's the harm in connecting each day, paying gratitude, asking for support, praying to God, Source, the Universe, whomever is listening? Look what we have to gain.

You want to make a difference today—do something kind for someone. Hold a door open, buy someone's coffee, give them a Tim's card, smile, make eye contact—it's just that simple. You want to make a difference in the world? It starts with one small gesture. It starts at home, and it starts in your neighbourhood, it starts within. You do something to light yourself up, then someone around you will feel lit up, who lights up another, who lights up another, and it goes on and on, and on.

I wish I could track the beautiful energy flow beginning from one simple connection and smile.

Let's be honest, all anyone really wants is to feel seen, heard, and paid attention to. My brother reminds me of this all the time. He's an expert at paying attention to people. We must take care of each other and show our love to one another, even when someone is being an asshole, *ESPECIALLY* when someone is being an asshole.

Have you ever heard this joke?

Every family has an asshole. If you're not sure who it is,

it's probably you. In other words, don't be a jerk. Don't be an ass. It hurts people's feelings and then contaminates the energy surrounding it. It's toxic and hurtful to your own self. It's not worth it; come back to love. God knows, I get sucked in being a jerk sometimes. It's so tempting to talk trash, gossip, and be nasty. It never fails, talking about people makes you feel poorly afterwards. Remember, always take the high road.

It reminds me of this teaching where they're trying to remind us to be mindful of the words we say. Our words are like feathers in a pillowcase. Once you let those feathers out... those words out, you won't be able to ever put them back into that pillow. But in some cases, the words can stay with someone, and you'll never really know their full impact.

Be energetically and emotionally responsible. I think that we must not only teach this to our children, but we also need to remind ourselves. I have a dear friend who can lovingly remind me of this and I can hear her say it. There was a time she just didn't partake in my childish, what I thought was harmless, jabbing about someone. It's not harmless and she lovingly reminded me of that. It's not kind, and others can feel your negative energy whether you think they can or not. And, to top it off, it's just a nasty habit to be harsh, judgmental and unkind.

How do you stop it? Eckhart Tolle says, "What do you do when you have a hot pan in your hand? You drop it."

Stop doing it. Make a choice not to engage. Change the topic. If you have a problem, go to the person and have the courage to open up your heart.

Connect, have a conversation and make the choice to change, and then let it go.

CHAPTER THIRTY-FOUR
GONE TO SHIT

June 28, 2022
10:26 a.m.

Well, everything has gone to shit this morning. Bella and I had words last night before she went to her baseball game. Walt woke us up at 1:35 a.m., so he slept with John, and I moved to his bed, and then my alarm went off at 5:45 a.m., and I literally picked up my phone, turned it off.

It's Tuesday. I can't stand Tuesdays. John said good morning to me with a cup of tea at 7:30 a.m., and got the kids up, and I went straight into real estate situations that needed to be worked out, not now, but right now. I haven't showered, I haven't done my Mandarin, I certainly haven't done yoga, and I'm sitting in a big load of my problems, both in reality and the ones that I'm creating in my head.

It's tough to snap out of moods like these. When I'm not the one in them, I can easily give someone a pep talk.

Today, I don't want to do that. I want to wallow. I want to feel sad. And, I want to make up stories in my head, and I wanna believe them. Even writing this, I can feel the intensity in my body. My mind is making up stories about almost anything in my life right now, my relationships, work situations, friendships, and I'm finding myself grasping onto things I can't and ultimately have no control over.

Why do we always want what we can't have? Why do I often want to be anywhere but here and now? What's up with me? Is it just my internal addiction to the feeling of uneasiness, and creating drama? Or am I just processing past patterns and habits that need to be healed? Why do I seem to be programmed to want to be drawn to the dark, rather than rise up to the light today? What is different today than yesterday when my day started out on a lower note, but my spirits were lifted by John and a simple cup of tea? Why didn't the simple cup of tea work this morning?

I was reading the beginning of my memoir last night, and I was so disappointed. I thought it was scattered, unfocused, with long, rambling sentences. The talk in my head was so negative. I kept trying to figure out, why am I doing this and how is this going to end up? And, I started wondering if there's a purpose to this? And then I started thinking that once I finish this on my birthday, maybe I'll just sit with it for a bit, and see how it blossoms. Yeah, I've committed to writing every day for seventy-four days, maybe I won't put all of the days into my memoir. I don't know.

You see, when I start getting all up in my head, this is what it looks like for me. I feel uptight; I worry—everything gets unclear. I feel sad, and I feel like everything sucks.

John just called and asked how I was. He said, "Let me cheer you up!" He told a stupid joke that wasn't even funny. So, not even funny that it's not even worth sharing here. Its lack of funny made me laugh.

You know, I asked him, "Am I too much?"

He simply said, "No, not to me."

CHAPTER THIRTY-FIVE
HEALING

June 29, 2022
6:24 a.m.

Today is the last day of school for Bella, Millie and Sam. John surprised them last night and filled their lunches with Lunchables, chocolate treats, fish crackers, Oreos and Sprite. Can you believe it! They were so excited! Bella lost in her baseball playoffs last night, so she came home a little blue. She was also blaming herself because she hit a ball someone caught, and the runner on second didn't tag up. Ahh... so it was a... I guess a double play... is that what you...? Yeah, I think it was a double play. I told her that's the joy of learning how to play the game. Anyway, they're all still figuring out the rules.

This morning, I lit my three candles for authenticity, joy and love. I've been in and out of a funk lately. Yesterday, I ended up going back and reading some more of the writing that I had been creating, and you know what... it lifted my spirits. I decided I must be on the right track if reading some of my pages made me feel a little bit better.

I'm reflecting on my inner state of being. And, I'm pretty sure I'm anxious because of my piano exam coming up. I was telling John yesterday that when the end is near, in something, I start procrastinating. I would never think I was a procrastinator, but obviously, I am. When I start getting closer to the final countdown, I start to shut down.

Today, I have my piano and Mandarin lessons. I'll practice about an hour right before I come home from the gym. I think that's what I'll do on the day of the exam—really warm up and have a full practice before the exam. As for the gym, John is trying to get me to commit to three days a week of lifting weights. He wants me to build muscle and strengthen my body. He says there's nothing better for mental health than being active. I know he's right. That being said, he just brought me a green tea and snuck off to the gym. He loves getting to the gym bright and early, then straight to work. He likes getting a great jump start to the day. Truly, the only bad thing about getting up early in the morning is that you have to get up. Once I'm up, I feel like I'm the Queen of the World! I can do anything! The trick is, though, you have to go to bed early. You need to get enough sleep to function at a higher level.

We protect sleep in our household. The girls have been giving us grief about it, wanting to stay up later and later, but we've put our foot down. Getting to bed by 9 p.m.ish is almost like medicine for the body, mind, heart, and soul. I realize some people are night owls, but for our family, early to bed and early to rise works the best.

Stacey, my lovely sister-in-law from Calgary, messaged me yesterday and said that Anne Bérubé is coming to Saskatoon tomorrow. I believe she's on her book tour to help promote The Burnout Antidote. Melissa, my dear friend, first introduced me to Anne's teachings when

I was about to give birth to Walt. I ended up missing Anne's workshop at an 'I Am Gathering' event in Saskatoon. As usual, thoughtful Melissa came to visit me afterwards and brought me a signed copy of her other book, Be Feel Think Do. I loved reading this book—it was wonderful. I was so inspired by it; I actually ended up creating a song after reading it. I've always wanted to go to one of her retreats; maybe I'll put that on my bucket list.

> *Speak to me, speak to me.*
> *I am listening, I am listening.*
> *Speak to me.*
> *How can I be? How can I be?*
> *I am listening, I am listening.*
> *Speak to me.*

Ellen Nasser, 'Speak to Me' [unreleased version]

Now, as I'm writing this, it should be on my list to read it again. As I think about my own life, I seem to be more of a Feel, Do, Be, Think, I don't know. Stacey said Anne's talk was amazing and that I should go when she comes to Saskatoon tomorrow. When I get a message like that, I listen. There are no coincidences.

I ended up meeting and seeing Anne in Banff at another I Am Gathering event where she was a speaker, along with Nova Whiteman, Dandapani and Neale Donald Walsch. They were all amazing in their own ways. I'm really feeling the need for a spiritual mentor, and I'm curious of where this will end up, and who it will be?

I've a number of wonderful mentors in my life. I've been so incredibly blessed to have worked closely with Tara Preston over the years, learned from Belinda Davidson's online course and coaching, Dr. Shefali's 'Conscious Parent Course'. I also go for acupuncture quite regularly at Traditional Chinese Medicine Centre, with Dr. Li. Eckhart

Tolle's six-month online course, as well as a few in-person retreats. And then, of course, all my yoga—it's helped me navigate and transform. And, I've had years of cranial sacral sessions with Susan Pulvermacher, and sessions with my sister-in-law May Nasser, and energy healings with Melissa Hewison, and, of course, intuitive card readings with Jessica Elfar. And then I've had my music...

I am listening, I am listening.
Speak to me.

Ellen Nasser, 'Speak to Me' [unreleased version]

CHAPTER THIRTY-SIX
LAST DAY OF SCHOOL

June 30, 2022
6:12 a.m.

It's official, the kids had their last day of school yesterday. Hard to believe that everyone has wrapped up another successful year of school. Bella ended up biking to school yesterday and then went to a friend's house right after. Mille had soccer and went to her friend's house, so our house was moderately quiet. I told John I didn't like them not being home to celebrate the last day of school, and John said, "Ellen, this is just the beginning." He's always so level-headed and rational about things. It's true, they're going to start wanting to hang out with their friends, and naturally, I'll be on the sidelines praying for them. I hope to God they choose wonderful people to spend their time with. I hope they're leaders... no, they don't even have to be leaders, I hope they listen to their own hearts. I've said it over and over, but that is my only wish for them is to listen to their own heart. May they live their lives in love rather than fear, and may they connect with their spirit, keeping a "joie de vivre." Joie de vivre, does that sound like I have children in French Immersion? "Joie de vivre!" Ha! Ha!

I emptied the backpacks and washed them, put all the recycling away, made supper and felt nostalgic. The boys were here, but it didn't feel the same. John and I went out for a hot tub, and the boys were jumping and wrestling on the trampoline, and Sam yelled back to us, "This is a perfect family, right, Mom?" Oh, he makes us laugh. He is so funny! Yeah, get the sisters outta here, this is a perfect family, right, Mom?

Oh my gosh, okay, here is a perfect song to help celebrate summer. Crank it up!

> *No matter how your day was, no matter how the time flies,*
> *You never seem to be far, always crossin' my mind.*
> *Sitting by the fire, staring at the skyline.*
> *Get over here, you're my only one, baby, you're mine.*
> *The sun is setting, now the moon is bright.*
> *The stars aligning, tuck the kids in tight...*
>
> Elly Thorn, 'You Should Be You'

As you know, our family grew up on Anderson Lake in Saltcoats, Saskatchewan. When I was performing as Elly Thorn, I went to the Canadian Country Music Awards. No, don't get excited, I went as a spectator. I went to take in the Country Music Week. And when I got there, I really felt like I belonged. I met so many amazing people, and I loved the country music scene, and I thought this was the best thing ever. And, I thought I was home. It's all a bit of a blur, but there was this walkway between these two convention centres, and the acoustics were amazing, so I started humming and writing this song. I was thinking about my childhood and growing up on the lake. I just love looking at the water. I don't really like swimming. I tried to get into it last year, but my body seriously wants to sink. Like... like, I actually can't believe how our kids swim. It seems to come so naturally to them.

> *I know it isn't easy, baby, when we fight.*
> *'Cause you're living with a lady who is always right.*
> *But I feel the fire burnin', sweep me off my feet.*
> *Call 'er a night, you should be you, and I will be me.*
>
> *No matter how your day was, no matter how the time flies…*
> *You never seem to be far, always crossin' my mind.*
> *Sitting by the fire, staring at the skyline.*
> *Get over here, you're my only one, baby, you're mine.*
> *Get over here, you're my only one, baby, you're mine.*
> *Get over here, you're my only one, baby, you're mine.*

Elly Thorn, 'You Should Be You'

CHAPTER THIRTY-SEVEN
CANADA DAY

July 1, 2022
8:04 a.m.

Happy Canada Day. I'm so grateful to be living on this beautiful land, Treaty 6, and for the life we have created here in Saskatchewan.

You never know what a day will bring, and yesterday morning brought the grand opening of the Nutrien Tower downtown at River Landing. John asked me to come with him; he and his family were visionaries of the project that broke ground about six years ago.

Calm the world, no, calm myself.
Starts within and nowhere else.
Calm the world, no, calm myself.
Starts within and nowhere else.
Call your teachers and your guiding stars,
ask your angels to arrive.
We are all so beautiful.
Beautiful, right now.
Beautiful, right now.

We had booked our babysitter to come and watch the kids, so that we could leave by 8:45 a.m. Her kids ended up at a camp, not happening, so she asked if she could bring her kids to our house. Yes, yes, and yes. Never a question. I also had two possessions that day—I had to organize.

So, when we walked into the Nutrien Tower, we were blessed with First Nations singing, dancing and drumming—they said the drumming was the heartbeat of Mother Earth. That resonated so deeply with me. They were so talented.

Once we got up to the very top of the building, it was the most breathtaking view of our city. The visiting started; the ceremony thereafter. They had an Elder come and bless the building and the land. She brought different colours of fabric to honour the Grandmothers of the world and bless the building with yellow. She said yellow was like the sun, and the sun never lets us down. She reminded us of how little control we have of the weather and how we must honour our land. She was so lovely and so inspiring. She brought tobacco, and I believe she said that it had to be offered to the ground.

I'm very moved by a ceremony like this. It's all energy, and I can feel it. Literally eighteen floors down below, and fifteen years ago... where John proposed to me. We had no idea that this development would be in our future—it's nothing short of a magical love story.

We're blessed; Canada is a beautiful place to call home.

Subconscious and the conscious,
divine light throughout our souls.
We are all so beautiful.
Beautiful, right now.
Beautiful right now.

Ellen Nasser, 'Beautiful Right Now'

Yesterday, I was daydreaming about the good old days in Saltcoats on Canada Day. We'd call it going across the lake. I can remember, um… going across the lake to watch people play baseball. If there was a foul ball and the kids returned it, we'd get fifty cents. The Moms were selling homemade pies. Ahh, there were white freezies and chewing like… ahh… do you remember the white baseball gumballs from the concession stands? They were white, yellow and orange. I always got the white ones because I was allergic to artificial colour; it made me hyper. We'd play on the swings, and my all-time favourite was playing bingo and loving every minute of it. I would go when Grandpa was working his shift. And, I remembered thinking he looked funny with the wrap around his waist, to hold bingo cards, and collect money. He always bought us kids some cards to play.

Walt ran in… Can I have a popsicle?" It's like déjà vu. I said, "No, because you already had one, have a banana or yogurt. Your tummy must be hungry."

"No, it's only hungwee for popsicles."

I said, "Ahh, okay, just because it's Canada Day."

I can see it all now, don't worry—all my crappy parenting is perfectly evident, especially when I'm writing it down like this. Picture me with curlers in my hair, fuzzy slippers, my pink housecoat, chain smoking with a martini… bright early in the morning, Mama's writing a book, git outta here. I don't care what you eat for breakfast, eat anything. Eat the whole damn box, for all I care. Just git outta here. Git outta Mommy's magical closet; this is where all her morning magic happens!

No, just seems to be something I say to begin the negotiations. Ugh. But it's Canada Day. This is a little bit of the discussions John and I have had over the years.

I would say, "But John… you know when the kids want something, it's a special occasion, oh but it's Canada Day, oh but it's their birthday, oh but it's their birthday week, oh but it's their cousin's birthday, or oh it's the Easter Bunny's birthday, it's Christmas, oh it's Christmas holidays, it's the weekend, oh but it's…."

"What, Ellen, what is it?"

"Um, Thursday?"

Insert John's eye roll here.

"Yes, it's one of those days of the week that ends with word 'day'."

Hold your head up, say a prayer.
Taking chances, start somewhere.
Anything worth something you'll pay a price for.

Don't always search, and wish and hope
for something more.
We've got to laugh more often, don't sweat small stuff.

Here and now, come on make, make this count.
Anything worth something you'll pay a price for…

Don't always search, and wish and hope for something,
something more.

And…
Open your heart, and let somebody in.
We don't know how lucky we are.

Open your heart, and let somebody in.
We don't know how lucky we are.

Open your heart, let somebody in.
We don't know how lucky we are.

You know those people who put away their fancy dresses and tea sets to save them for a special occasion? I'm the complete opposite; I'm a walking special occasion. Apparently, I used to say it so much to the kids, as a toddler barely speaking, Bella used to say, "Peh show cassion, peh show cassion."

And, I can remember my Dad would often say it to me, and we'd laugh. He'd say, "peh show cassion."

You know what? Every day is a "peh show cassion."

CHAPTER THIRTY-EIGHT
FUN AND FAMILY

July 2, 2022
9:09 a.m.

We had such a full day yesterday of fun and family. We went down to the Kay Nasser Plaza to celebrate Canada Day, but it was really windy and cold. We ended up getting treats at The Shoppe. Cotton candy, ice cream served in these mini balls, coffees, teas, gummies, pastries, soft drinks, waffle cones, it's quite the little shop. No shortage of sugar, that's for sure.

As we left, one of my nieces misplaced her phone, so we retraced our steps and ended up finding it tucked between her seat and the floor. Here's another great lesson: When you're out and about, always turn your ringer on because if you lose your phone, someone will at least be able to hear it ring. More phone hints that I learned from my friend, Linnea. On your settings, parents can set a time limit on their kids' apps. During the school year and week, we have a forty-five-minute a day limit, and once the kids hit that limit, it just shuts down. Insert evil laugh here. But seriously, now that it's summer, they're trying to negotiate for up to two hours. We'll see what happens. The kids really complained at first, but honestly, once they started realizing that they had to use their online time wisely, it really worked.

The third phone secret is: turn the location function on your kid's phone, no matter what. Then you'll always be able to track their phone. I just learned of this one the other day; neighbour, Shannon, told me that one, she's very smart.

Being a parent in this day and age is challenging, and can feel lonely; the wheel feels like it's been reinvented. I struggle to keep up.

> *I'm alone... and it's cold.*
> *I'm alone... waiting for you.*
> *I'm alone... and it's cold. I'm alone... waiting for you.*

I wrote this song in the dead of winter when I was very pregnant with Sam, pulling Bella and Millie around in the sled, around this little pond named after my Great Uncle, in the area we live. I felt completely alone. I don't know if in the lyrics I was talking to John, talking to Mom or Dad, or to God. I just felt sad, empty, and dark.

Now, years later, I listen to those lyrics again and I wonder if I was talking to myself? Searching for... trying to comfort... longing for... waiting for... me? I don't know, I wonder.

> *It was a night like this when I see the skyline glowing.*
> *I could just get carried away.*
> *Wish all your worries away.*
>
> *So, say something on this cold and lonely night.*
> *Say something... anything will make it right.*
>
> *I'm alone... and it's cold.*

All alone.
Waiting for you.
I'm alone... and it's cold.
I'm alone.
Waiting for you.
I'm alone... and it's cold.
All alone.
I'm alone... and it's cold.
All alone.
Waiting for you.

Elly Thorn, 'Waiting for You'

CHAPTER THIRTY-NINE
LUMINOUS AND SCRITCHY

July 3, 2022
9:24 a.m.

Millie just came in and asked where our makeup wipes are. Auntie Kriti took her out for her birthday shop yesterday, and the older girls put mascara on her. Millie went along with it for a bit, but now has woken up and really wants it off her eyes. She's not impressed.

These tween years are interesting. I don't think I went through the tweens in our small town. I wouldn't have imagined putting mascara on the summer of grade five, but hey… that was just me. I can remember having a big crush, though, cranking up 'A Whole New World', sitting on a small rug at the side of our bunk beds and belting it out, pretending my crush, Chad, was Aladdin. I can remember pretending to be Jasmine and poking my head from behind and around Aladdin's shoulder, batting my big, animated eyes. That was my kind of playing, I suppose.

I also remember listening to 'The Greatest Man I Never Knew' and bawling. You know that song? I don't know, I think it was Reba McEntire. Anyways, I had all the feels; I was feeling heartbroken that no one had a crush on me. I had to count on sports and being funny, so that's how I got attention growing up. No real attention came from any of my crushes. No one has to feel sorry for me. It's just the way it was in my adolescent years. I actually look back and think it was kinda sweet because I didn't think I wasn't crush-worthy. I remember someone at the rink one time calling me "scritchy redhead," and I didn't know what that meant. I still don't know.

Hold on, I'll Google it.

Oh My Gosh! I had NO idea what it meant. I'm actually laughing out loud. I think I was racing around the rink, probably wildly laughing, and she was older. She was probably like in her fifties, and she was being funny with me. Because... I have... like... we... I have fun with people. And, I haven't forgotten it, though. She called me, "Scritchy redhead... Oh, aren't you a scritchy redhead. Get over here, you little scritchy redhead." Ready to hear the definition?

Scratchy, itchy, prickly.

I'd rather be luminous, thank you very much.

I hold on to both of those words. I think the bottom line is... is that we have to love ourselves. It's truly not any of your business what anyone says about you. Let all the comments go, the "scritchy" comments, the luminous comments, at the end of the day, neither really matter.

CHAPTER FORTY
PiNCH ME

July 4, 2022
7:18 a.m.

The kids are basically in "pinch-me" mode. They can't believe that they have almost three months off of summer holidays.

Bella said last night that her mind wants to think her summer break is almost over, like it's only a long weekend or something like that, but of course, she gets a really long holiday. They work so hard throughout the year, I'm happy that they have the summer off. We have been toying with Bella going to some summer swimming camps, but have decided against it. It's funny, Auntie Kriti took them shopping the other day, and when they returned, Bella looked like she grew an inch at the mall. She needs some time to catch her breath for the summer, hang out with her friends, go on family trips, give her body a rest from all of her training that she has been doing. She's been going full swing with her sports for years, sometimes a break is best for everyone. She is one of those people that was born with so much drive. Bella is just so determined and powerful that when she puts her mind to something, there's absolutely no stopping her.

The conversations we've had at this point are something else. She has emotional intelligence; she tries to phrase things so that we can have open conversations about our feelings and how what we said to each other may not have been the best way to go about it. We talk, we grow, we forgive, we reset. She has been such an amazing daughter to grow with. I've learned so much from her.

To be honest, from all of our kids. One day, she woke up wanted to take her babysitting course and asked what we thought. And, just like that, she was online, she had signed herself up and was taking the course. It's fascinating the way she just gets things done. She turns thirteen in August, and she already has a list of things she wants to do/get for her birthday, including redesigning her room herself and getting a new hairdo.

CHAPTER FORTY-ONE
BiRTHDAYS

July 5, 2022
6:43 a.m.

One month until I turn forty. It's hard to believe that it's almost here. You know, I've never been the biggest birthday person. I love making fusses for other people, but not myself. If you can imagine, I feel a bit shy with my birthday. I don't really want people going out of their way to celebrate me, and I've always been a bit strange accepting gifts.

As a child, my Mom would make our birthdays very special; she'd bake a cake and often fill the table with food and treats we loved. I can remember in my later years, one of my siblings joked that my birthday was the worst one because the table was full of like my favourite things: fruits and veggies. It's true, my cake would be like angel food cake with whipped cream and raspberries from the garden, or sliced peaches. And, there'd be bowls of fresh blueberries and Saskatoons that Grandpa picked. The raspberries and strawberries from the garden, and gummies. There would also be chocolate—and, ahh... even typing this is making me crave all of my things!

Another special birthday was when I was singing on Norwegian Cruise Lines, and I turned twenty-three. I remember waking up and opening my corridor door, and it was fully decorated with balloons and streamers. I couldn't believe my eyes, and it meant so much to me. The entire cast got me a little gift, and for some reason, it has stuck with me all of these years later. For over six months, these people were family to me. We all cared about each other, but I couldn't believe my birthday door and all my treats. I can even remember some of the presents: Alaskan moose socks, Alaskan-dipped Oreos, earrings, only to name a few. It warmed my heart just thinking about that and them; what a beautiful group of people.

It was a very magical and challenging time of my life. I was feeling very mature and doing all these things that grown-ups would do, but I was still so young, performing, living my own life, sailing the ocean, very independent, and having experiences I'd never dreamed of. What a time of adventure and freedom. I still can't believe I completed that contract. Once I got home, nothing was the same. I ended up going back to Victoria for January, February, March and I was serving tables, and I was super depressed.

The person I was with, I thought I was going to marry, and that didn't work out. And, I found myself back in Saskatoon, living in my parents' basement, just in time to try to pull myself together for my brother's wedding in April.

Funny story about how Lee and Kriti met. Kriti and I were working at Pharmasave on Central Avenue, where we became fast friends. She jokes that when we first met, she couldn't believe how bubbly I was. She said that I was just happy all the time. We laughed and laughed, and we even laughed about putting milk away in the fridges. Anyway, I had recently graduated from High School, and I was getting my grad photos developed at the pharmacy—words our children will never say—and we were looking through the pictures, and I actually remember what picture I was looking at, and Kriti said, "Ooooooh, who's that? Looks like my future husband!"

Of course, she was joking, but was she really? She was looking at my brother Lee. Kriti ended up coming over to our house to get ready for a date she was going on. She was going to do her hair and makeup at our house, and Lee was there and couldn't stop flirting with her. I guess the feeling was mutual; the two of them were ridiculous. They now have two little girls and have been together for over twenty years. It's hard to believe.

Now, back to Johnny and how he and I met. It was the end of August, and there was this wine tasting at The Granary where I used to serve, and the manager, Steve, asked if I wanted to play some live music on the patio. It rained and got cancelled, and then it cleared up and it was back on, and then they cancelled me again, and then it rained again, it was this all afternoon long, and I had a bit of a cold, and I was so depressed. And, ahh... You know my Mom, and Cheryl, and I ended up going to the wine tasting even though I wasn't playing at it anymore. And, Mom said, "You know, I just... I think it's a good idea to show up, and just enjoy it, whether you're playing or not, have a glass of wine, support it." So, I said, "Alright." I went, but wasn't in the mood.

And, I walked into The Granary lounge, and the doors... the double doors were open to the... the patio. I looked around the room, and my eyes were drawn to a table on the patio. I can see it now; it was over to the left.

And, I said, "Mom, look at him."

She nodded in John's direction, "Him?"

"Yeah, isn't he cute?"

"Looks a little long in the tooth to me."

And, I said, "What does that mean?"

She's like, "Old."

I started laughing.

We enjoyed a glass of wine; I was still sniffling away and kinda mopey. We started leaving through the lounge, and a friend stopped me, and gave me a big hug and said, "Hi Ellen, I heard you're back in Saskatoon and single."

Ugh.

She told me that she was doing this speed dating night and she was putting on... ahh... ahh... it was like ahh... it was... There was a pub and wondered if I'd be interested in going. And, I said to her, "No, I'd sooner drop dead." Then, she laughed and at the end of the table. I heard, "Hey, why don't we skip the speed dating and you just give me your number right now?"

Oh My Gosh—it was the guy from the patio! They had moved, the entire group, into the lounge, and he wanted my number.

You have to remember, I had been in a long-term, long-distance relationship, been dumped many times, with most guys running for the hills because all I could talk about was marriage and wanting four babies. I couldn't believe my eyes, or ears, it was him. That hunk. He wanted MY number.

So, I asked Lisa, "What's he like?"

And, she said, "Who John? Oh, he's like a big, cuddly teddy bear."

I told Lisa, "Well, if he wants my number, he can ask for it properly."

Insert my heart racing like crazy, are you kidding me? Are you kidding me? Are you kidding me? I turned to leave, and John followed me out. We started walking past the bar, and we were visiting, and then we stopped at this little area where people... the servers come to pick up the drinks. And, he was so funny, and that smile. Honestly, I couldn't stop looking at his smile. And we... I took out this piece of paper from that receipt thing, there's a receipt thing right by the bar, and he took out some paper, and I wrote down my phone number on it. And, I said... just about as we were about to part... I said, "Oh, I was just wondering where you were headed." He said, "Oh, I was going outside to have a smoke." He mentioned he likes to have the odd cigarette when he drinks.

I said, "Ugh, I'm a singer, I don't date smokers."

And, he said, "Oh, well, then I just quit."

Even typing this makes me laugh... almost sixteen years later.

John just walked into my closet sanctuary and said, "Why are you laughing?"

We were talking about weddings at the gym the other day, and my friend A for Apple asked me how long John and I dated before we got married. I said it ended up being two years, but as I told you earlier, he started designing my ring at about six months. I told her most guys dating me were running for the hills. A for Apple said, "Except John—while everyone was running for the hills, Johnny was runnin' to the jewellers."

Typing that makes me cry. Reading it makes me cry.

> *How am I to know, how am I to know?*
> *If I should keep you or let you go?*
> *Should I wait around, let the story unfold?*
> *How am I to know, how am I to know.*
>
> *I wish this story was brand, spankin' new.*
> *But I have been here, I have worn these old, haggard shoes.*
> *Had my mind made up,*
> *thought my dreams were comin' true.*
>
> *Then how was I to know, how was I to know?*
> *That you... you'd be the stars in my sky.*
> *And, you... you'd light up my life.*
> *No, I never felt, no I never felt... so alive.*
>
> *How was I to know, how was I to know?*
> *Before I met you, someone stole my glow.*
> *Then that warm August night, out on the patio...*
> *How was I to know, how was I to know?*
>
> *That you... you'd be the stars in my sky.*
> *And, you... you'd light up my life.*
> *No, I never felt, no I never felt... so alive.*
>
> *How was I to know, how was I to know?*
> *If I should keep you, or let you go... let you go.*
> *Should I wait around, let the story unfold?*
>
> *I'm forever yours, that's how I know.*
> *I'm forever yours, I'm forever yours...*
> *I'm forever yours, that's how I know.*
> *That's how I know, that's how I know.*

Ellen Nasser, 'How Am I to Know' [unreleased version]

One more thing, umm, we were cleaning up... I can't remember, something in the closet... or whatever, and I opened up this... I don't know if it was like an old wallet or something, and the little piece of crumpled paper was tucked away, and it was... that night, I gave him my phone number. He's kept it all of these years.

CHAPTER FORTY-TWO
IN A MOOD

July 6, 2022
6:57 a.m.

*T*here haven't been too many days where I have woken up and not wanted to sit down and write. Well, today is one of them. I think the whole idea around devotion and commitment to something is that you just get up and do it anyway. A lot of the time, the beauty shows up after you don't feel like it.

It's a very rainy day. John gave me a cup of tea before he went to the gym this morning. Sofi just came and snuggled in beside me. So, what's different about this morning than yesterday morning? I ask myself. I have all the things that typically make me feel good, so what gives? I don't know, and that's the stuff I'm curious about. I know it'll pass, because it always passes, but it's interesting to know why I woke up in a bit of a foul mood, besides the fact that I'm human. I went to bed at a decent time. I had a good sleep. And, I don't remember having a weird dream. And, I didn't eat anything weird before bed. I fell asleep in a pleasant mood. So, what gives?

Sofi just took a deep breath and rested her head on my lap. Even she feels my rotten energy this morning. Come on, Ellen, shift.

Deep breath.

My piano exam is on Saturday. I practiced again last night for an hour. I think I'm about 90% there. It feels like a lot of pressure, but I seem to be the only one putting it on myself. I must remind myself how far I've come. It's been a huge amount of work and a big commitment. Commitment—that word again. Devotion. Every day, I show up. Sometimes it's magical, and sometimes it's not.

When I'm in a mood like this, I sit and I think about everything that isn't great in my life. It's all a ripple effect. I just went to my phone to find a quote that I saw yesterday that lit me up: *If you want to feel rich, just count all the things that you have that money can't buy.* I think this is why these early mornings have lit me up so much. I get this quiet time to reflect and enjoy. It's my creativity. When the pros say things like it's all in the journey, they're right. The journey of this is where the healing is, where the magic shows up, where the revealing happens. Once August 5th comes and goes, I don't even know what will happen. Is this the end? There, I've written about my first forty years, I can die happy now. My kids will have some stories and will hopefully have my voice forever.

Oh my gosh, I didn't tell you. Yesterday, after my writing session, I went to my phone to look up a song that I once started and never finished. I found pieces of music back from 2014. I'm going to add them to this audiobook for the kids to hear.

The boys came in, and I was listening and crying. There's this one clip where Sam is about two months old and Bella, Millie and I are sitting around writing his love song. I actually think Bella inspired me for a part of the song where it says, "his eyes wide open."

It's really neat to see how the music and how my songs evolve, and I feel like that's how God is watching us. Just slowly observing and watching us learn, and transition, and transform. Even listening to 'Song for Sam' now, I would still make some changes to it. My music and songs are never really complete. My friend tBone reminded me of this quote: "Art is never finished, only abandoned." It's all just a constant work in progress.

We are all a constant work in progress. I'm not proud to say it, but I've written people off in the past. People, for whatever reason, I just didn't want to be around. Then I happen to see them again and I'm taken aback that they aren't the same person I thought I knew. Maybe I'm not the same person I was? Well, I know that's a fact. Who knows what people are going through? I have to remind myself time and time again to be more gentle and less judgmental. Everybody has a story and healing to do. Things change, people change, the only constant thing is change. All I know is that we're all on this journey together, and it's so easy to get into a funk and write people off and blame people for this and the other thing. Situations will inevitably arise, but I want to try to meet them graciously and face-on. Some things will be worth a conversation, others won't. You'll know which ones are worth it.

Music and creating makes me feel so good—that's why I do it. The sun is now peeking out through the clouds. Sam is awake and excited to buy a Lego set today, the cleaners are coming, and I have a final piano lesson before my exam on Saturday.

I'm excited.

I'm so grateful for the gift of music.

I'm eternally grateful for my inner drive and passion.

I am blessed.

Wow! What a shift from where I started at 6:57 this morning.

Nothing prepares you, and nobody can...

God knows I'll keep you, as long as I can.

> *Rock-a-bye baby, rock-a-bye boy.*
> *Rock-a-bye baby, rock-a-bye boy.*
> *Rock-a-bye baby, rock-a-bye boy.*
> *Rock-a-bye baby, you're my every joy.*
> *Rock-a-bye baby, you're my every joy.*
>
> Ellen Kolenick, 'Song for Sam'

CHAPTER FORTY-THREE
ADDING UP

July 7, 2022
6:23 a.m.

I got a message from Guitar Playin' Gray yesterday, and he said he will likely play on my *Stillness* album. It's still blowing my mind because everything is starting to add up as I keep journaling on.

I pulled two cards yesterday, and they were "Expression" and "Nurture." That's why I want to create this: To express and nurture.

Last night, I thought of one of the first songs I ever wrote. I was nineteen years old and I recorded this song with my sister Amy singing and my brother Danny on the dobro.

> *If someone could teach me*
> *how to love you like you love me,*
> *I'd feel better.*

Ellen Kolenick, 'If Only'

I was singing with my sister, Amy, at the time and had these four songs I created while I was performing with Saskatchewan Express. I was dating one of my brother's friends—we'll call him... ahh... Music Man. Ha! Ha! Ha! The minute I said, "Music Man," I thought of "Music Man, do you know? Ha! Ha! Ha! Ha! Ha!" It's John Mulaney's umm... music video about making music and how music's here, music's there, music... music's everywhere. And, it's this... Oh... It's absolutely hysterical, and there's kids in it. And, it's ahh... I can't even remember the actor. You have to Google it, John Mulaney, Music Man.

The four songs included:

+ Stay Rain
+ Stranger
+ If Only
+ Patiently Waiting

When I think back to how long my producer Bart McKay has been in my life, it's wild. I recorded my first four songs in his old studio, over twenty years ago.

Last night I watched a spry fella on Rich Roll being interviewed. He's 100 years old and is all about eating plant-based food for longevity. John and I were then discussing... Hmmm... Would a person want quality or quantity of life? Quality all the way for me, and if eating more of my favourite foods is where it's at bring on the veggies, bring on the fruits, bring on the farmers markets!

CHAPTER FORTY-FOUR
DO A GOOD JOB OF IT

July 8, 2022
7:04 a.m.

I've been thinking about my music an awful lot lately. I can't believe it'll all be woven into this creation. I can't believe I have so many songs. I wouldn't have thought I had that many. Fifty-eight at this point, and you're going to hear them all. It's unbelievable. I may have more before this is complete because some are brewing. I can feel it.

Wow! Since I haven't been able to fully discuss this with anyone, just little bits and pieces with my chosen few. I keep having this feeling like it'll be a scrapbook of my life. I am going to let the pieces fall where they may. I trust, I trust, I trust. On August 6th, the day after my birthday, actually on my friend Bruce's birthday, I will look into what the next steps will be. But right now, it's writing and music, and that's all I want to do.

I no longer feel shame for being an "expressive." I don't feel embarrassed by it anymore. We need them in our world, just like we need you in our world, and everything that makes you—you.

I was born like this. I can remember when I was younger, I would write my parents notes and letters when I'd get into trouble, apologizing, and telling them how much I loved them, wanting to... you know, plan special surprises for their anniversary and birthdays. At about nineteen years old, my little love letters turned into songwriting, and now it's coming out in a book. Who would have ever known? When you're a third-born, first daughter, a Leo with a passion and drive to connect with others through healing and expression—I suppose this is what you get. Me.

Not everyone is the same; that's why the world is such a beautiful place. Some people's dream is to work in a daycare, and I thank God for them every day. Some people dream of saving our planet, and I thank God for them every day. I can remember my Dad telling me, "You can be anything you want. Just whatever you do, do a good job of it."

I can remember, I made him a Father's Day card in my "slapdash" ways. Just basically folding over a piece of paper, scribbling on it, obviously at an age where a little more care could/should have been considered. When I gave it to him, he looked a bit annoyed and disappointed. I knew, and he knew. He didn't say much, but I figured it out pretty darn quickly that he wasn't overly impressed.

Dad, not much of a fisherman, oddly enough, ended up going away on a fishing trip with two of our relatives, and while he was away, I wanted to create him something special to try to make up for my shoddy first attempt. I took my time, I paid so much attention to detail, and drew this fishing boat in the water with he and two other guys. When he returned, I gave it to him and he loved it so much. For some reason, I can remember seeing it around the house, maybe in his bedside table, or on the top of the drawer of my old dresser—it was kept for a long time, and I remember how special we both felt about it.

Dad valued effort. He loved people with passion and the ability to show up, especially when the going got tough. He loved a big heart, admired courage, and simply anything we kids did. With Dad, you never had to *BE* the best or win, that was a bonus, you just had to show up, be prepared and *DO* your best. That obviously stayed with me for a lifetime, and that's how we try to be with our kids. Yes, school is important, but we aren't totally attached to the end results of everything, especially not in these younger years of the kids getting their footing, and exploring different ways of self-expression. John's and my goal is to help guide them and support them and nurture them to be who they are meant to be. I can remember when we started out parenting, we had an idea of who *we wanted* them to be. We quickly realized that we aren't here to dictate that. We all have our own journeys; our kids are in a completely different time. When I was growing up in Saltcoats... it's apples and oranges, so I have to be able to go with the flow and be flexible with how life shows up for all of us.

> *It's late night and I'm awake,*
> *with the hum the vessel makes.*
> *My feet are planted to the ground,*
> *though I can't stand still.*
>
> *I don't mind my stay,*
> *but I miss you more each day.*
> *I'm learning lots about myself,*
> *but some things never change.*
>
> *I miss you more each day.*
> *It's time I come back home,*

I don't know why I roamed so far.
I always look for more,
never know just what for,
and don't know why.

Alone, my mind is racing,
alone, my heart aching.
Home, home, home... home, home, home.
It's time I come back home,

I don't know why I roamed so far.
I always look for more,
never know just what for,
and don't know why.
Alone, my mind is racing.
Alone, my heart aching.

Ellen Kolenick, 'Come Back Home'

CHAPTER FORTY-FIVE
EXAM TiME

July 9, 2022
6:31 a.m.

Guess what? This morning is my piano exam, and I don't feel like it. I have this dull ache in my lower back—I know it's the tension and anxiety of the exam. When I was younger, and I had figure skating tests and competitions, it would almost be like I got myself sick on purpose. I loved figure skating, but it really didn't come easily. I had such a true passion to perform, but I resembled Bambi in the forest learning how to walk when I was on the ice.

As I sit here, I'm noticing my nervous bowel, the pain in the back of my right shoulder blade, my tight solar plexus and shallow breathing. My head is telling me that I should be doing better, but that doesn't necessarily help me. Someone once gave me an example of it's like reading a book on how to run a marathon. Once you finish the book, you technically know how to run a marathon, but you can't just put the book down and go run the race. The next step is putting it into practice. Right, you now have the tools, and it's time to put it into practice. I think that's why I love challenging myself like this. I'm using the tools I've acquired over the years to try and manage my nerves, thoughts, emotions and breath in a situation where I feel stressed. It's not about passing or failing for me; I know I'll pass; that's not the thing. I've put in the work, and I know I'm a beautiful piano player; it's managing what comes up for me. It's trying to get comfortable with the uncomfortable. It's the pausing, the expanding of my lungs, the holding of my breath and breathing intentionally. It's my practice that I've been doing every morning. The lighting of my candles, the spraying of my Aura Spray, the repetition of Melissa's prayer... the daily creation of mine. It's using all these tools that will evolve and change and shift over the years, but the continual choice to come home and align each and every morning.

I also have made a note that I'm not checking my phone this morning. Not at all. I don't want any distractions. You know, people may giggle at this because it's only my Level Six piano exam, but it's all relative. A person can't downplay someone else's stress. Someone may feel stressed performing spine surgery, someone else may feel stressed performing on stage. You know someone else may feel the pain smashing up their bike, and then someone may feel the pain of smashing up their motorhome. It's still their pain, their anxiety and their stress.

7:50 a.m. Time to do some yoga and practice each song three times before I head over to Martin's house. Oh heck, I'll write a prayer, why not?

Dear Creator of All Beings,

Thank you for another beautiful day. I humbly ask you for calm, grounded energy to surround me as I write my exam. I am so grateful for the gift of music and for a l of the healing it's done for me over the years. I ask for my roots to be connected and grounded to our beautiful Mother Earth, and also for abundance of the divine, heavenly energy to flow through my chakras as I play. Surround me, dear loving Lord, with focused energy. May my heart be open and share light with all who I meet today. Please remind me why I am here and give me the courage to be my authentic self in all aspects of my life. May I listen to my heart surround myself with people who I feel good around. Thank you for John and for our beautiful children. May I continue to rise up and dance in high vibrational energy. I ask for awareness and attention to detail as I enter this exam, may I also be in the flow of music and expression, surrendering to the moment. Thank you for ten beautiful fingers, thank you for our beautiful life, thank you for my beautiful eyes and mind that I may see the beauty more often than not. Sending love and gratitude out into the world, now and always. May we laugh, smile and enjoy the day!

Thank you, thank you, thank you. Amen.

Wish me luck!

CHAPTER FORTY-SIX
WELL, THAT SUCKED

July 10, 2022
9:35 a.m.

Well, that sucked. My exam didn't go as well as I hoped. I wish that wasn't the opening sentence of this morning's entry, but it's just a fact. Oh, I was so nervous, and it got the worst of me as 10:30 a.m. slowly approached. I'm not an overly anxious person, so now I have compassion and empathy for those who are.

I can't believe that I feel so worked up playing Royal Conservatory of Music. There's no bullshit with Royal Conservatory of Music, there's no in-between. You either know your stuff or you don't. There's no kinda knowing the music, or kinda understanding the scales, or sorta learning the intervals. This music I'm playing and that I've been immersed in has been around for hundreds of years, and it holds such prestige. I hold these works of art in high esteem, and I want to play them well, I want to honour the music.

It's funny, a person can razzle-dazzle their way through lots of things. If you're onstage and hit the ditch singing, or if the band messes up, you can easily get back on track, often without the audience even having a clue. With me playing RCM music, if I hit the ditch, I'm the only one driving, and to make it worse, I'm the only person in the vehicle. I'm alone, vulnerable, and totally out of my comfort zone. If I don't know my music, there's no one to hide behind. It's all on me, and I feel it. If I don't know my music, there's no one to distract the adjudicator, no guitar player to look at, no one to secretly blame. I'm helpless. It's me all by myself, and I either sink or swim. I have to musically find my way out. Oh, my goodness, and that is what I've been doing. I've been musically finding my own way out.

Wow, anyways, I had probably played all my pieces a thousand times, and when I sat down to play my Etude in C Major, it was filled with staccato notes. And, staccato notes are those short, bouncy notes. My hand jumped literally off the piano like I had touched a hot stove. I never played it so poorly in my life. And, to make matters worse, I thought that was going to be one of my best pieces. The mind and nerves are something else. When I was driving to Martin's house in the morning, I could literally feel my hands and fingers starting to get heavy. I can't believe that I am so uncomfortable with these exams. A friend of mine said it's good for me to get comfortable with the uncomfortable. But John also said that... I don't know, he thought, maybe it's a little too stressful for me. Both my Mandarin and music are challenging for my brain, and I like it because I enjoy evolving. Practicing being at an elite level in piano and Mandarin lights me up. It's fun! I would rather do something like that for an hour and a half a day than sit on my phone and feel numb.

I'm using language and music as medicine. Both are solo projects, besides my teachers, of course, and they keep me learning and lighting up different parts of my brain, all the while showing our kids that ultimately, we are all limitless. It's empowering.

I say to the kids all the time, "If Mom can learn Mandarin, anyone can do anything!"

CHAPTER FORTY-SEVEN
A NOTHING DAY

July 11, 2022
6:45 a.m.

Yesterday was a beautiful day. John and I were both a bit draggy from a big weekend, but sometimes a nothing day is the nicest thing ever. We let Bella go to a friend's cabin for a couple of nights, which was a first, so I was very happy to have all four of my little birdies back under one roof. Johnny took the boys to a movie, Millie just biked around the neighbourhood for a bit, and I went over to my Mom's in the morning and had a great visit with her and Gigi.

Since it was just the three of us, we had a big talk about my project. Mom couldn't believe that John didn't know. There's only twenty-five days left of writing, so I may as well not blow it now. I read them some of my writings from the beginning, and it felt so healing for me. We laughed and cried, talking about our time together growing up as neighbours on the lake. They really are such cherished memories for all of us. I really wanted to create a life like that for our children, where we're surrounded by amazing family and people. I told Mom that I'm adding all my music, and it's starting to unfold, better than I could ever imagine.

We talked about grief and the healing process. My Gigi had a sweet little four-year-old boy named Danny. One day, he was complaining of a sore throat, so Gigi and Bumpa took him to get him checked. It was obvious the little guy needed to get his tonsils out. So, they booked a surgery to get them removed in Yorkton. What they didn't know was that Polio was going through the hospital. Little Danny ended up catching Polio, and the virus got into his lungs, and he died.

> *And when I close my eyes, I see you in my mind.*
> *I thank God that you are mine.*
> *I would die a million times.*
> *Over again my love, for you over and over again.*
> *Over again, my lovely.*
> *Over again.*
> *And again, and again and again.*
> *Over again, my lovely.*
> *Over again.*
> *And again, and again, and again.*
>
> Ellen Kolenick, 'Over Again'

Gigi is ninety-seven years old and still grieves her son. My Mom was only six months old and can still remember feeling the pain surrounding the loss. Gigi said that Mom was the reason she could keep going, which explains their lifelong bond.

They say everything happens for a reason, but sometimes I just can't wrap my head around it. I am so glad that they know about my writing secret because it's nice to be able to share some of my stories with them. We started talking about some of the logistics of my memoir and the idea of changing some names and situations just for privacy and/or get some permission from the people I mention. I think that's a good idea. Is that what people do? I'm going to keep in the flow of writing and cross that bridge when I get to it.

Well, I'm booked in at the studio with Bart tomorrow. He's going to finish up my music. I just need to go through all of my songs to make sure I have them all. The kids are at sports camp this week, so it's absolutely perfect. They'll be running and jumping—I'll be creating, which makes me feel like I'm running and jumping. And, I'm winding down work this week. Two weeks off! I'm so excited, I really feel like I need to put my feet up.

CHAPTER FORTY-EIGHT
SUMMER PLANS

July 13, 2022
6:15 a.m.

Walt was up 5 a.m. and now is cuddled up in our bed. I managed to sneak out to my closet sanctuary.

Why did I choose our closet? Because the kids always seem to sense me when I get up. Even walking down the hallway, I can hear them stirring when I walk on by. This way, I can just literally roll outta bed and not worry about disturbing anyone, besides my Sofer Wofer. She always gets disturbed and is happy to follow me. Pitter, padder, pitter, padder into the closet.

We are just ironing out our summer plans and I believe the kids and I are now going to fly to Summerland, and then John will bring out the vehicle to meet us. Apparently, rentals are really difficult to find, so this will be good because we really want to have a vehicle there. I'm really looking forward to this holiday with our family. It also sounds like my Mom and my brother's family are also going to join us for a week, so that'll be wonderful. I'm sure we will have lots of adventures. I'm trying to figure out if we should bring our bikes, just bring a few, rent them all. I'm also going to miss my puppy, but Auntie Julie promises to spoil her. I've been talking about "Auntie Julie" with Sofi all week, so that she knows who she is when she comes to pick her up. I told her that Auntie will take her for lots of walks and even for ice cream at Beppies, if she's an extra good girl.

我的狗狗, 我的狗狗。
(Wǒ de gǒugou, wǒ de gǒugou.)
I have a puppy, 叫 Sofi,called Sofi.
(jiào Sofi)
What colour is she?
What colour is she?
What 颜色 is she? 我的 Sofi,my Sofi.
(What yánsè is she? Wǒ de Sofi, my Sofi.)
Is she yellow, like the sun?
Is she 黃色, 像太阳?
(Is she huángsè, xiàng tàiyáng?)
No! 不不不, 不不不, No Taeyang No Taeyang No!
(No! Bù be bù, bù be bù, No be No be No!)
不不不, 不不不, No be No be No!
(Bù be bù, bù be bù, No be No be No!)

Yesterday was a magical day. I spent most of it in the studio working on some songs. Bart and I had a chat about my vision, and I'm excited to see this completed. I know I still have twenty-three days of writing left, but I'm going to start editing my entries. I'm at 76,063 words, and I don't think I'll want more than 80,000. On the other hand, I won't want to edit too much if editing is what someone else will do. Also, on the other hand, I really have to be careful of who I choose to edit this, because I want these stories to have my touches in my own words, especially for our kids, that's the whole point, you know. So, whoever I choose, they'll have to know the way I communicate, and I want it to be so cuthentic to who I am. I have a few more songs to weave into these writings, but overall, I think I have a good idea of how this is gonna flow. It's been a lot of work, but it's worth it.

Hey, hey!
What colour is she?
What colour is she?
What 颜色 is she? 我的 Sofi,my Sofi.
(What yánsè is she? Wǒ de Sofi, my Sofi.)
She is white and brown, the 可爱狗狗 in town.
(She is white and brown, the kě'ài gǒugou in town.)
She is white, 她又白、
(She is white, tā yòu bái、)
and brown, 又棕,
(and brown, yòu zōng.)
The 可爱狗狗 in town.
(The kě'ài gǒugou in town.)
I said the 可爱狗狗 in town.
(I said the kě'ài gǒugou in town.)
I said the cutest puppy, 可爱狗狗；
(I said the cutest puppy, kě'ài gǒugou;)
The cutest puppy, 可爱狗狗；
(the cutest puppy, kě'ài gǒugou;)
The cutest puppy, 可爱狗狗in town.
(The cutest puppy, kě'ài gǒugou in town.)

Ellen Nasser, 'Sofi De Gē'

CHAPTER FORTY-NINE
THE LEAKER LEAKS AGAIN

July 14, 2022
6:32 a.m.

Well, I've done exactly what I didn't want to do, and I've told a few more people about my secret morning writings. The people I've told are very supportive; I find most people are. My friend said that I've inspired her and that she, too, wants to write some stories and lessons for her kids. Another person said I have a lot of verve. I'd never heard that word before. There are some people who have commented on the logistics of it, and that's what I don't like because it gets me outta the flow. I'm nervous about that, too. Who is going to publish it? Will anyone want to publish it? How am I going to create all of this with my songs? Will I just have to release all of my music again under Ellen Nasser? I need a few cheerleaders because I'm starting to feel a bit fatigued. I know I can do it; I can get through. I just have problems at the very end of things.

Last night, we ended up having another family over. We had a late dinner and ordered some Vietnamese food, kids swam, and I had a couple of beers. Do you think I felt like waking up this morning and writing? Nope, not even a little, not even a bit. It's kinda like going to the gym though. Now that I'm up and creating, it does feel good.

> *Sometimes we love too much.*
> *Sometimes we're scared of that stuff.*
> *At times, we wake up wondering what happened.*
> *Our minds are spinning out of control.*
> *We need to stop and ask ourselves a question.*
> *What is this all for?*
>
> Ellen Kolenick, 'At Times'

CHAPTER FIFTY
THE DINO WAR

July 15, 2022
7:15 a.m.

Bella and I were talking about the ups and downs of friendships. She's at an age where there are lots of emotions, lots of big emotions, and many of her friends are trying to make each other jealous.

Now that I write that, I don't think it's really necessarily an age thing because I can still feel all those emotions myself. I can also feel myself getting angry and wanting to be in like... Momma Bear protector mode when I hear about all this stuff. I know I have to take a deep breath and step back. I want to protect her and make sure that no one ever hurts her, but I also know that's unattainable. And, look at what I'm doing—some of my greatest breakthroughs and creations have come from a broken heart. And, no one could have saved me from it. And, not just romantically, but even a friendship floating away, leaving me wondering what I did wrong. It's not easy, but it's necessary for the transformation.

Bella and I were talking as we packed and tidied her room. Just chatting about life and how hurt she feels. I told her that I've been in her shoes many, many times. It's not the greatest feeling; she's not alone. It's funny, as we were tidying her room, there was the little piece of art in her closet that said, "She needed a *HERO*, so that's what she became. She needed a *HERO*, so that's what she became." What a profound message.

As much as I want to save our children from pain, I know I can't be their saviour. They have to be their own hero; they have to use their own tools, their own wisdom to work and process through their own inevitable ups and downs. I can't always be the one to fix this or fix that. And, you know... I don't want them to think I can fix everything for them because I can't. I don't know what's supposed to be fixed or not.

If my Mom could have saved me from watching my Dad take his last breath, she would have in a second. But if she would've, I don't think I would've been here today, healing the way that I am through writing and music. You see, only God and Source knows the great big picture, and we have to trust he knows what he's doing. We have to have faith that everything is done in His divine timing. We have to trust that we're experiencing everything this life is supposed to be for us.

I so deeply believe my job is to keep healing, cultivating peace and finding joy, and the rest will just fall where it may.

John is going to leave tomorrow for Summerland. He's going to drive and take lots of our stuff out. If you can believe it, a few days ago, John got an email with a deal on a small private plane that was going to Kelowna. He said it's at a massively discounted rate and only flies nine one way. We were out for ice cream with friends, and they said, "Aren't you guys going to Kelowna on Sunday? Why don't you snag this?"

John asked what I thought of it, and we pounced on it. He said it's part of my birthday gift. So, Mom, Kriti and her girls, me and our four are flying out Sunday morning. Both John and Lee are driving their own vehicles in convoy to meet us there.

Walt just came in with his arms crossed and said he wants his Dino. He said he hasn't gotten Dino for 100 days... 100 days. It's only been one day, but who's counting? Bless his heart, he's not taking this well. A consequence. I think this is his first real punishment. He'd been a bit feistier than usual, and I'm having problems disciplining him. He's our baby, he's a ball of energy, he's been nothing but amazing as far as rolling with the punches and keeping up with our circus. Poor kid. I have this internal struggle with wanting the kids to feel freedom and joy in their childhood, but I also want them to know there are boundaries and rules.

Back to Walt, he smacked Sam on the way to sports camp and then got in trouble and then kicked the console of Papa's car. He was holding his beloved Dino, and I took it away from him and said he couldn't have it for two days. It's been tough. Tougher on me than him. That was yesterday morning, so when I picked them up after sports camp, he asked for Dino back, and I said, "No." And, I asked him if he remembered why?

"'Cause I hurt Papa caw."

Yup, 'cause he hurt Papa's car. And then we talked about if he keeps being physical and rough, he may hurt someone or something, and people won't want to play with him. We got home and he asked for it again... and again... and again.

"I want my Dino! I said, sowwwwwy... please!" Walt wailed, followed by yelling and huge crocodile tears. Then Sam and Millie started feeling really sorry for him and started begging me to give it back to him. Nope, can't do it. Then I lose at parenting, again!

Instead, we talked about it more, and I had Dino whisper in my ear. "I miss Walt's little hands so much and want to play with him so badly, but I understand that we have to wait until the end of tomorrow because Walt hit someone and kicked his Papa's car. I know it's for the best. I can wait until tomorrow."

Fast forward to this morning, John was making snacks for the kids' lunches, and Walt had another massive cry because Dino was up on the shelf watching us get ready for the day. Now, even John looked over at me and gave me the eyes, looking at Dino, and he said... he gave me the eyes to say, "Can he put Dino in Walt's lunch to surprise him?" Ahh! And Bella and Millie and Sam were pleading... So, everybody caught what was going on, and the older kids looked at John and me, and they were pleading. And, I nodded, Ahh... Okay.

Actually, full stop. No! No! No! Not... Not okay! I said to myself, "We must stay strong!" I said, "No!" and I meant no.

So, I secretly got John's attention again and made sure the three older kids saw me, and I just shook my head no. Walt can't get it back sooner than what we agreed upon, or else the lesson will go out the window. Wow, I'm learning how to parent, dammit.

So again, I said out loud, "Walt, Dino will travel with Dad all day long in his vehicle, and when you're done your sports camp, Dino will be waiting for you."

Parenting is so hard. Seriously.

Everyone in the family wants Mr. Walt to get his Dino back—we all can't handle it.

So, I'm just waiting, patiently waiting.
I know I said it's over, but I'm still waiting for you.
I'm just waiting, patiently waiting
I know I said it's over, but I'm still holding out for you.

It's been a great lesson for all of us. I haven't been the greatest at follow-through, and I'm sure you've noticed. John will yell and say something extreme like, "You're grounded for a month." Which in my opinion, is quite a harsh punishment for, say, not bringing up your dirty dishes from the basement. And then I snap at him because I want us to try and parent consciously. Isn't that awesome? Good Lord and good luck, kids!

For real, though, what I'm learning is that parents have to be on the same page together at all times. Fine, you can argue and disagree behind closed doors, but I can remember my Mom and Dad saying that there needs to be a united front. I've grown up hearing and watching that, but I really have to try to put it into practice. It only makes sense for parents to parent together. It's work, and it won't work if one parent thinks they have all the answers. It only works if you're working together.

I'm just waiting, patiently waiting.
I know I said it's over, but I'm still waiting for you.

I'm just waiting, patiently waiting.
I know I said it's over, but I'm lost without you.

Ellen Nasser, 'Patiently Waiting' [unreleased version]

CHAPTER FIFTY-ONE
WAITING ON UNCLE LATE

July 16, 2022
6:25 a.m.

Yesterday was a big day. I'm starting to share my secret project with a few more people because I want to get everything lined up and complete it. I ended up having a call with Carla, Auntie Moomoo's author friend, and read her the beginning of my book. She really liked it. I talked to her and explained how this all came about and what my intentions are.

Do you remember the owner of Mano's where we had Mom's birthday lunch? Well, we recently heard Manoli passed away. I just can't believe it. After we had that nice visit with him, we heard he had gotten sick with cancer and quickly passed. He was only seventy years old.

And that day, he told us he'd probably work at the restaurant forever; he loved it. He said, "Why not?" He felt no need to retire. He could holiday and run the restaurant—he thought that sounded like a great plan.

I've been reminding the kids that if they find a job that they really have a passion for, they honestly won't feel like they're working a day in their lives. I'm sure most people don't realize that, but it's true. It's even true with this project. I have a passion for it. It's much easier to get up bright and early on a Saturday morning because I'm excited about what I'm doing. There's a fire.

Bart is finishing up my music. I've been in touch with Carla, and she's going to connect me with a literary agent—oh yes, I just wrote that and I have never heard of that in my life. I'm thinking I'll let my family know about it sooner than later. I told Fabulous about it yesterday, and I just sat and cried with her. She gets me, she knows where I'm coming from. She has been helping us so much lately, I just keep thanking my lucky stars that she can help us with our family. We work so well together. With both John and I working full-time, we need another set of hands, and are beyond grateful for her wanting and choosing to be a part of our lives.

John and I packed for a long-time last night. I think we're ready to leave tomorrow morning. John and Lee are leaving at 8 a.m. today. Fishy, the Fishiest Fish of All, will be in Penticton once we arrive. We will literally overlap for a few hours. I can't wait to see her. She said, even if we just get one quick hug, it'll be great. Remember, she was in the chat group the morning this project got started—she and Australia Eric.

It's funny how some people just stay in your life forever, others come and go. Even hearing about Manoli passing away made this project ever more relevant for me. I told Bella what I was up to, and the response was, "Woah, Mom, this is so cool." Made me feel like it was so worth it.

Oh, my goodness, John is belly aching, he's about to leave and walked past our mirror and said, "My Gawd, my ear hair is outta control."

I'll tell you, these magnifying mirrors don't lie. Of course, I started laughing, like really hard, because he is so pissed off about it. He said, "I should have an ear hair transplant to the top of my head."

I couldn't stop laughing, and he's like, "What?"

I said, "Sorry, I just reread something in my journal, and it's funny, that's all."

I hope this conversation translates well because in real life it was *EXTRA* funny. Anyway, he's pacing around waiting for Lee to text him back. They're driving convoy, and John loves being the boss. Then, in true John Nasser style, he comes to the closet and abruptly says, "That's it, I'm leaving."

I laughed and I asked him what's up, and he said he has to leave, and Lee hasn't messaged him back. I asked him what their plan was, and he said, "To leave at 8 a.m."

John, it's 7:31 a.m. I thought, am I missing something? He laughed and said, "Okay then, I'm gonna go get a coffee, want one?"

Yes, please, a 1,000 times, yes please.

As he leaves, he says, "By the way, I turned down the A/C for you."

Wow! Was I supposed to thank him? Um, thank you, thank you, John, for not turning it down all week as I froze into a frozen turd. Thank you, thank you, John, for turning it down as you leave town? I followed up and said, "Honestly, I'd like to talk to you about that. It's so cold in our house, John, that I can barely feel the tip of my nose, and the one nostril—it's actually stuffed. Like my body is absolutely freezing cold, John."

He said, "Yeah, that's why I turned it down for you."

For me… Wow, he's leaving the house for two weeks. So, I said to him, "I just wanted to get this straight, you turned down the A/C for me, as you're heading out the door, but you couldn't turn it down *for me*, the past three days as I've been sitting here freezing my ass off?"

So, we banter back and forth like this as we always do, and he can't wipe the smirk off his face because it's the stupidest argument in the world. So, he follows up, "Oh, I'm so sorry, Ellen, I can't control how hot I get."

To which I followed up with, "Yes, John, I can't imagine having someone not respect your body temperature."

He laughed and I laughed, and he goes, "Shush, or else you're not getting your coffee."

This basically sums us up, most of the time. It's funny and stupid all at the same time.

I love him, but I really don't think he and I would have been good for anyone else. We *aren't* a total match made in heaven; that's for sure. I'm not even sure if that even exists, but for the most part, we do have fun together. We don't take each other too seriously, and it seems to work for the most part.

Did I tell you that when Dad officiated our marriage, instead of saying you may now kiss your bride, he said, "You may now… *smooch*."

Dad had a great sense of humour, and so does John. Okay, I'll go smooch my bubs goodbye. And, just like that, he showed up in my closet with my decaf latte, and I told him I was *just about* to come and see him off. We had another little visit. And then, Bella poked her head out of her bedroom and asked why Dad was still here, and he said, "Ahh, I'm waiting for Uncle Late." That made us all laugh. He's such an ass.

I just went downstairs to say bye to Lee and John, and of course, I was telling Lee what Johnny had just called him. Lee had a good laugh and said, "We said 8 a.m. What?!—Were we on Newfoundland time?"

Off they go. It was 8:01 a.m.

> *I like coffee, tea is fine.*
> *I've got a man that I call mine, that I call mine.*
> *You know, I love coffee, tea is fine*
> *I've got a man that I call mine.*
> *I like chocolate, vanilla's alright.*
> *I've got a man that tucks me in at night, if that's alright.*
> *You know I love chocolate, vanilla's alright.*
> *I've got a man that tucks me in at night.*
> *I like a nice cold drink in hot sunny weather.*
> *Hangin' with my babe makes it that much better.*
>
> Ellen Nasser, 'Hangin' With My Babe' [unreleased version]

CHAPTER FIFTY-TWO
READY TO ROLL

July 17, 2022
6:09 a.m.

John and Lee have made it to Vernon. We had a big day of swimming and friends, now we need to be at the airport by 8:30 a.m. I can't believe we're off to Summerland.

Carla sent me some contacts for my memoir yesterday. I read all of the names, and I was drawn to one in particular, let's call her Julie. I pulled her photo up online and loved her smile and energy. Funny thing, Bella came and said, "Oh! Who's that?" And then boys came and asked about her. Now, even typing about it, I'm getting the urge to diarrhea. Crap, I spelled it wrong again. I thought the one thing I'd figured out in writing this book was how to spell that word. It's funny, this is how I want to spell it. D I A R R E A H A. Every time. Ha! Ha! I have diarreHA—clearly not... Ha! Ha! Clearly not a laughing matter.

I've been doing my research on Julie, and I sincerely hope she chooses to work with me because she offers so much creative support and knowledge in so many different aspects of the media arts. I have many ideas. Dare I say it, I've even dreamed of writing a musical one day? There, I said it. A combination of my songs and stories, I also have these other ideas about books. I just have this feeling she'd be a wonderful contact. If I could wake up every day of my life and be creative in the arts, I would. I'm putting it out there—Julie will be my literary agent.

The thing is, though, this isn't my first rodeo in something like this. You know, rejection. Rejection and I are like old acquaintances. I wouldn't say friends, but we definitely know of each other.

Figure Skating – Rejection was there.
Dating – Rejection was there.
Friendships – Rejection was there.
Auditions – Rejection was frequently there.
Job Interviews – Rejection was there.
Listing Houses – Rejection was there.
Radio Play – Rejection was there.
Radio Tracker – Rejection was there.

With my performing life, I have auditioned and been turned down so many times—I can't even keep track anymore. I've had to have thick skin over the years. It doesn't always work out the way *I think* it should. So, if Julie and I don't hit it off, that's okay, I'm a 100% certain there is a literary agent out there waiting for me. Like John, he was waiting for me. I had to go through a lot of heartache to find him. But now, I have a collection of music that I would have never had... had I wouldn't have gone through the pain and loss. I don't regret any of it. Not for a second. Okay, maybe for a second... but certainly not more than a few seconds.

Group chat buzzing away! Kriti just texted: "We are up! Cab coming at 8 a.m." Mom and I both answered: "Wa-hooooo!"

On that note, maybe I should start wrapping this up in the morning. I'm going to miss Sofi so much. She's been my co-writer. The minute I wrote that; she let out a big sigh. Auntie Julie is coming... Oh, dang it! I wouldn't have named a literary agent Julie had I remembered Auntie Julie, puppy sitter. Ahh! It's okay... whatever! Auntie Julie is coming to pick up Sofi on her way home from the lake.

My next entries aren't going to be in my closet sanctuary. My writing partner won't be with me, my Priestess Aura Spray is gone, and I'm going to finish up my project with Lover Aura Spray. Oh my gosh, the only constant thing is change. I'm a bit nervous, of course, thinking how this creating is going to all pan out with a house full of family, in Summerland.

I can do it.

CHAPTER FIFTY-THREE
SUMMERLAND

July 18, 2022
6:56 a.m.

We arrived in Summerland. I woke up and started my meditation on the balcony with the sun shining and a few raindrops sprinkling. I moved inside because God turned up the tap a bit. It's now raining, but I've never witnessed such a peaceful sign from Mother Nature.

> *You came in like the rain,*
> *felt so refreshed.*
> *I forgot about the pain.*
> *But now you're gone,*
> *and the sun is here to stay.*
> *I can't believe we're through,*
> *in the blink of an eye.*
> *The clouds began to move,*
> *and now you're gone.*
> *And I have myself to blame,*
> *I want the rain. Give me the rain.*

> Ellen Nasser, 'Stay Rain' [unreleased version]

The drops are gently falling from the sky, and the sun is peeking through the clouds, and it's the most beautiful thing. I feel like this morning is the validation that life can be so many things simultaneously. I guess a person doesn't just feel one thing and one thing only. This morning is so peaceful and calm. I'm sitting here and feeling so blessed that I'm having problems putting it all into words.

Mom is in a huge bedroom with a vaulted ceiling, letting all the kids bunk with her. Kriti and Lee are in another bedroom across the open deck in a separate area, and John and I slept in a bedroom with Walt on an air mattress. I joked and I said, "It's the summer of John, Ellen and Walt." John followed up with, "It's our Waliday!"

As I mentioned, the kids are going to a summer sailing camp with John's cousin hosting, and John, Walt, and I will be visiting New York together. I'm going to turn forty and then the next day fly off to Connecticut. Seems strange to think I won't be writing to let you know what happens in New York. I have this daydream that I'm going to meet up with one of the literary agents Carla sent me, and I'll just pop by their office to say hello. We'll have a chat about life and all things creative, and she'll say, "Ellen, sounds like a great project. Yes, let's work together on this."

I read a little bit out loud to Mom the other night, and Sam walked by and heard what I was reading. He heard his name and came over and smiled and said, "Is this… is this real? Did I say that? Did I do that? What is that?"

The smile on his face melted my heart. I could already tell he loved it.

Kriti just came by the kitchen table where I'm writing, and she said that she and Lee had been up since 6 a.m. They've exercised and are ready for the day. She was complaining about how inflexible she is, and we both laughed because we knew that if she stretched every morning for about ten minutes, she'd notice a world of difference. Little Emily just walked up to me and asked what the Wi-Fi and password are—I showed her where to find it, and Millie zipped by and said, "Oh Emily, don't ask my Mom that—she's not good at that stuff." Sam and Walt are fighting over the iPad on the couch; John is meditating and journaling in the corner of the room. It's 7:24 a.m., and our vacation household is buzzing.

I was so happy to get to see my dear Fishy and her beautiful family yesterday. What are the chances of them being here, from the Yukon, for a wedding and then us being able to sneak in a couple of hours of beach time? I told her what I was up to; I told her my secret, and she wasn't surprised at all.

We are all now having a morning squabble about what the perfect temperature for a vacation house should be. Really? This shit follows us everywhere we go. There was a fresh rain, beautiful breeze, and I'm up against John and Mom this morning discussing the A/C. I'm not gonna win.

Oh, my Lord, I won. I actually won. The A/C is off, the windows are all open, the fresh air is breezing through.

"Sorry guys, I'm in heaven."

Kriti said, "Don't be sorry, Ellen, we're *all* in heaven."

Let our summer vacation begin.

> *I don't know, how to love you.*
> *Like I'm supposed to.*
> *Like I used to.*
> *I don't know how I'm supposed to hold you.*
> *Haven't got the slightest clue.*

When it's really not you.
What's easier?
Losing someone one day?
Or one day at a time?
What's easier?
Losing you or losing my mind.

Goodbye, old friend.
Please forgive me while I cry.
Wasn't ready to say bye, old friend.
How selfish am I?

Goodbye, my love.
Not ready for this show.
But I must let you know my love.
My world, you will hold.
My world, you will hold.
My world, you will hold.
My world, you will hold.

I must surrender and let go.

Ellen Nasser, 'Surrender' with lyrics [unreleased version]

CHAPTER FIFTY-FOUR
DEEP BREATH ELLEN

July 19, 2022
6:59 a.m.

We spent most of the day with John in a work meeting and us wandering around the Orchard Mall. The kids all wanted to buy something, and I swear we won't set foot in a mall again, on this vacation. It was complete chaos, to say the least. I counted about four times that I had to talk myself out of a complete breakdown.

Momma ended up buying some Italian pasta and sauces, we picked up zucchinis and fresh cherries at a fresh fruit stand and had a lovely dinner. You wouldn't believe the gentle breeze and sun pouring into this guest house. No doubt, yesterday morning's rain added to the beauty of it. Everything here is so lush and vibrant.

My morning practices have gone to the dogs.

I've been setting my alarm for 6:30 a.m. and enjoying a bit of a sleep-in. The problem is, the kids are up so early.

I'm sitting at the kitchen island, and Sam is eating Froot Loops, Walt is on the iPad and John is journaling, and Mom is closing the blinds, prepping for a very hot day. Now, cousin Emily is up.

Sam says, "Mom... Mom, is Subway the most healthiest fast-food store?"

I asked, "Why?"

"I don't know, because I really love it."

Next, enters cousin Molly and Millie.

I think the key thing to creating is to actua ly have the physical space to create in. I am missing my closet sanctuary and writing partner. Like I said, at the beginning of this project, with creativity, you need to carve out the time, and guard it with your life. I know I'm trying to take one day at a time, one moment at a time, but vacationing and keeping your daily practices is a challenge. I haven't exercised for two days. I just asked Mom if she wanted to go for a walk along the beach because if I don't move my body soon, I'm gonna lose it.

Okay, I just announced to all the kids that nobody gets technology until 10 a.m. Nobody... nobody gets technology until 10 a.m. Maybe that'll encourage a sleep-in. Walt walked over to me in a huff and said, "You said dares no tecnimology, git off your compter den."

Deep breath, Ellen. John and I have yelled at most of the kids, and it's not even 7:30 a.m. yet. Anyone else's family holidcys feel like this?

I told my family about my project. If you can imagine. I told them all. I'm so glad I didn't tell everyone right off the hop. When I shared it, I felt the energy shift a bit.

It's been such a big undertaking, and now everything is different. Or is it? Maybe I'm just being moody and dramatic. Maybe I should've waited to share it until I was actually done? Hard to say, but I suppose it doesn't matter anymore; it's out now. It was fun, though, having this big, little secret and creating *without* people knowing about it. That definitely added to the magic of it all.

There've been some good in sharing it, too. It inspired some people—and I think that's incredible. Also, Kriti reminded me of a song I had forgotten about, so I'll be sure to plunk it in somewhere. Can you believe it? I had this cute song called "Mr. Painter." I actually forgot about it altogether, so I must go back to my writings and see where it'll fit.

Hopefully, I'm going to send off my submission to a publisher in New York by this Wednesday. I'm also second-guessing all of that, you know, doubting myself and everything else I'm doing. On my "I am limitless days," and rainbows and unicorns flying outta my butt, everything is great. And, I talk about being courageous and listening to my heart, but on other days, when I feel scared and closed off, I feel petrified to share my soul. I need to ask myself, what am I scared of? What is the worst thing that could happen?

When I shared a bit of my story, some commented, some took it personally, tried to change my story to suit them, and I didn't like it. I'm reminded, I'm not sharing my stories to get a stamp of approval from anyone, really, on how I choose to live my life. Also, my songs on the radio are one thing, my memoir stories and piano compositions are another. These are truly a piece of my soul. If you want to know who I am or what I'm like, this is it. You got it; I've let you in. That's why I need to breathe deeply and sit with this. I need to feel into it and make sure this is *really* what I want to do.

Rejection is a real thing in my life and likely a real thing in yours. The more you put yourself out there, it seems the higher chances for rejection. In all honesty, I don't want my memoir to be rejected by a publisher. That'll suck!

Dear Creator of All Beings,

I ask you to support me while I finish the creation of this memoir. Please hold and support me so I can continue writing from my heart, and so this can be used to its highest good. I humbly ask you to surround me with light as I explore where it's supposed to land. Bless every single heart who listens or reads this, fill them with love, inspiration and a deep knowing that they too are limitless and they're not alone. I ask for the wings it needs to soar, whi e grounding me to the core of the Earth. Please continue to bless our family with abundance, may I choose to live in the flow of creativity, inner peace and joy. Amen.

CHAPTER FIFTY-FIVE
REGAINING ORDER

July 20, 2022
6:59 a.m.

It was a beautiful day yesterday. I finally decided I needed to do some of the things I do every day in order to feel good, or else I'm not going to feel good on our vacay. We all exercised, and it felt amazing. There's a really steep hill up to the house we're renting, so Mom recommended that the kids all walk up and down it three times, so I liked that and made the announcement. When they all stopped bellyaching about it, they ran up and said I had the worst idea ever. I threw Grandma under the bus. I told them it wasn't my idea; it was Grandma's. However, my idea is to do it every single day while we're staying here. They all groaned, almost in harmony. Mom, Kriti and I power walked for forty-five minutes. There are so many hills. We came back up to the house and made a picnic for the beach. Turkey and ham sandwiches with mayo, lettuce and pickles, and then a bunch of peanut butter and syrup. And then we had various kinds of sparkling bubblies and, of course, some cherries and watermelon.

From there, the family all went out on Skaha Lake with our friends from Calgary. I ended up going to find a place to record a voice-over of me reading the first few pages of my book. When I submit this to Julie today, I want to send my cover letter, fifty pages, a couple of family pictures, and this trailer of me reading my memoir, including my music throughout. When I finished recording it, everyone was out on the boat, so I just started walking towards Skaha Marina. I ended up running out of juice both figuratively and physically at about the Safeway. I stopped to buy some raspberries and a water. I ended up going next door to a Telus to charge my phone because I thought I'll be outta luck if my phone dies because I didn't have my purse on me. Anywcys, I ended up having a chat with a nice guy there, and we talked about life, Penticton versus the Prairies, and we ended up talking about meditation and how healing it is. He said he really didn't know where to start with it, so I recommend he read *The Untethered Soul* by Michael Singer and to listen to Eckhart Tolle's audiobook of *The Power of Now*, and then we breathed together with our hands on our hearts. It was beautiful, and then John picked me up, and off we went.

Andrew emailed my voice over to tBone in Saskatoon, and it was divine timing that tBone could get it done because he is leaving town. My dear lawyer friend Flora from Calgary is the one that's here right now, and she's having a look at my cover letter this morning, and then I'll send it all off to Julie by noon. I can't believe it. Now I just need to follow up with good vibes. After I send it, I'll just sit and see what happens. It seems silly, but I'll just keep writing, finish up my project, and celebrate my birthday. I know on the website they say to expect a significant wait time for a response, and John also reminded me that I shouldn't hang my hat on one literary agent, to which I answered, "Well, I hung my hat on *one guy* and look where that got me."

John's trying to save me from rejection and disappointment; he doesn't want to see me get hurt. I also know that meeting with her next week, when we happen to be in New York, is a total long shot, but I can try.

Today was Mom and Dad's Anniversary. We're going to surprise her and take her out to a winery for either lunch or dinner. The kids can play, and we'll have some food and celebrate. Even though Dad's no longer earthbound, he's still with us. He's making that very obvious. We must celebrate them and their love for each other.

Seems like everyone is sleeping in a bit longer today, praise the Lord. I'm certain the sun, water and outdoors make everyone sleep better.

CHAPTER FIFTY-SIX
WHAT'S SO STRANGE ABOUT THAT?

July 21, 2022
9:16 a.m.

My Grandpa would have been ninety-nine years old today. Happy heavenly birthday, Grandpa!

Yesterday started off a bit rough—my sweet niece Emily barfed, but bounced back really well. We think she may have had heat stroke from the day before. The Dads took the other girls, Bella, Millie and Molly, to Penticton to get some more groceries, wine, and get John's tire on his bike fixed up, picked up a new shower head and got Millie some new sandals. While they were in town, the girls got their nails done, so they were excited about that.

It seems like on vacations, my entries are more newsy updates than my deep thoughts and feelings. Maybe it's because I'm missing the cocoon of my sanctuary.

I also wonder if it's because my secret is out and my family knows what I'm up to. Hard to say. The one thing is, when I woke up at home, it was nice and early, and I could just sneak into my closet without anyone really knowing I was awake. Here I'm sleeping in, and I'm trying to write on the floor of the bedroom we're staying in... missing my Sofi Wofi, and it's just different.

Yesterday's workout was a walk along the streets in the hills in Summerland, and it was absolutely glorious. Each time we climbed up another street, the views of the mountains and lake were even that much more spectacular than the last. Before we left, a huge black and yellow butterfly was at the front door. My Mom and I were visiting. There was traffic buzzing by on the busier streets. We were talking to an Albertan who had been living in Summerland for ten years and just loves it. And then we walked over to a bench that looked out over everything. The grape trees, the houses, the mountains, Okanagan Lake—it was truly breathtaking.

And, then my Mom said, "Ellen, did you hear that?"

Remember, it was my Mom and Dad's anniversary yesterday, and her sign that Dad is near, is *always* the mourning dove. I stopped and listened very carefully, and there was no doubt about it, the dove was singing to Mom. We could hear him singing faintly, far away and near the lake in the lower part of the landscape. He sang, and sang, and sang.

"Happy 48th Anniversary, Toots."

It was Dad. We came back, and as we started walking up to the front door, guess who welcomed us back home— the butterfly.

When we told my brother about it, he said, "Yeah, Dad is

really making it known he's with us on this holiday. The signs are everywhere."

I sent my submission to Julie yesterday. I'm nervous, but I couldn't have done it without Lee's help. I know it's a long shot, but I'm happy I did it. Dad would be so proud that I said yes to this and had the courage to follow through.

Okay, I've circled back. I just drove John to Penticton to go gravel biking. He said that he admired that I was able to get this project done. He told me that some people may roll their eyes at me for creating a memoir at forty years old—who does that, he said. But I said to him, if he could tell me the magical age in order to have "permission" to write my own memoir, please do let me know. I also told him that he would have to promise that I would live healthily enough to be able to write my memoir, *and* remember all the stories, and all of the magic.

He said I was right on that one. He said to just go for it!

We agreed that there are going to be people who roll their eyes and paint me however they wish to paint me—but it really isn't any of my business what people think about me. I have a promise to myself that I'm going to continue to be true to *myself*.

I love fiercely, and I feel my best creating and connecting. I sent my preview for a few of my friends, and they've messaged back and sent voice memos telling me it's so beautiful. A few of my pals said that it didn't even matter what the rest of the world thinks about it, because it's going to be such a beautiful treasure for our kids and family. Goosebumps. They also said that they want to create something like this for their own families. Goosebumps, on top of my goosebumps.

What did I say from the very beginning? If it inspired one person, then mission accomplished. I haven't even completed this yet, and mission is accomplished. I can't wait to do the voiceover and tell my story with my music.

John and I were laughing about my email to Julie—he said, I really don't want to burst your bubble, but I'm guessing there's a 95% chance that this woman won't ever get back to you. He said even higher. He can't believe I'm trying to get a meeting with her this week, when we happen to be in New York.

He laughed and said, "Oh, hey Julie, super accomplished woman living your big, important life in NYC. I just happen to be in the city, and I was just hoping you could... you could work your big, important life around our kids' summer holidays."

John's like, "Don't you think the minute Julie says she'll meet you for a coffee, you'd be on the first flight out?" I sheepishly agreed. I guess it doesn't *have* to be the week of August 8th, but why not kill two birds with one stone, right?

So, this is why John and I work. We try to manage each other as far as our heads getting too caught up in the clouds. It's sure been a journey of growth, that's for sure. He's proud of me and he enjoys my quirkiness—but I don't think I'm really that quirky.

He commented, "You hugged the stranger at Telus after you both listened to your meditation music and breathed deeply together?"

Yes... yes, I did... and what is so strange about that?

He said, "My point exactly."

Every time I walked by,
the expression on your face,
told me you thought you maybe knew me
another time, another place.
Every time I saw you,
I thought you were someone I knew,
but I was wrong. (I was wrong.)
You're just a stranger;
Someone I don't know at all.
Someone I only see when we pass in the hall.
You don't know me, you're just a stranger, that's all.

Every time we say hello, the next word is goodbye.
It's never more than that, and I always questioned why.
Every time that we touched,
thought you were someone I could trust.
But I was wrong. (I was wrong.)
You're just a stranger;
Someone I don't know at all.
Someone I only see when we pass in the hall.
You don't know me, you're just a stranger, that's all.

When we moved in together,
thought I'd get to know you better.
But now you're just a stranger,
that's all.
You're just a stranger;
Someone I don't know at all.
Someone I only see when we pass in the hall.
You don't know me, you're just a stranger, that's all.

You're just a stranger;
Someone I don't know at all.
Someone I only see when we pass in the hall.
You don't know me.
You don't know me.
You don't know me.
You're just a stranger, that's all.

Ellen Nasser, 'Stranger' [unreleased version]

CHAPTER FIFTY-SEVEN
MOMMY MEDITATING

July 22, 2022
7:59 a.m.

Being woken up with your kids fighting is the most annoying thing ever. It may be the worst thing than waking up to SNOOZE. SNOOZE = Barf. Waking up to your kids fighting = Barf. Same barf, different pile. Barf!

I think it was mostly the boys, but somehow Millie got involved, as she tends to do. And she is reporting it to us, so John got everybody up and out the door. The last thing I heard him say was, "I know it's not your fault, Millie, but you're coming too, and we're all going to explore Summerland."

So off they went—the three littles are with Dad, and I'm trying to start fresh, again.

These summer holidays are amazing in many, many ways, but honestly, I'm pooped. We've had so much fun at the beach, driving around, John cycling, kids getting their nails done, hiking, shopping, getting lots of treats and ice cream, eating out, but... whoa, it is exhausting. I think Bella would have rathered us only be away for a week, instead of two; she's getting to be at that age, but this is good for us to have a change of scenery and enjoy some family time.

Millie just peeked her head over my shoulder—John let her stay after all. She just said, "I meditated with Grandma, and it was boring."

Millie asked, "What time are we leaving for Vernon?"

"Noon", I said.

I'm excited. We're going to meet one of John's colleagues, have a BBQ and check out Vernon. I've never been there, and I've heard it's also really quite beautiful.

So, Flora from Calgary just messaged me photos of when the kids were really young, holidaying in Penticton years ago. It's just proof that time flies without us even noticing, and the nudge that what I'm doing makes sense. In the photos she just sent, Sam was toddling around in a diaper, and the girls were so extra precious and so little. It was probably six years ago, and it seems like yesterday.

When you think about it, six years ago—life was so different. Your life was so different. Six years ago, I bet you had friends who aren't even your friends anymore. You might have friends who used to be married. Maybe friends who have moved houses a few times. You may even have friends who have passed away. In another text my sister just wrote, "Oh, wow, the kids look so grown up." Nothing ever stays the same. The thing we must remember is that there's always so much beauty right now, but also so much awaiting for us on the other side.

I can barely type with all the action around me. It's so important to claim that time and space, and soon the kids will start respecting it. When Sam and Walt were around two years old, they'd say, "Mommy meditating."

I can remember John said he never thought his two-year-old would be saying a phrase like that. It's been essential for my mental health and emotional health. It starts with one deep breath.

Well, I just had a little hissy fit because I heard of death incidents happening to kids because of social media, and I made Bella take TikTok off her phone. I don't even really know what TikTok and Snap are; I can't even work them. And, yes, I just wrote that. I have a love/hate with these phones.

This morning, it's an obvious hate.

CHAPTER FIFTY-EIGHT
SOCIAL

July 23, 2022
7:38 a.m.

We had such a big discussion about social media, YouTube and TikTok yesterday. I'm getting so tired of it, and I've voiced my opinion loud and clear.

I feel I can make conscious decisions on where and what to look at it and what to post. I get it, I know why many of us are on social media, it feels good to connect, be entertained, be inspired, but the children's brains aren't developed enough to make sense of this stuff, and there's no real way to monitor it. It's a chance to unwind, relax, have your kids be entertained for a bit, but the reality is, it's not good unmonitored.

I don't know about your kids, but after ours are online for a considerable amount of time, they turn into absolute monsters. Have you watched *Social Dilemma*? It's worth a watch.

My Mom hit it on the nose. She said if used unconsciously, the internet robs our children of their innocence. I couldn't agree more. So, at the end of the day, I think conversations need to be had around this topic.

I asked Lee how many families have talked about the importance of monitoring this? He doubted that many had. This is a new topic for many of us parenting in this time, and I think time limits and boundaries need to be set, not only for the kids, but for all of us.

I deleted Facebook and Instagram for the rest of our holiday here to prove a point. Do I miss it? Not overly. I do enjoy posting a picture and some news about real estate or music, but to be honest, it's more of an addiction—the constant checking of what? What am I checking? I love using it as a way to express and advertise for real estate, but I also know it's more negative than positive.

I think that Eckhart would say; It all depends on how it's being used.

What am I looking for? What am I looking at? Is the device being used with awareness? These are important questions to ask. If the phones and apps are being used consciously, as far as I'm concerned, there isn't a problem, basically, like most things in life. Our three younger kids don't have access to these apps, and they won't for a very long time because we've learned our lesson with our eldest.

We didn't end up going to Vernon because one of the host kids had the stomach flu. We ended up going for a drive, and it was awesome. Kriti remembered they visited this sweet little beach the last time they were here, called Manitou Beach. It was the perfect amount of shade, and trees, and people. There was a man selling

Italian gelato, and it might have been the best choco-late gelato I've ever had. Wow, it was amazing. We had another picnic on the beach, and then the rain started—with the sun still shining. Heavenly. At one point, I was treading water in the lake, surrounded by divine Mother Nature, the mountains, the blue sky, the sunshine, va-cation, family, the sprinkling of the rain. I was stewing about some recent work situations, and I thought to myself, "If I can't be happy and content right here, right now, there's no chance I can ever be happy."

Calm the world, no, calm myself.
Starts within and nowhere else.
Calm the world, no, calm myself.
Starts within and nowhere else.
Call your teachers and your guiding stars,
ask your angels to arrive.
We are all so beautiful.
Beautiful, right now. Beautiful, right now.

Calm the world, no, calm myself.
Starts within and nowhere else.
Calm the world, no, calm myself.
Starts within and nowhere else.
We are all connected; we all hold the secret.
We are all so beautiful.
Beautiful, right now. Beautiful, right now.

Ellen Nasser, 'Beautiful Right Now' [unreleased version]

Honestly, the awareness of your mental health is the key to everything. It's the foundation of everything in your life—your mental health and your health. You can have all the education and all the monetary success in the world, but if you don't have your health and mental health, you don't have anything. If you can't see the positivity and light, all the money and surface successes in the world won't change that. You'll be rich and miserable.

All the worldly trappings are of no value unless you hold

the secret of inner peace. No matter where you travel or who you're with, whatever luxurious temporary distraction you indulge in, at the end of the day, you're still stuck with yourself. It doesn't just go away.

My advice is, take the time to heal. It's not easy. It's messy, and you must look at the parts of you that you don't necessarily *like* and *learn* to love them.

CHAPTER FIFTY-NINE
PONTOON TiME

July 24, 2022
8:15 a.m.

Yesterday, we rented a pontoon boat for a couple of hours out on Skaha Lake. Mom treated me for my birthday—it was so much fun! We're taking birthday week to a whole new level on this one.

I'm ready, I can feel it in my feet.
I'm ready, I can feel it in my heartbeat.

Don't you know when it snows down below,
the flowers still are growin'.
Don't you know when it all falls apart,
there's a deeper knowin'.

Every time I say goodbye, I want you to stay.
With thoughts in my mind, if I wanted it this way.
Try to get some sleep, but it's just no use.
Tossin' all night long, only thinkin' 'bout you.

John was the captain, and we cruised around the lake tubing and let the kids fly off the double-decker slide. It was a fantastic way to finish our holiday with the Kolenicks and Grandma leaving tomorrow. Ohhh... do we have sad kids. Kriti said we ended our holiday with a grand slam. We've had so much fun together.

I messaged my piano teacher, Martin and said, "Dare I ask? Are the marks in?"

I got an 87 on my piano exam. I can't believe it. I feel so happy about it, but I also realize how much work I still have to do. To you who are studying/studied Royal Conservatory of Music—Bravo! It's no easy task, especially for a tired Mom.

I miss my piano and my puppy, but we are having such a lovely time. Millie said she's ready to leave and misses her house and friends, though. I get it, she's our homebody. Bella and the boys are happy to hang out for a few more days. Especially Bella, because one of her dear friends is moving to Summerland. What are the chances? And, they'll be able to hang out for a few days.

Yesterday we went to our first winery, Dirty Laundry. I'm hoping we can visit Covert Farms this week.

I met a gal on a floating dock in the middle of the water who said, in her opinion, the best way to live life is to reside in Banff or Canmore all year round and summer in Penticton. I think she might be onto something.

Did you know that you have to be employed in Banff to buy a property there? I thought that was interesting. Canmore doesn't have any rules like that, not ye¯, at least.

Anyways, we're off to a waterfall hike—can't wait!

> *I'm ready, I can feel it in my feet,*
> *I'm ready, I can feel it.*
> *Don't you know when it snows down below,*
> *the flowers are growin'.*
> *Don't you know when it all falls apart,*
> *there's a deeper knowin'.*
> *I'm ready, I can feel it.*
> *So ready, I can feel it.*
> *I'm ready, I can feel it.*
> *So ready, I can feel it.*
>
> Ellen Nasser, 'Feel It in My Feet' [unreleased version]

CHAPTER SIXTY
PLANTiNG SEEDS

July 25, 2022
7:46 a.m.

John is cycling the Kettle Valley Railway bike trail between Penticton and Kelowna. He's back into riding and feeling good. He'd been off for a few months due to a sore back, so I'm glad he's back at 'er.

Our company left, so we shuffled the bed situation and have four kids sleeping in the dark room—if you can believe it, they're still sleeping. We're planning to meet a new friend and her two boys at the Summerland Beach, and then I'm not sure what the rest of our plans are today.

The waterfall hike yesterday was absolutely beautiful—it was about an hour and a half, and the kids loved it. There was an area where you could plunge in the mountain water if you wanted. You know—I wanted! It was freezing cold.

Bella and I are still in conversations about social media, and I think it's so important to have breaks and discussions. It's healthy to recharge and log off. It feels so good to me, so I can imagine it feels good for Bella, too—she just doesn't realize it, yet.

Millie ended up getting a timeout yesterday, and I ended up laying in bed with her, and we both fell asleep. After we woke up, we drove to Oliver, to this really neat outdoor gathering place where there were mist sprayers, a theatre in the round and, of course, little wine stores and restaurants. Our friend said my goal should be to play there this time next year, for his wife's birthday... oh, my gosh, a solo show. The very thought of that gives me nervous bowel. I don't think I could get a solo show together, by this time next year.

My friend simply said, "Get practicing!"

This is what I mean. It's like I have all these cheerleaders throughout my life that continuously push me into my secret desires. I would love nothing more than to have a solo show and to be able to set up and play and connect, anytime, anywhere in the world. Well, I suppose I'll have to talk to Martin about this. What songs would be in my setlist? It's funny, I would also sprinkle a few of my favourite Royal Conservatory pieces, I love The Beatles, of course, my own compositions, my radio songs, my spiritual creations...

And then my friend Flora just said, "Why don't you also read a bit of your book?"

Planting seeds, planting seeds... my cheerleaders are always planting seeds.

Honestly, I just don't know if I could do it, but, strange enough, before we went on holiday, Lee suggested,

"Why don't you learn a bunch of popular songs and just play them for your enjoyment?"

I suppose all signs are pointing to a One-Woman Show, I don't know—we'll see.

Walt is up, and his first words this morning are, "Mom, where's my minion?"

I don't even know what he's talking about... he's now searching our bedroom and came out with a white plastic hanger. Next question: "Where's Dad?" Walt loves his Dad. He thinks he's pretty cool.

Oh, and I forgot to tell you the other day, if all I hear is crickets from Julie, I decided I'm going to edit my work and get it ready to send out to fifty publishers this fall. You know, make a job out of it. When I told John about this, he said, "How about making it forty publishers?" I like that idea. *First Forty* (the original title of this book) being sent out to forty publishers. If no one wants it, that's okay. I've come to terms with it. I'll just finish it up for our family and maybe some other friends who want to listen to it. Actually, it'll be a wonderful welcome home gift for my clients. A gift card to their favourite restaurant, a scented candle, Epsom salts for their bath and a link to my book. Hmmm, Bella still thinks I should publish a hard copy. We'll see...

CHAPTER SIXTY-ONE
REJECTION

July 26, 2022
8:42 a.m.

I had a dream last night about a childhood crush who I just adored over the course of my life and even into adolescence. Even though we moved, again in my teenage years, I still emailed and borderline hounded him. He really didn't seem to like me at all, but I was completely smitten. My Dad always taught me to never toy with other people's emotions, and as I think back, this guy never did that. He never strung me along, not at all. He just didn't really like me that way. And, looking back, it's so embarrassingly obvious, but I always come on way too strong.

So yesterday, I was all ready to go to the beach with my new Okanagan friend, and we had a plan, and she and her kids were going to come to our rental, and then we would walk down to the beach together. She said she'd come at 9:30 a.m., and I got everyone up, packed lunch, sunscreen on... was waiting.

9:30, 9:45…

"Girls, girls look out the kitchen window to see if she's there, okay!"

9:48…

At that point, I text to make sure I didn't get our wires crossed, I didn't want her waiting for us at the beach or something like that.

So, I wrote, "You were planning to come here first, right? At 9:30 a.m.? No rush, I just wanted to touch base."

She wrote back, "Yes… But, on WEDNESDAY!"

Oh, my Lord, oh my Lord—that's so me. Today is Tuesday.

When I told John, he laughed and he said, "Ellen, that's so you. He said I just always come into relationships guns a-blazin'. No clue of the rules. Rules?!" That's the thing with me, I… I don't… I'm not even aware of the rules. I just love and show affection like a dog. I'm excitable. I… I… I never really… Umm… See the writing on the wall. I… I come in way too fast.

And, when crushes didn't respond to my phone calls or emails, I honestly thought, "Maybe they just didn't get them for some strange cyber reason, I don't know." I suppose I'm a bit naïve and ignorant that way. More often than not, I'm full of hope.

Anyways, my new friend just laughed and said we'll see you tomorrow. And, it's all good.

I think these morning writings have me reflecting on other things in my life, like unreciprocated love and unfoldings. I think I've had more than my share. And, no,

I'm not being a victim here; I'm just reflecting and stating the obvious. It's no wonder I have the courage to do stuff like this because what's the worst-case scenario—no one likes it? Too late, my most important people already do like it.

I'm sad and a bit discouraged that Julie hasn't been back in touch. Sure, of course, I am. Are there 1,000 reasons why she hasn't been in touch? Well, probably, there are. She may be on holidays, she may have turned off her emails for a few weeks, she may be having knee surgery, she may be celebrating a wedding anniversary, her Mom may be sick, her brother's kids may need her attention, and heck, she… I… she… she… she might even be out Christmas shopping. The list could go on and on. Also, she just might not be that interested in my project. I thought she'd email back right away, but that's in true Ellen style. No matter how much rejection I encounter, each new project, each new relationship, I truly believe that everyone will love it as much as I do.

Bella asked me yesterday, "Momma, has Julie responded?"

I said, "Nope."

She followed up with, "No, not yet, don't jinx it, Mom."

Not everything you do in life is an immediate home run. Many things in life take so much time, effort, nurturing and, of course, a little bit of luck.

> *Tell your friends you've gone away,*
> *they don't need to know we are here.*
> *No one needs to know it, my only hope is,*
> *you and I to do a little mistletoein'.*
> *Lights are out, the tree is up, magic's in the air.*

Christmas time is,
Christmas time is here.

Grab your jacket, off we go,
for a sleigh ride in the snow.
The snow is fallin', love is calling.
Bring your mittens and your toque.
All I need is you.
Love is calling.
Christmas in your arms feels right.
Feels so right, it feels right.
Here we are, just you and me.
Cuddled up near the fire.
No one needs to know it, my only hope is,
you and I to do a little mistletoein'.
Rest your eyes, the day is done.
Magic's in the air.

Christmas time is,
Christmas time is here.

Grab your jacket off we go,
for a sleigh ride in the snow.
The snow is falling, love is calling.
Bring your mittens and your toque.
All I need is you.
Love is calling.
Christmas in your arms feels right.
Feels so right, it feels right.
Right here, right now, it's true.
There is no one else but you.
Nothing written on my list.
Cover me in your sweet kiss.
Grab your jacket off we go.
For a sleigh ride in the snow.
The snow is falling, love is calling.
All I need is... you.
Christmas in your arms feels right.

Elly Thorn, 'Christmas in Your Arms'

CHAPTER SIXTY-TWO
I THINK I LOST MY CANDY

July 27, 2022
8:10 a.m.

Nine more days of writing. Hard to believe this is coming to an end. It feels like I should just keep going, but I need a rest. I'm looking forward to turning forty and sitting with it for a bit.

Yesterday was so full of fun and celebration for our sweet family friend Nina. We had lunch at Loco Landing, which is this little amusement park for kids, in Penticton, and then spent the afternoon boating, and tubing, and enjoying. Their family made a delicious meal, and we were all laughing at the summer adventures we've had together over the years.

I've basically shared the preview of my book with most of my family and friends.

I have a question for the parents out there. When do you feel the most relaxed? Is it at home when your kids are at school? Is it in your workplace when your kids are at school? Is it on a three-day getaway with your significant other, when your kids are at home and at school?

Or is it on a family vacation when we are all together? Said no parent, ever. Just joking you guys!

We were driving back to Summerland last night after our big day, and John said he was just wiped. And, remember, John and I have almost twelve years between us in age, so he is a little older. These family holidays are a massive undertaking, and of course, my phone doesn't stop just because I'm away. I'm still managing real estate, but sometimes it'd be nice to just turn everything off. Once Lee is licensed, I may just forward my number to him and have a total break.

I can't believe all four of our kids are still sleeping. It's like the good old days when the three of them would all sleep together in one of our upstairs bedrooms at our Collins house, while Walt was in the crib in the other bedroom; now it's the four of them all together. It's pretty awesome.

I'm feeling all the feels lately. I am loving it out here in BC, but I think Sofi has to come next time. It's too long without her.

Oh, sad day—rejection again, Walt just got an email from his gymnastics assessment saying that he wasn't chosen for the competitive gymnastics. When I think about it, it's not really a shock, considering he's built like a linebacker. I'm still thinking a couple of years of gymnastics is a good idea for Walt, just to get him some agility and balance.

On that note, I can hear Mr. Walt's voice, he's up for the day.

And, now Sam just walked in, barely awake with a BIG concern, "Mom, I think I lost my candy."

What candy, I'm wondering? I had forgotten they got a treat bag from a birthday party yesterday. This isn't the biggest concern, as there never seems to be a shortage of treats or candy.

He's back, and he repeated, "I lost my candy."

I said, "Well, Sam, what do you want to do?"

"I don't know, play on the iPad?" Oh, Sam.

Now, Millie is up, walking into our bedroom, yawning, and plunking herself into our messy sheets.

She asked what time it was.

I said, "Almost 9 a.m., you guys had a really good sleep-in."

Sam is back, "Mom, I even lost the iPad!"

CHAPTER SIXTY-THREE
GRATEFUL

July 28, 2022
8:11 a.m.

> *Couple of years now, we made it somehow.*
> *Take a bow—full disclosure,*
> *it's getting closer to being over.*
> *Something I overlooked,*
> *got our trip booked was gonna be off the hook.*
> *I can't handle this, baby, just cancel it.*
> *You said, baby, what's eight more days?*
> *We can fight 'n cry in the sun or rain.*
> *Pack your bags and get on the plane.*
> *I know I can't make you stay.*
> *Baby, just give me eight more days.*
> *Sitting on the airplane, headed to the States,*
> *you always get your way...*
>
> Elly Thorn, 'Eight More Days'

Yesterday was a full day of sun and sand. Being a natural redhead, and someone who doesn't load on the sunscreen, except I put sunscreen on my face every day. I'm a bit fried. When I was little, I tried to tan so badly. I can remember dousing my body with oil, wanting to be anything but the freckle-covered, stark white gal that I am. And, on top of that, I can remember begging Mom to get me a two-piece bathing suit. She finally caved, and I can remember it plain as day. Picture this. Blue and white striped bottoms with a thick, white fabric at the waist that I could fold down, and hike up a little bit, you know, to make it a little extra fancy. The top was this blue sports bra with the words "Lifeguard on Duty", which, I might add, couldn't be further from the truth. Swimmers we are not. I get tuckered out after about ten consecutive strokes and always feel afraid that I'm going to run into something.

When John and I were first engaged, actually, I don't even know if we were engaged, but my parents took all of us kids and our spouses to Hawaii. And, we rented a condo with a pool, and John jumped in and started swimming. We all couldn't believe our eyes; he swam so beautifully. By the time we left, Lee had named John, "JohnaFIN", for the rest of the trip. JohnaFIN, he still calls him this, like all these years later.

Sounds like we'll get up nice and early tomorrow and hit the road so that we can have dinner with our Calgary family. The boys have mentioned a couple of times this week how much they love their Calgary boy cousins. I am so blessed to have the most beautiful nieces and nephews. We have such a flock of them.

Thursday, wow, my favourite day of the week. Today is Thursday. We ordered take-out dinner from Shaughnessy Cove last night and it was delicious—of course, our new Okanagan friend recommended it, she's a total font of knowledge. If anyone is ever going to travel to this beautiful part of Canada, be sure to follow her. She's on Instagram as "Little Okanagan Adventures." It's especially awesome if you have little ones.

Well, just like that—everyone is up. We went to find one of our favourite coffee shops the other day in Naramata, but it had turned into a high tea house. When we walked in, an Angela Morgan painting was hanging on the wall—again, another sign. I have to confirm the size I'm treating myself for my birthday present.

Yesterday, I said to John for every single day that we wake up feeling healthy and have our four strong, beautiful and capable children by our side, we must give thanks. Like, real, genuine, heartfelt thanks.

> *Pack your bags and get on the plane.*
> *I know I can't make you stay.*
> *Baby, just give me eight more days.*
>
> Elly Thorn, 'Eight More Days'

CHAPTER SIXTY-FOUR
BiRTH

July 29, 2022
7:49 a.m.

Last night, my beautiful cousin Kakey gave birth to a precious baby girl.

It took me back to our births and how they all progressed just like my Starbucks orders and piano lessons. Our childbirths were such amazing journeys for both John and I, as I know they are for most people.

What I realized by the end of my birthing chapter there was the power of positive thinking. By the time we had Walt, who was eleven days overdue, which apparently isn't typical of a fourth child, is that there is power in the words we choose. We ended up hiring a lovely doula who helped us shift some of our typical words. She used the word "waves" instead of "contractions"—she explained what was actually happening internally as each "wave or sensation" was going to come. She gave John some tools to really help support the labour process and actually feel a part and have a role. It was unbelievable.

With Walt, every time a "sensation" came, I can remember standing over at a window in the hospital, overlooking out into this beautiful courtyard with the afternoon sun pouring in, and John was holding my hips in his strong hands, just lightly pushing up and providing me such relief. It was such a blessing to have him wanting to be so involved in our final birth.

And, feeling his strength, supporting me both physically and emotionally was something we had never shared before. It was truly amazing. We had beautiful calming music; I can still almost hear it in my mind. And, on the way to the hospital, we stopped and picked up white birthing pants and shirt. Just some comfies to have at the hospital. We packed some natural sprays created by beautiful Melissa, of course, meditated that morning to consciously set the tone for the day. I remember the sun, how the light was pouring in. A person never knows what will actually happen during the labour and birthing of their newborn.

When we first got pregnant with Bella, we talked about what our birthing plan would be, and both of us just nervously laughed and unknowingly and ignorantly said, "Well, really, no plan, just to you know, God willing deliver a baby safely into the world." Like, we didn't have a plan. There was very little discussion about anything after that. Neither one of us were interested in discussing it. We also really didn't think that we had a say on what was going to happen on that day. If all went well, I would have an epidural because that's just what I thought a person having a baby did, and I had no idea what I was doing and trusted the professionals, and I trusted they knew what they were doing. So, I didn't really ask any questions, and I didn't really think about anything, and I really didn't think much more about it.

When we got pregnant with Millie—the epidural took to only half of my body. Once I delivered Millie, I tried to get up and go to the washroom, but my one leg shot out like a chicken. It scared me… it scared me a lot. I told John for our next baby, God willing, I would try to give birth naturally, still in the safety of the hospital, but perhaps without any medications. And, that's how we welcomed our Sam. In January with those eyes wide opened and those eyelashes and no medication.

And, when Walt came, I wanted to make some more educated choices. So, I asked John if he would do this with me, and he said, "Yes." We made a plan, we read some books, we healed and reflected on my past pregnancies and labours. We talked about my pain and some of the feelings I felt that weren't seen or heard. And, John and I grew so much with the pregnancy of Walt. John showed up for me like you wouldn't believe. We both knew that this was our last time at this, and he really wanted to support me. I had to work through the shame I felt of not having enough milk for our babies, trying to listen to every single person and their dog about what was good for *my* health and *our* children.

How over and over, I would abandon myself and ignore my deep knowing of how to nurture our children, trying to please others around me. My mind running wild, trying to people-please—a pattern I'm starting to notice and heal.

Our children and pregnancies were a spiritual journey for us. Everyone has their own stories about how their children came to them. Others have their own journey of not being able to have them, others have their journeys of working through having them and not wanting them, and feeling societal pressure to have them. Others have journeys of losing them.

I used to be one of those people who would say—oh, you have to have kids, they're the best! Ignorantly, not having a clue of what some people were actually going through. Better yet, I had no idea if people actually wanted to have children. Obviously, I did, it was my dream, but I'm realizing it's not *everybody's* dream.

I have made it perfectly 100% clear to our children that whatever they choose is their own decision. My life has absolutely flourished with each one of these children, blessing our lives—I have grown immensely as a human being, evolving with each bambino.

That's my journey, it's not necessarily Bella's or Millie's or Sam's or Walt's.

They are all so deeply loved.

CHAPTER SIXTY-FIVE
NO OFFENCE

July 30, 2022
8:47 a.m.

Well, that's two nights in a row I haven't slept well—must be a sign it's time to get back to our bed.

We spent the night in Calgary with my brother and beautiful sister-in-law Stacey and their two boys. The kids had a wonderful cousin play, and we had a nice visit. The kids were very tired last night, in fact over-tired and rangy, so I slept with Sam, and John slept with Walt. Divide and conquer. It worked for the kids; they went to sleep quickly, except I couldn't sleep.

I dreamt that I was hearing my childhood alarm clock going off. I can remember it was light pink and had an annoying tick, tick, tick, tick, and the sound of the alarm was actually startling. I was wondering if it was a sign I shouldn't be doing this project, or else a sign I shouldn't have drank my three-pineapple vodka Nutrls. Blah...

Needless to say, I felt drunk and my mind was racing, and of course, I don't like that feeling. I don't sleep well when I drink, and that's a fact. Last night it was 4:10 a.m., and I'm certain I tossed for at least an hour. I usually sleep like a baby right through the night, but not with alcohol in my system.

Sam is up, sneezed and is asking me questions.

"Mom, how is your mouth connected to your nose?"

"I'm not sure."

"I hope you're not offended, but even Millie knows this answer."

"Well, tell me then."

"I think your mouth has a tiny hole at the back of your mouth, where there's that tiny ball, and you know what I'm talking about? And then there is a hole that goes up to your nose. So, they're connected."

Barely a beat.

"Mom, if there was a movie with just one song in it, would it be a musical? Or would it have to have more than two songs?"

I'm not sure what makes a musical a musical—I should know stuff like this.

I can feel Sam staring at me in the morning darkness out of the basement room.

"I can see your shadow in Dad's shadow. Is that weird? No offence. Your shadow looks like Dad's a bit, but your head is more triangle, no offence."

He is in this "no offence" phase, which is really cracking all of us up because most things he says are actually really offensive, and true, I might add, but he thinks he can get away with saying things if he says no offence.

Now he is up and getting dressed.

"Mom, Mom, why did you pack me mostly Walt's underwear?"

I answered, "Sorry, they're basically the same, though."

He's quiet.

"No, mine are more mature underwear."

I can hear the smile in his words—Sam's a funny guy.

Now I just said to him, "Do you know how funny you are?"

Sam said, "No, how? Did Dad look like me when he was a kid?"

Oh boy, and now he's dressed and just like that, he opened the door and left.

Pause.

He's such a feisty little thing; they all are in their own ways.

Upstairs, I hear Walt say, "Hi Sam!"

I hear cousins say, "Hi Sammy Whammy."

Now Millie is up, and I am thinking it's a really good thing most of my morning journals were written, tucked away in my sanctuary. I don't think I would have been able to get much done otherwise.

Walt just poked his head in my room, stuck out his tongue, and wiggled his body, yelling, "Daddy was sleeping with me!" Oh, the excitement and I've barely opened my eyes. I'm guessing we'll be home by 5 p.m. I am so ready for our bed, a snuggle with Sofer Wofer and our piano. I'm tired. I think I'm hungover.

I've let many people in my inner circle know about what I've been up to, and I've decided I'm going to post about my writing on my birthday. I'm still off social media, but Karyn Kimberley, my content manager, has sent me a bunch of questions for me to answer. I love that because she's in charge of everything, but everything is still coming from my own heart... You know. She's going to line up my posts for the few weeks, and I don't mind having a little break from it all. It's busy with the kiddos at home.

CHAPTER SIXTY-SIX
TRUST THE PROCESS

July 31, 2022
5:55 a.m.

Walty got me up this morning at 5:15 a.m. He's now tucked back in and cuddled in our bed. I'm up now, not a chance I can go back to sleep. Oh, it feels good to be back in my closet sanctuary and have my co-writer, of course, cuddled up on my lap.

We had such a nice welcome back dinner at Mom's last night. All of her food tasted extra good. I'll take the kids over to see Nana and Bumpa this afternoon. They've been missing them, especially these past couple of years.

We've had a few days at home now to rest. I have a possession later this morning and then a house evaluation. I'm hoping to get done as much work as possible so that I can enjoy New York and my birthday week. All the kids have swimming lessons booked this week, but for the most part, I'm just going to let them chill. I can't believe tomorrow is August. Where did July go?

On our drive home from Penticton, I followed up with Julie for a third time. Ew, cringey, I know. Is a third follow-up too much? Probably. Do I look desperate? Most definitely. Will I email a fourth time? It's quite possible. I never really know what the magical number of contacts is. Even with real estate, it's a bit of a guessing game. How much is too much, how little is too little?

In the email, I told her that I understood there's a fine line between showing my tenacity, ambition and drive, and also being annoying and overbearing. John said she probably has an assistant reading her emails like Anne Hathaway's character in *The Devil Wears Prada*. He also wondered why I'm putting all my eggs in one basket. I didn't have an answer. If she doesn't respond by the end of August, then I'll probably shop my book around to others—if they all say no, then I'll stay the path, record the audio for our family and possibly self-publish it for anyone else interested. I also think it's neat, though, to show the kids the process of devoting yourself to something, sticking it out, getting rejected, but still enjoying the process regardless of the outcome. These are important life lessons.

I want them to know it sucks, though, too. It's not like I'm invincible; it still hurts.

CHAPTER SIXTY-SEVEN
NO CRACK

August 1, 2022
9:24 a.m.

Julie responded. Maybe three emails was too much. Ugh. Maybe I annoyed her? Maybe she just didn't like my project? She said she's not taking on anything new at the moment. It was mostly a thank you, but no thank you, but there seemed to be a little crack left open. John read the email and said, "Nope. There's no crack."

I said, "Sure, there's a crack, I can sense it. She's expecting me to write back."

He said, "Nope, no crack, Ellen—not a chance. That was a fully closed door."

Then he proceeded to go to our sliding door in our ensuite and demonstrated his take on the door being closed. He said, "Ellen, this is Julie sliding the door totally shut... this is you sneaking your foot in there at the last possible second. Ellen, there's no crack; her intention was to close the door shut." And then, as he said, "Shut," he shut the door. Of course, on that note, and basically as he was demonstrating the closing of the sliding door, I was composing one more measly email, which made John laugh. I told him, "I just wanna thank her, send her my funny Christmas video, and tell her about a couple more creative ideas I have brewing in me."

Sent. Ahh...

The beginning of the season,
I'm so full of Christmas Spirit.
By the end of sweet November,
all my plans are crystal clear.
This year will be different.
I'll feel centered, I'll feel calm.
I'll give my hubs a list "to do"
I'll have time to write this song.

Unpacking all the boxes,
CHRISTMAS, they are marked.
And then about 2 hours in,
it looks like Christmas barfed.
The four kids running round the house,
I told myself I wouldn't yell...
Mommy's favourite ornament is smashed up on the floor.
Johnny's frozen with the tree and banging at the door.
"Move your shoes!" He's gonna lose it.
Kids out of the way!
All my Christmas expectations, POOF on the first day.

Are we having fun, fun, fun?
Christmas has begun, gun, gun.
Am I the only one, one, one...
It's December one, one, one.

To the mall for Santa pics,
To Lawson Heights it's more quiet.
Enchanted Forest on our list,
stop at Tim's for hot chocolate.

Later bedtimes, too much dessert,
calendars and Christmas concerts.

Thinking, planning, shopping, wrapping.
Thinking, planning, shopping, wrapping.
Thinking, planning, shopping, wrapping.

By mid-month, I'm about to scream:
no more parties, no more treats,
no more concerts, no more candy...
It's not good when mom ain't happy.
We're right on track with two big fights,
the next big one on Christmas night.
Kick that elf into next week,
time to book more therapy.

Setting boundaries is fun, fun, fun...
Especially for mom, mom, mom.
Am I the only one, one, one?
Put eggnog in my rum, rum, rum.

The Teachers! The TEACHERS! THE TEACHERS!!!
I can't forget the teachers...
Is a Starbucks card enough?
Our kids are home for 14 days, straight...
They deserve a million bucks.

Baking, EATING, spending, spinning.
Baking, EATING, spending, spinning.
Baking, EATING, spending, spinning.

I'll take my doggie for a run, run, run...
Right, it's – 41, one, one.
Never mind, I'll have a rum, rum, rum, rum.
Make it two instead of one.
Am I the only one, one, one?
Is Christmas almost done, done, done?
Next year will be fun, fun, fun
We'll try Christmas in the SUN.
Jingle all the way!

Elly Thorn, 'Am I The Only One'

Ahh… then I re-read it—I tend to re-read things *after* I hit send. That's not normal, trust me, I know that. Oh dear. I asked her to meet me for a little quick visit in NYC and hope that she'll point me in the WRITE direction. Do you know how I spelt right? And, I wasn't trying to be funny. I said, "Point me in the W-R-I-T-E direction."

I told John, and he said, "Ahh, of course, you did."

Again, I'm reminded of the importance of cheerleaders. I had the biggest and brightest, and the best, and he died a year ago last June. I have to say that I am missing him as I write this memoir.

I've sent out my nine-minute audiobook to people in my life, and the responses have meant the world to me. So, I'm glad I didn't share this until now, and now, it's basically done. And, I'll admit I've really enjoyed having this extra support by the end. But, ahh… the things we say to each other along the way—the things that can stay with a person for a lifetime.

I received three emails last night that meant so much to me. All three saying they couldn't wait to hear more, and one person even suggested that this might be a good CBC audiobook series. What! What a sweet idea—now who do I know at CBC?

Anyways, besides Julie's email this morning, I received another that admired my creative fire. Wow, my creative fire. How inspiring. Hearing those words alone will push me to the end.

I just checked my email—well, that just sucked. Julie emailed again, "So sorry, but I am not taking any new projects, so won't be able to meet."

Okay, now that's a closed door. Even I know that one.

I even felt the breeze of the door being slammed in my face. Yup! No need for anyone else to put eyes on this one.

I told John, and he said, "Oh, you just got turned down from one of the top agents out there, and you're feeling sorry for yourself?"

That's his way of cheerleading. He pushes me and supports me, but he also kinda cringes because he can't believe I have the courage to do what I do.

CHAPTER SIXTY-EIGHT
STORMS

August 2, 2022
8:13 a.m.

Last night it poured like you wouldn't believe. The ball diamond behind our house was like a lake. The lightning and the thunder were rolling and flashing. We were literally in the eye of the storm. It woke the middles up. Sam and Millie were so nervous, and to be honest, so was I. I like storms if I'm safely inside—but last night the hail was pounding against the windows, and it was kinda scary.

Speaking of storms and explosions, Bella had a friend over for a sleepover, and one of their *RED* drinks from the Circle K store exploded onto our cream-coloured carpet in the basement. By that point, John was already upstairs getting ready for bed. I had to breathe so deeply on that one. I don't usually get too upset over spills of any kind because I know accidents happen, but *RED* on our new *CREAM* carpet kinda had me feeling like that storm. I couldn't believe my eyes. They had opened the drink, and it exploded like a volcano, everywhere. They called me, and I seriously... I had to take a minute... I knew our carpet cleaner was outta town. I know, only words a real estate agent says. But their first instinct was to start rubbing it, and so they were rubbing and rubbing, and then they called me, and I came downstairs and said, "Stop rubbing!" And, we quickly googled what to do. And, it said to use 2/3 cup of vinegar and the rest warm water. Saturate and blot. And, of course, we don't have any vinegar, so I asked them to run across the street to ask our neighbour for some. Let's call her Neighbour Wendy. My Lord, what an undertaking. I can feel my forearms this morning from saturating and blotting. They apologized so many times. Ahh, the poor girls.

Okay, speaking of arm workouts. I'm off to the gym, first day back in a couple of weeks. I also have to remember to get the kids' health forms signed, so that they can go on their sailing trip. Speaking of which, I think Walt has an eye infection; he woke up this morning all gooey.

Kids have swimming lessons today, and I have to get packing again. Neither John nor I feel like leaving again. I think we're bigger homebodies than we'd like to admit.

On that note—we got a beautiful invitation from our dearest friends Eric and Cameron, who are getting married next fall in Australia—count me in! I can't wait to be a part of their special day. I've always wanted to see that beautiful continent.

Yup, lots going on today.

CHAPTER SIXTY-NINE
PHONE WARS

August 3, 2022
7:13 a.m.

I sent my little preview to Gray because I wanted him to have an idea of what my project was all about. I woke up to an email from him saying that I'm funny. Naturally, I had to show John that email. I was lighting my candles to sit down and write, of course, being back in my closet sanctuary, and John came by and I said to him, "I told you I was funny."

And, he said, "Yes."

Pause.

And then he looks at me and says, "Could you please not set our clothes on fire?"

I think we're *both* funny.

It was a big day of packing yesterday. John has decided

that everybody has to take a carry-on *ONLY* because we aren't going to lose our luggage, God knows where. It's like a make-work project for me. The kids don't have carry-on luggage, so naturally, a normal person would go out and *buy* some. I told him that the kids are going to need carry-ons soon, but nope, not this trip—this was not the trip the Nasser kids were going to get their own carry-ons. This one is not going to happen. So, John decides to call on the neighbours and my family and go door-to-door collecting carry-ons. With parents like us, our kids have no hope.

So, Bella has negotiated to get her phone back today, and we have figured out all the conditions. We proposed thirty minutes of Instagram, thirty minutes of TikTok and thirty minutes of Snapchat. Once she's used up all of her time, it's automatically done for the day. Since it is summer, though, she tried negotiating for two hours, but we shut her down. So, in the negotiation, she got super complainy and whiny, then outta nowhere, John reveals his, what we called, Inspector Gadget arms, reaches over the kitchen island and steals her phone and says it's gone for another two days. Guess that's the end of that conversation. It's actually been a battle in the Nasser household, but Bella is a strong contender. She's empowered and logical, which works wonders for her case. She followed up with, "You know, I can see my stubborn ways have gotten in the way of getting what I want, and I apologize."

I... I'd call that an apology. Then she's beer whispering to me on the side, "Mom, can you please get me my phone back from Dad?"

She's hilarious.

Bella has proposed that she gets an hour and a half a day in the summer, but she can allocate where the time is spent. I think that's fair, actually. If she wants to spend all the time say on Instagram, she can be the boss of it. She knows the boundaries around it, and we're trying to basically teach her the importance of cherishing more the real-life relationships and steering clear of the online bullshit.

We also have been talking about intentional posts, and for her to know when to stop scrolling. Isn't this a conversation we all need to have?

Anyways, these are such important conversations; even John and I must check in because before you know it, we've been on our phones *way more* than we're proud of. Phones are a gross addiction. There, I said it.

Everything is such a learning experience; parenting included. Mom came over, and we finished packing up the suitcases together upstairs, snuck in some yoga in the hallway, as the boys were having a "time-out" for smacking and pinching each other. And, John made a beautiful dinner of fresh salad, baked potatoes, and chicken skewers. Mom and I had a cocktail, and I got to play some piano, and the evening ended up WAY better than last evening—fingers crossed the carpet cleaner can make it today. I feel like I have one more piano composition in me before I complete this project. We'll see.

CHAPTER SEVENTY
AUTHENTICALLY CONNECT

August 4, 2022
1:56 p.m.

What the actual?! Wow, what a magical sleep-in... I woke up at 8:19 a.m.—no alarm. John had already left to cycle to work. Didn't meditate or ground myself before I bolted to the gym. Actually, had a great workout, mostly on my abs because we were all laughing so hard at life and each other, and then I came home, got ready to head over to a listing presentation with Lee.

I'm sitting down to do my entry, and I can't believe the time of day. All is well, I must be gentle on myself, especially on summer holidays with the kids home. Millie and a truckload of cousins and friends just came down the stairs, asking to go over to their friends' house. I told them they could, but grab some veggies before they go because we all know there's way too many Slurpees throughout the summer.

When we were out for dinner last night, at our friend's house, I was talking to another friend that I hadn't seen for a while. Whenever we connect, we often have a good chat about life. She reminded me that we may not even notice it, but we're all gently touching each other's hearts with words, gestures, small looks and random acts of kindness. She said we're all so beautifully unique, needing one another to do what we are called to do. She reminded me that without listening to our hearts, the whole entire world suffers. It's actually our duty to show up, it's our responsibility to listen to our hearts, and we need to live our authentic lives. It's as simple as that.

By the way, this friend... she's my birthday twin.

CHAPTER SEVENTY-ONE
THIS IS FORTY!

August 5, 2022
6:40 a.m.

*T*his is forty. Nothing feels different. Hard to believe that I've written my way to forty. I wasn't planning any of this—it just happened, and here I am.

Mom surprised me with a beautiful birthday dinner and two cakes. Of course, she made my favourite... carrot cake. I had a full work day, and I arrived at Mom's in a bad mood. Millie and Emily made me the sweetest hand-made birthday cards, which I loved, and Mom spoiled me from one of my favourite shops—Indigo. Life is good.

It's crazy, the card she gave me opened with, "I love watching you write the story of your life." Isn't that funny, she found a card that said that? We all know it's no coincidence.

As I sit here in my closet sanctuary with my candle-light and my puppy cuddled on my lap, wrapped in the toastiness of my pink housecoat, that I think I've had for thirteen years, I'm thinking about how blessed I am. Hold on, I'm gonna open the card that John put on my bedside table before he snuck off to the gym. I heard him in the upstairs hallway, and then he snuck back into our bedroom and he put this card on my bedside table, but as he placed it, he accidentally clanked my incense holder with the card falling on the ground. He burst out laughing. I just looked at him, and... anybody that knows John... he has this most distinct, infectious giggle. Anyway, he jumped on the bed, and hugged me and said, "I tried!"

He told me to go back to sleep so he could try again. He gave me a big hug and kiss and said we'll talk when he gets back from the gym. The card, in his handwriting, it opens with, *Dearest Best Friend.*

I can remember in the days leading up to Dad dying, my Mom said to my Dad gently, "Peeps, who needs any other friends when you have the best friend in the world?"

That's my John, he's my best friend. Sure, he drives me bonkers, and I'm sure I drive him bonkers, too, but I wouldn't be who I am without him and the role that he's played. He has taught me so many things, and I know I'm stronger and more empowered because of his love and support. We seem to inspire each other, and I know that's a true gift.

His card ended with, *"I'm so happy you chose me to share your life with."*

The love that we first knew,
when we were 22,
Completely changed.
Running fro and to,
barely getting through,

the day-to-day.
I know we don't have the time for this
but it's weighing on my mind.
It's a choice to be together
I need to know what you decide.
I choose us.
To make more time.
Not choose everything around us.
Start with you and I.
I know you've changed, so have I.
I'm choosing right now, not forever.
Love you one day at a time.
This is you and me.
Not everything we dreamed,
but we have it all.
Wanna feel you on my neck,
some time to reconnect
and slow the clock.
It really isn't fair of me feeling incomplete.
Thinking just because I say it more,
your love is not as deep.
I choose us.
To make more time.
Not choose everything around us.
Start with you and I.
I know you've changed, so have I.
I'm choosing right now, not forever.
Love you one day at a time.
Life is full of changes, things we can't control.
We hold onto each other, afraid of letting go.
Do you choose us?
To make more time.
Not choose everything around us.
Start with you and I.
I know you've changed, so have I.
I'm choosing right now, not forever.
I'm choosing right now, not forever.
Love you one day at a time.

Ellen Nasser, 'One Day at a Time' [unreleased version]

"Well, John, thank you, thank you for choosing me and waiting for *me*."

I asked him if he wanted to read my memoir before I publish it, and he said no, he didn't have to. And, I asked him if he was sure. I said, "What... what if I wrote something you didn't like?" He just simply said, "Ellen."

He trusts me.

I know John doesn't complete me; I'm long past the idea of thinking someone else will complete me. I know that I must love myself and feel complete on my own. I get it.

I told John this morning that forty feels like a big number. And, he said he thinks forty to fifty was his best decade yet. He assures me I'll love my forties.

I just took a moment to open an email from my dearest Fishy. If you can believe it, she created a video for me, and my heart could just burst. She had many people from the Canadian College of Performing Arts share a message to me of one of their favourite memories of me. Wow. Now, I'm bawling.

You know, it's connection that we all need the most. It's how we feel inside that shapes our outside existence.

On that note, Flora from Calgary just messaged me. I love her, too. I have a big call today, a call at 9 a.m. with my editor from Toronto. We'll see how that goes. If he can help clean up this project a bit, I'll be thrilled. I just want to make sure that... like I said, I still want to have my voice and my goal isn't to have it perfect; I just want to have it to share with whomever wants to hear it.

Elly Thorn, 'There's a Heaven'

My childhood friend Jenn just emailed me yesterday, and she said she was walking around the park in Toronto listening to the nine-minute preview of my audiobook, and she was crying. She said she was going to listen and cry again. I just got goosebumps writing that because that's exactly what I've been doing. Listening, writing, crying, rinse and repeat... for seventy-four days.

I'm tired. I have one final song that I need to share in my project. I wasn't sure how this was going to end, but it's the last song that has to be shared. I can remember years ago hearing of the story about a young family that was killed by a drunk driver around New Year's, and this song came through me. It was about five years ago, and our children were at a similar age as their children. It was around the holiday, and the news brought me to my knees. It's called 'There's a Heaven.'

When I heard the latest news,
I felt a sense of peace.
The little girl had found her way;
they're together now, at least.
You know there's something, a somewhere
beyond this life.
'Cause if there's nothing, really nothing—
How on earth can we survive?
Our hearts are broken; it turns to anger
And all you really want to do is escape
But hold on tight 'cause there's a heaven,
just you wait.

Elly Thorn, 'There's a Heaven'

The Mom who passed away in the accident, her brother wrote a book. His name is Chad Mierau, the book is called *Surviving the Crash*. I've heard people say that everyone has a story and it should be told. I couldn't agree more. After I read this book, I knew I had to share my light, too. Chad not only chose to forgive the drunk driver who killed his sister and her beautiful family, he has become friends with the family, whose mother was convicted. The families are working together to try to connect and educate others on driving under the influence. Through his healing, he has found inner peace and knowing that all will be well.

I know the grief never really goes away, but the healing process is such a gift. I also have a deep knowing that all will be well. We just need to keep living our own truth and sharing our light, and love, and joy, and sometimes pain with others.

To our four beautiful children, continue a deep love for the relationships in your lives. May you nurture them and be strong enough to let go of the ones that need a little space. May you learn from all of them and know that you can always make the choice to heal and repair things. Remember to take time for people you meet on the street, for your neighbours and for your pets. It's the simplest things that fill my cup; it'll likely be the same for you.

Fishy came over yesterday, and while her three girls were swimming, we were talking about our first time and how we should/could talk to our children about sex. I cringed like a little kid and said, "What, are we really starting those conversations now? Fisher, are you kidding me!" I suppose if we are, I better get cracking.

Ahh... Fisher said you know they have started the conversations and mentioned that she has learned a lot by watching Kristen Bell and her ways of sexucl education for her kids. I'm now gonna look into her videos and see how I can open the doors to these conversat ons around our house. But Fisher said she told her girls, "Did you know the only job of the clitoris is to feel pleasure?"

I almost died.

Why am I so immature? I shouldn't be. I have four kids, and now I'm... I'm forty. I'm a grown... I'm an actual grown-up. This shouldn't make me feel like saying, "Eeeeww-www!" And my face turning red at the same time. But it does. I'm a little old-fashioned in some ways. Maybe now I'm forty, there's an expansion of vocabulary and maturity. That can be my birthday wish today.

Fisher giggled over my reaction, and she said, "Are you kidding me?!"

I suppose... she's right; if I can write and share my heart and soul, I should be able to say the word 'clitoris' to our young children without being shell-shocked. Baby steps. We all have our things.

I just happen to have many things. So, I said to Fisher, if a clitoris' only function is for pleasure, then maybe my book should be called, *I Want to Live My Life Like a Clitoris, My Only Function is for Pleasure*. And, we both laughed at that, and now, I'm going to keep going 'cause I'm on a roll.

And then I said, "How about this: *Choosing An Existence Full of Pleasure, Just Like My Clitoris.*

CHAPTER SEVENTY-TWO
FINISHING STRONG

August 6, 2022
4:17 a.m.

I'm basically finishing this project the way it began.

Yesterday was full of visits, texts, drop-offs, flowers, FaceTimes, and I couldn't feel more blessed. I worked until about 3 p.m., and then we ordered in some pizza. We'll do some more celebrating on our travels. The kids are so excited, and I'll be there, too. Once I get there. Heck, I may be even excited, once I get to the airport.

I had a really good chat with an editor from Toronto—his name is Chris. We connected yesterday, and after I finish up this morning's writing, I'm going to email this all to him. He recommended I enjoy a nice break, and I couldn't agree more.

I asked him what this is called, and he said a manuscript—who knew?! I feel blessed to be guided by someone who actually does know, someone who is in this literary world. All I really knew was the gentle nudge I felt in my heart, Monday morning of the May Long Weekend. And, all I had to do was show up and write. Show up and write, no matter what.

One of my beautiful nieces sent me a birthday text saying she thanked God for an Auntie like me. I love Leah Violet so much. She's like a kindred spirit. Another niece messaged and said she hopes the last morning of writing is a great start to a new chapter in my life. I can't explain how being surrounded by all of these vibrant and radiant nieces and nephews has filled and inspired my heart. They all feel like they're mine... Jeez Louise—I feel like they're ours.

Truly does take a village, and we are so lucky to have surrounded ourselves with a community like ours.

I sincerely hope these words touch your heart and that you remember the reason we're all here... when it's to connect, and experience, enjoy, and most importantly, to heal, and love.

I remember a yoga teacher used to say at the end of the class, "The light in me bows to the light in you."

Thank you for being a part of my journey... I love you.

Thank you for the first forty, here's to the next.

CHAPTER SEVENTY-THREE
A FEW MONTHS LATER

It seems like I went balls out writing this book, and then everything kinda went to shit after that.

The more I wrote about the magic, the more I felt it, the more I felt it, the more I noticed it. Once my secret was out and I stopped writing, the magic seemed to disappear. I felt totally deflated.

In all honesty, our trip was mostly a flop.

As we were heading to board the plane in Calgary, Sam ran to the top of the escalator, thank God that no one else was on it but our family, and he caught the top of his carry-on on the stair, and it tumbled down *ass over tea kettle*. Is that even a saying? Anyways, almost instantaneously and on cue, Walt then pushed his carry-on, remember, not actually our carry-ons but the collection of the neighbourhoods and family members, and sent it down right after Sam's—both crashing at the bottom of the escalator where Bella and Millie were. Thankfully, no one was hurt.

John lost it—and rightfully so.

Our kids are full-on. This stage of life is so full-on.

I couldn't even comprehend what happened because I couldn't fathom the series of events and the stupidity of it all. Everyone got a blast. We all cooled down and boarded the flight like a normal family, ready for their summer holiday.

Five hours, Calgary to Boston, the kids were good as gold. Hallelujah!

But once we finally landed in Boston, we waited two hours on the tarmac for the airport employees to find the stairs to connect to the plane, to let us exit the craft. In the meantime, I was trying to keep a positive disposition because I knew the minute I blew a fuse, the rest of the family would be sure to follow. Remember, we'd been up since 4:30 a.m. Saskatchewan time. We were ticking time bombs.

We finally broke free of the claustrophobic airplane only to wait in the Boston airport to pick up our rental vehicle. By this point, the kids were starting to fade fast. Next life, I'm going to be one of those Mom's who packs a purse full of snacks. I always admire those Mom's who have literally everything in their bags. Pen... pen... blue or black or red...? I got... Does anybody have a piece of... gum... gum... Tic-Tacs... orange ones or the white ones...? Umm... I leaked... Does anyone have a tampon or... or... or maxi pad... Do you want the... Do you want the four-hour or the eight-hour? I got the real thick ones, too... and the... or just the pantyliner... Does ahh.... Oh! Shoot! Oh, are you okay... Oh... Umm... my child's knee is bleeding... Do you... Poly... Polysporin... Do you have Polysporin...? Do you... I have a little kit in here, I could stitch that up quick. Oh, dear... a wet nap... I gotta wet nap... I got a bag here... Do you... Oh, I gotta... I got a little washcloth... I can just get a little bit of water here and a bit of soap... Do you have any... a... oh... a... a... umm... hand...handsani... got it... got it... hand sanitizer? A snack... Do you need a snack...? I have tons of snacks in here... I've got everything... granola bar, Fruit by the Foot, Ahh... fish crackers... I got... I got... umm... Made Good if you wanna a little bit of healthier things... Ahh.... I got some protein here... I gotta... I gotta... steak.... I gotta steak... meat... rare or medium rare... I can do whatever... Ha! Ha!

Anyway... we finally arrived at our destination 10:30 p.m., considerably late for our dinner prepared by John's relative.

Happy Birthday to me, I couldn't wait to get to New York City.

Then, Millie got an earache—a whopping earache.

New York would have to wait.

John, Walt and I ended up sticking around Stonington just in case her ear flared up again. We could hardly dump old Milster at the relatives and run off gallivanting to the Big Apple. So, to top it off, we had no place to stay because we didn't plan on needing accommodation. Do you know what happens to all the lovely hotels located in Connecticut in August? You know... that's right, correct. BINGO! They all get booked up *WAY* in advance. Who knew?!

So, John, Walt and I just hopped from one crappy motel to the next, making sure Walt was happy because this trip, after all, was all about him. Poor little guy had to stick around with us while his siblings were at Sailing Camp. But we had fun—we filled each day with drives, treats, museums, aquarium, zoo, restaurants, movies.

It was our "Waliday!" And what a wonderful Waliday it was. Walt basked in being the center of attention for a week; he never experienced one-on-one time like this, with us, in his entire life. We spoiled him, and he loved it. In fact, John even let him buy two stuffed animals at the Providence Zoo. That never would have happened in real life with all four kids in tow. Walt bought Parrot and named it Parrot and Owly the Owl.

Homeward bound—what a schlep.

Once we settled back into life and got the kids back at school, I got the edited version of my manuscript back. Editor Chris did a beautiful job of making sense of my seventy-four days of verbal, dare I say it again, still can't spell it—diarrhea. Not even joking. But as I read it, I wanted to clean it up even a little bit more. As usual, I asked myself:

Who knew writing a book would be so much work?

Who knew travelling with four kids would be so challenging?

Who knew turning forty would be so full of angst and crisis?

Who knew? Who knew? Who knew?

Well, I think most people know many of these answers. In fact, I'm really starting to realize that I am the one who's late to the party. Who knew?

✦ ✦ ✦

John and I went out for dinner with one of his friends, and we were talking about life and eventually, my manuscript. I talked about the process and my grief, and the overwhelm with many parts of my self-inflicted existence lately, feeling kind of mopey. I ordered two Grand Marniers, along with my tea, which didn't help. John's friend alluded to the fact that "people like me" don't really have any business feeling sorry for themselves.

That stung.

Like, what could I possibly have to complain about? Look at my life. Look at everything in it.

Right, smack in my face.

It was my fear, plain as day. This was my fear of creating this project.

I took everything he was saying personally and felt incredibly embarrassed and unseen. I argued a bit and then stood straight up to storm out of the restaurant.

I had a flashback to a memory years ago when I reacted the exact same way. I was drained from overworking, and someone started insulting the real estate industry and said I had a "joke" of a job.

I can remember they said that they'd never use a real estate agent. Following up with, what do you actually do? Measure a house, take some photos and put a sign in the yard?

I can totally remember it all. I can remember where I was. I can remember the people beside me.

It was like déjà vu. Once I heard this, I tried to, once again, do a dramatic exit, but this time it was different.

It was different, and no, it's not because it was years later and I was more mature and self-aware.

No, it was truly only different because I wasn't on the outside of the table, and I was stuck in the booth, and nobody was moving out of my way, so I couldn't do a dramatic hissy fit and exit.

Dang it!

So, I had to sit my ass back down and face my fear. There it was, so uncomfortable and right in front of me. My fear delivered with a side of linguine.

Tears filled my eyes thinking about the loss of my Dad and the lack of support I seemed to be getting. My neck felt red and blotchy as it typically does when I'm revved up. I could feel the blood pulsing in my eardrums and I could feel the blood swirling in the sides of my neck. I was reading way too much into the tones and body language. I wasn't giving this guy any benefit of the doubt. It was all my pain. All of my hurt. All of my fears. I was hurt. He hurt my feelings. I felt embarrassed... embarrassed for sharing my heart, and especially mad at myself for having those two drinks and totally letting my guard down.

Yes, I'm blessed. There's no doubt about it. Most days, I feel so much gratitude that my heart feels like it could overflow.

The truth is, though, I've grown to learn that pain is all relative. We all feel it, no matter what our lives may look like to everyone else. No matter who we're married to, no matter how talented we are, no matter what the facade is, we all feel the same stuff.

Also, I've learned that there's no Pain Police, there's no

official Judge of Pain saying:

Okay, now this person's life is so crappy 'cause they have this, that and the other thing.

Therefore, they're allowed to have pain. But no, not you, ma'am—you're not allowed to have pain. You aren't worthy of feeling the pain. Your pain is real pain.

Not this person. They look like they have too much, their house is too fancy! If they indeed have pain, which they shouldn't because look at all the nice things they have. It's not real. Look at the car they drive, or the jewelry they have. They can't feel those emotions, and they especially can't express them. Sorry, I'm the... I'm the Judge of Pain. I'll let you know if you're worthy.

No, it doesn't work like that. Your pain is your pain, and it's the real deal to you. Just like your grief is your grief. It's all relative. It's all worthy of compassion, and please don't feel like you can't feel what you're feeling—because it's all valid and it's all real.

So, my conclusion, as a forty-year-old woman, is that we're all doing the best we can. We're experiencing life here on earth on our own journeys and paths. And, we need each other for constant growth and self-realization.

I'm actually so grateful for this somewhat painful interaction. I needed to experience this exchange with John's friend because I indeed really had nothing to fear. I needed John's friend to play his role in order for me to fully embrace this next chapter of unapologetically expressing myself to everyone around me. It was essential to work through this as another layer of my ongoing transformation.

It's complicated and it's magical all at once.

Ahh, I do know, more now than ever, the more compassion I have for myself and others, the better I feel.

Time and time again, it's evident that I keep circling back to the choices I make, whether they are big or small.

Because I do have a choice, and remember, so do you.

P.S. John ended up reading my entire manuscript. I did give him a due date that he had to finish it by, and I'm sure that annoyed him. Once he finished it, I fished for a compliment. I said, "Soooo... what'd you think, John?" And, he said he liked it.

But he really didn't need to read it because he is indeed living my manuscript. He said he knows all of my stories from the seventy-four days because he was right there along with me. He commented on what a ton of work it was, and he couldn't believe I secretly wrote it in our closet. The funny part is... is we both agreed I could write every day of my life and not ever run out of material. No truer words were ever spoken.

It is a circus, but it's our circus.

John leaned in for a hug, quietly saying, "You know, I'm proud of you, Ellen. It takes a lot of courage to express and share your heart like that."

He's right... It did.

Cheerleaders, thank you for cheering me on!

I'm so glad I chose to do it. I made the choice.

CHAPTER SEVENTY-FOUR
3 DAYS TO 100

Can you believe it?

Over two and a half years later, and I find myself almost ready to release this audiobook—or should I say, Musi-moir to the world. I've never worked on a creative en-deavour like this to such depth and magnitude in my life. To say it took on a life of its own is just the truth. There's no chance I was going to circle back and add another chapter at this point, but what can I say... Gigi changed the end of my story by writing the end of hers.

Biography of Peg Thorsness (nee Wood)
Written by Peg Thorsness, 2016

My mother's parents immigrated from Sweden to Min-nesota, U.S.A., in 1904. They homesteaded in the Yellow Grass, Saskatchewan area. My father's parents were from Iowa and homesteaded in the same area.

My parents, Ruth Flodin and Frank Wood, met and mar-ried, and were together for 63 years until my father's death. I was born in 1924, the seventh in a family of seventeen children. There were six girls and eleven boys, which included two sets of identical twin boys. To say that times were hard would be an understatement, but some of my fondest memories are of my childhood. We were taught to respect and support one another, to share and take turns and say our prayers at night. Even to this day, I marvel at the amazing person Mom was. She was always dependable, capable and resourceful. Her unwavering faith gave her great strength. She was still living at home when she died at 95 years of age, dearly loved and sadly missed.

By the time I was old enough for high school, we were living in Regina. I attended Scott Collegiate and graduated in 1942. I then attended U of S (University of Saskatchewan) in Saskatoon for one year on a bursary from the College of Engineering. That summer, I signed up to work in a munitions plant in Ajax, Ontario. Representatives came to campus to interview students and provided train fare and barracks for those who worked on the assembly line rolling T.N.T. pellets for anti-aircraft guns. I remember thinking of family members overseas fighting the war and feeling I should be doing much more. However, I returned home and attended Normal School that fall. I received my teaching certificate at Easter when I was asked to go to teach at a rural school near Pilot Butte. After taking summer school classes, I took a teaching position in Lake Valley for one year and then moved to Bredenbury to teach in 1945. It was there that I met Wilf, who had returned from air force duties overseas, serving as the pilot of a Lancaster bomber. He and his father were the new owners of a local hardware store. Wilf and I were married in 1946. I moved into the family home to take over for his younger sister Shirley, who was leaving to study nursing. She had been caring for her younger brother and father following the death of their mother.

In 1948, we moved to Saltcoats to operate a second hardware store. Wilf was a dedicated and hard-working entrepreneur, and the business expanded over the years to a chain of 5 stores in 5 different towns.

Saltcoats was home for the next 66 years. We were blessed with four children, two boys and two girls. Tragically, we lost Danny, our firstborn, during the polio epidemic in 1952, the year the vaccine was discovered. He was not quite 4 years old. That seemed like the end of our world, but eventually life did go on.

In 1960, we moved into a new home that we had built on the lake shore. It was a great source of pleasure for us where we enjoyed the beauty of nature and all that the lake had to offer year-round; boating, swimming, skiing, skating and ski-doing. We also had a huge garden, sometimes two, keeping us supplied with vegetables, both eaten fresh and frozen for the winter. In addition, Wilf was a terrific hunter, and there was always an abundance of birds, game and fish on hand for those "free meals" he loved to have prepared for the family and any guests he could round up.

One of the joys of our life was when our oldest daughter, Wanda, a Registered Nurse, and her husband, Peter, a lawyer with Legal Aid, built their home beside us and raised their four children. They were there for almost 20 years, and it was a sad day when they left following Peter's judicial appointment to Estevan before moving on to Saskatoon.

Holidays were fun, travelling in our motor home to many parts of Canada and the United States. We also travelled to various other countries over the years: The British Isles, Jamaica, Bahamas and Nigeria, stopping in Rome and Zurich on route.

We were community-minded, partaking in many things: town council, park board, air cadets, housing authority, legion and legion auxiliary. We were also volunteers at Lakeside Manor Care Home. We were members of and regularly attended the Saltcoats United Church. I was a Session member for many years and at times taught Sunday school and led C.G.I.T. (Canadian Girls in Training). I was a member of the U.C.W. (United Church Women) for over 50 years and received my 50-year membership pin from the Legion auxiliary. These two memberships allowed for ample baking, sandwich-making and tea serving over the decades.

Our son Robert graduated from the U of S (University of Saskatchewan) with a B.A. (Bachelor of Arts) in History and also completed his M.B.A. (Master of Business Administration). He has one son who is presently studying Engineering at U of S (University of Saskatchewan). He and his wife, Cheryl, also reside in Saskatoon.

Our youngest daughter, Myrna, is a physiotherapist and moved to Calgary after graduation, where she met her husband, Jack and continues to reside. They have three children, which gives me a total of eight grandchildren. Not only Wanda and Peter, but three of their children have homes here in Saskatoon. Between them, they have seven of my eight great-grandchildren to light up my life!

Sadly, Wilf passed away in April, a year ago, just 4 months after we moved to Riverside. I am so thankful to be here with my family. They are a big part of my life. I very much appreciate the beautiful river view, the services provided and especially the friendly residents here. I am certain I could not be in a better place.

✦ ✦ ✦

As Gigi's 100th birthday was drawing near, the excitement was growing, and growing for all of us. We couldn't believe that Gigi was actually turning 100 years old on October 16. Unbelievable.

If you knew our Gigi, our Grandma, lovingly called Gigi after us four Kolenick kids started procreating, you knew she was so special. She really was one of a kind.

Gigi's Mother, Ruth, who I'm named after, often said she

didn't feel a single pain when Gigi was born. Great-Grandma Ruth lived the last of her years in Saltcoats and then Saskatoon, where she passed away at 95 years old, and I can remember thinking that was incredible.

Both Great Grandma and Gigi were very proper and well-mannered women. When I was little, I can remember Gigi sharing with me, in her most respectful way, that she often wouldn't even know her mother was pregnant because she wore her homemade house dresses and apron. One day, when Gigi was eight years old, she came home from school to find Aunt Josie hanging clothes on the line, and Aunt Josie said:

"Go into the house and see what your Momma has!"

They went in to find a new baby sister named Mary Lou. Gigi and her sister Shirley couldn't believe their eyes, they didn't even know their mother was expecting, and were happy to find a baby sister after several boys had been born since Gigi.

We grew up hearing stories of those boys being born and put in shoe boxes placed on the open oven door to keep them warm. Gigi was twenty-one months old when Great Grandma gave birth to her third boy, followed by two sets of twin boys with another boy between the twins, that would make six baby boys in just a 5-year span. Can you even imagine?

When times were really challenging, for example, Great Grandma Ruth was known to sew some clothing for the kids out of the flour bags. She also made homemade braided rugs for the floor out of old cloth scraps. This was likely in a time where food and water were sparse, giving the children baths, one in, one out, one in, one out... and of course, rationing the water and warming it on the wood stove. Gigi could remember her mother saying that none of the children asked to be brought into this world. I remember Gigi told me that she remembered feeling terrible because one time, she said at supper, while ungratefully looking at her plate of cornmeal, "Awww, not mush again."

Great Grandma Ruth said, "Tonight, we'll eat it on our good dishes."

Gigi's sister Shirley remembered asking, "What are we going to do for supper?"

Great Grandma Ruth would gently say, "Don't worry, it will be okay," and somehow it always was, even if that meant fried cornmeal mush pancakes with syrup as a special treat. As for treats, Gigi told me they always had a birthday cake for each birthday, one each for the twins, and if they were really fortunate, they'd all get an orange for Christmas.

There's a story that some of them were driving into town in a makeshift vehicle, literally an old jalopy, and it tipped over; thankfully, no one was hurt, and the vehicle was set back upright and off they went.

Gigi said she rarely ever heard her mother raise her voice.

They had nothing. They came from nothing, but what they had was such a sense of family.

The crazy part is, Gigi remembered loving her childhood immensely. They were some of the happiest times of her life: the farm, her siblings, their freedom, the family, the energy.

She never looked her age. In fact, she never dyed her hair in her life. She was an absolute beauty through and through—her skin glowed, and we all commented, even as she was dying, just how beautiful she was. She played a huge role in all of our lives, especially as you know, as our neighbours growing up on the lake.

Gigi was always there, never loud or overbearing, never putting in her two cents, rarely judging or making comments. You always knew what you were gonna get with Gigi—and that was unconditional love.

Funny, last year when Gigi turned 99 years old, our family was away in Australia for Eric and Cameron's wedding, and she apparently said that she didn't think she's going to make it to 100. She said it off and on throughout the year. She wasn't being dramatic in the least; she was merely commenting and was in disbelief that she was nearing 100 years old.

I'm guessing she was feeling some pressure around it. I would have. It's a big deal, and we all knew it. We didn't want to get too carried away, though, because her heart had been acting up for most of the year, and more and more so within the past few months.

To be honest, any day could have been her last day in the months leading up to her birthday. She actually said to me a few times:

"I can't wait to see all of my family!"

And that day, she said she was so excited to see her son Danny and wondered if he'd be a child or a grown man.

If Mom would message, "Call Me." My heart would race thinking Gigi had passed away. Even writing this, though, I still wasn't ready to say goodbye to her; none of us were. Mom, Aunty Moomoo and Cheryl planned to have a beautiful turkey meal catered by Mano's. Remember, that's where Mom went for her 70th birthday lunch. Full circle. So, we decided to celebrate Gigi's birthday on Thanksgiving Weekend so that we could all be together.

The week leading up to Gigi's birthday wasn't very good. Mom ended up bringing Gigi to her place a few days before everyone planned to arrive. On the Wednesday evening, Walt, Sofi and I walked over to Mom's because I wanted to share the chapter where she and Grandpa lost their firstborn. I asked Gigi how she was feeling, and she said, "You know..." and just started laughing.

I told her that she sure looked wonderful, even though I knew she hadn't been feeling well at all, and she just said, "Your Mom brought me here and you know how she breathes life into me!" as she sipped a glass of wine and nibbled on her sour cream and onion ripple potato chips.

After we listened to the chapter and cried, Sofi got up on her knee—the first time that we can remember—and when it was time to leave, Sofi refused to come, leaning into Gigi's chest.

We were laughing and laughing. What was Sofi doing? She wouldn't leave her. I pulled and I pulled on her leash, and finally, I picked her up and she reluctantly came with me.

And then, after breakfast on Thursday, Gigi had another bad spell and Mom tucked her in for a few hours, and by afternoon, she was feeling better again and was happy to be up when Moomoo and Jack arrived from Calgary around suppertime.

As Gigi was getting ready for bed, she had another spell Thursday night, so Mom and Moomoo split the night sleeping with her. By Friday morning, her condition deteriorated, and she was very weak and in considerable pain for the most of the day.

Saturday morning, and I received a text message from Mom saying:

"Gigi was horrible yesterday, lots of chest pain and shortness of breath. Myrna and I split the night in bed with her. If you can believe it, she's excited about the turkey dinner tonight. Not sure if she'll be able to sit up at this point, but we will see."

By 11:51 a.m., we were all heading over to Mom's to see Gigi and carry on with our birthday plans.

When we arrived, we immediately went to Gigi's room and were so pleased to see her sitting on the bedside, giggling and laughing with Amy. We couldn't believe our eyes. She was no longer having severe chest pain. She was downright giddy and beyond excited for her birthday. You can ask anyone. It was unbelievabe.

At one point, we left the room so she could rest, and we were so surprised to see her come out of her room dressed and ready to party. She was smiling and animated, and we were all thrilled by her appearance and energy. At one point, numerous family members said she almost seemed euphoric. It was hard to believe, considering the previous 24 hours. The house was ready and so full of people and love.

There were balloons, banners, gifts, there was a massive bouquet given to her, from us grandkids and another gorgeous bouquet of long-stemmed roses like the ones she held on her wedding day. Two beautiful birthday cakes, one angel food with chocolate whipped cream made by Cheryl, and the other burnt sugar chiffon, made by my Mom.

So, we got down to business and gave her... her cards and gifts. In fact, my sister-in-law Stacey had even applied to get birthday greetings from King Charles and Queen Camilla, as well as Mary Simon, our Governor General. Even they mark a century of living! What a wonderful idea, and boy, Gigi was sure pleased when she opened that royal gift.

Then some of us wrote and read some fond memories of her in our lives.

Here's my love letter to her:

> When I think about you, Gigi, I remember Saltcoats and all of our memories on the lake. The sunrises, the ducks swimming, the geese honking... Mother Nature at her finest.
>
> When I think about you, Gigi, I remember Grandpa and your constant love and connection with all four of us kids. I can remember you respecting Grandpa and making him homemade soup and sandwiches at lunchtime. I can remember the huge garden and feeling so proud of it, even though I had absolutely nothing to do with it. I can remember Grandpa taking me on a tour once and pointing out all the berries and lines of vegetables. I especially loved the raspberries, strawberries, black raspberries. They were located at the far end that year. The asparagus that was growing along the lake side of the garden, gently swaying in the wind, the rows of lettuce, and, of course, the "Earthy" smell of our cold room in the basement full of dirty red potatoes.
>
> When I think about you, Gigi, I think of all your delicious baking over the years. I remember going to your house, and it smelled a lot different than ours. I loved it. I could know where I was with my eyes closed. At your house, there were often gingersnaps, chocolate chip cookies, shortbread and gooey, decadent turtle cake in the pantry between the kitchen and the garage. I also remember a perfectly square, silver tin full of muffins. Sometimes bran, sometimes blueberry and often banana

muffins that were a bit sticky and kinda flat on the top—they were way different than Mom's banana muffins. You never put chocolate chips in yours, and yours tasted more like overripe bananas.

It's funny, when I think about you, Gigi, I think about the motorhome and, of course, the family reunions over August long weekend. I can remember my birthday being on yours and Grandpa's anniversary. I can remember feeling very special about that connection. I think about how we had to be so careful not to wreck anything in that motorhome. I can also remember being wild and taking photos with Lee in the back—both of us kicking each other, and posing with our fingers in our noses, and then bumping the blinds, which inevitably caused a ruckus, bringing you to the back to settle us down.

Gigi, I don't think you read many parenting books, but from my childhood eyes, you were stern, if needed be, but always so gentle and so kind. You didn't even have to say much; I can remember knowing that I should have known better.

When I think of you, Gigi, I remember how excited I would get thinking about a family dinner together, going to church and seeing you there, and visiting Great Auntie Jean and Great Uncle Keith in Bredenbury. I can remember supper with you guys would often include turnips, mashed potatoes, fine and crumbly dressing, goose with gravy, chicken, or sometimes fish that Grandpa caught, fresh asparagus, a tossed salad and a beautifully decorated lemon meringue or pie with vanilla ice cream. I can remember Happy Hours and the outbursts of laughter filling your kitchen. I can remember us kids running downstairs to the basement to get a pop. I can still remember that feeling.

I still feel it when I walk into your condo at Riverside Terrace.

I can also remember sometimes, after supper, Grandpa would play the organ. We also knew we had to respect your organ, too... and we had to ask before we could play it.

I can remember Grandpa playing Now is the Hour and noticing his crooked pinky finger as he played. I can remember watching his clunky, old and heavy hands on the keys. I can remember Amy and I "lying down" with Grandpa, and he would let us take out the little black comb that he carried in his breast pocket, and we would comb his hair, making it look so funny. Combing it forward, to the side and bringing the fine, greyish/white hair over his eyes and down the front of his face. He would doze off, gurgle and snore, which made Amy and I laugh even harder... and at some point, he'd say: "Now that's enough, settle down."

When I think about you, Gigi, I remember Mom and Dad smiling and laughing with you and Grandpa. I can remember feeling the energy of that relationship and being able to feel the mutual admiration and respect. I can remember all four of you being examples of love and commitment to each other and, of course, to us kids, too—each of you in your own impactful ways.

Our beautiful Gigi, from the bottom of my heart—I thank you for being such a huge part of my childhood and life. As a 42-year-old woman, I now can see you in yet another light. You always go about your way, living such a beautiful life of grace and quiet leadership. You are an example of strength and commitment. As a mother now, I don't know how you could have gone on after the loss of Danny and continued to live as such an example of love and faith.

It's no wonder when I think about you, Gigi, I think about our shared lives, nurturing foods, nourishment, family togetherness and with all of that, my senses just light up. As I looked at all these words, I noticed something... sight, taste, smell, hearing, but where was touch?

It's because experiencing your presence in my life has touched me on such a deep level. Happy 100th birthday, Gigi. I can't believe I'm even writing these words.

And after she hugged me, and said to me, "Don't you think you laid that on a little thick?"

"No, not in the least."

The family then sang, "Happy birthday to you, happy birthday to you, happy birthday dear Gigi, happy birthday to you... and many more! Hip Hip, Hooray! Hip Hip, Hooray! Hip Hip, Hooray!"

Gigi blew out the candles and said, "Well, thank you so much for everything... the wonderful cake and for all these beautiful grandchildren, and great grandchildren and children and all the children-in-laws."

Gigi died the next day.

We sipped at our mugs of coffee,
thoughtfully,
thoughtlessly.
Some intermingling of these opposites.
Was it a paradox or mystery... misery.
Words,
and no words.

'I love it here' she said.
Was it to me or to the place or space,
or to the world instead.

'I love it here' she said.
Was it to me or to the place or space,
to the yard.

Remembering all that was behind us
or this moment.
She said it in a whisper.
Her hand slipped into mine,
a gentle pleasure.
Speaking of love and gladness,
her hand slipped into mine,
a gentle pressure,
pressing joy and sadness.

'I love it here' she said.
Was it to me or to the place or space
or to the world instead.

'I love it here' she said.
Was it to me or to the place or space,
to the yard.

Remembering all that was behind us
or this moment.
She said it in a whisper.
She said it in a whisper.
She said it in a whisper.

Ellen Nasser, 'Whisper' [unreleased version]

AFTERWORD

Dear Bella, Millie, Sam, and Walt,

Parenting has been the greatest teacher of my life. I had no idea what I was stepping into—only that I would give everything I had. Every day, I try to meet it with openness, courage, and love.

I treasure your grace and forgiveness in the many moments when I'm not at my best.

I hardly remember who I was before you guys. Since the day you arrived, my life has overflowed with lessons, laughter, and the kind of love that remakes a person entirely.

Without your Dad, you wouldn't exist. Without your Dad, our life wouldn't exist. You are *all* my dream come true.

Though it is far from perfect, I would choose our life together again in a heartbeat—over and over again.

Always choose love. Always lead with it.

Love
—Mom—

ACKNOWLEDGMENTS

We have no idea how our actions are received in the world. While writing this book, I was acutely attuned to the magic and ripple effect of the choices I was making. To everyone who has crossed my path—held a door, offered a kind word or gesture, a shoulder to cry on, or an ear to listen—thank you. You will never fully understand the impact you've had on my life and on this artistic endeavor.

I would like to thank my team who helped bring this project to life—tBone, Ashley, and Jenn—as well as my early editors, Chris, Camille, and Lorraine. Without your patience, expertise, and unique talents, this book would not be what it is.

A special thank you to my early readers and connections, Alice and Carla, whose support and thoughtful editorial guidance were instrumental in shaping this work.

Thank you as well to the wonderful team at Rock + Bloom, and to my Mandarin teacher, Zoe, for her kindness and generosity along the way.

Rev. Walter Farquharson, thank you for the poem you sent me in memory of your beloved wife, Joan. Your words became the seed of "Whisper," one of the most meaningful songs I've ever created. It is an honour to carry a piece of your grief and grace into the world.

To my constantly evolving musical family—some of whom have been with me for what feels like a lifetime—thank you. Beginning with Wendy, who gave me my very first performing opportunity, and continuing with Carol, Janis and Jacques, Michiko, Tibor, and Angie. Bandmates and brilliant artists and musicians include Bart, Murray, tBone, Bruce, Scott, Carman, my sissy Amy and brother Danny, Shawn, Ross, Derek, Berkeley, Chad, Andrew, Sheldon, Sarah, Dave, Jenee, Zoe, Gord, Sam, Ryan, Brita, Hal, Dean, Grant, Mark, and wonderful Martin—and most recently, Jessica, Martin Jr., and dear Elyse.

To beautiful Melissa—thank you for being the first person I spilled the beans to. Then to Mom, Moomoo, and Gigi—telling you made it real. Once the beans were spilled, there was no going back.

My handsome John, I don't know what brought us together. I don't know what keeps us together. All I know is that at times it's not easy, but I love you more than you'll ever know. Whatever happens in this life, know that my love for you is a deep love, a true love, a forever love. I'm not sure how we work and how we continue to work—we just do. It definitely helps that I'm funny. And you're sorta funny too. Sorta.

To my beautiful Momma and siblings, thank you for allowing me to share my healing heart so openly and freely. Because we grew up in a family like ours, deep care for one another is all we've ever known. Mom, you and Dad created such a nurturing, safe, and loving space for all of us. Thank you for your devotion to our family.

Darling Eric and Fishy, thank you for the reminder of my dream, and for your love and constant connection.

Dad, we know you're with us. We can feel it. Please never stop protecting us, we are all listening.

Beautiful Gigi—you made up your mind you were going to be at your 100th birthday party and damn it, you delivered. What a gift you gave to all of us.

What a way to go.

Rooted in the prairies of Saskatchewan, Ellen Nasser has spent her life turning everyday moments into art—through song, story, and the written word.

A graduate of the Canadian College of Performing Arts, she began touring with Saskatchewan Express and performing with the Canadian Heritage Society's Spirit of a Nation showcase. Her creative path has carried her from small-town stages to television sets and symphony halls—performing with the Saskatoon Symphony Orchestra and the Victoria Symphony, singing on Norwegian Cruise Line, appearing on Corner Gas and Rabbit Fall, and sharing her music on country radio and beyond.

Now based in Saskatoon, Ellen brings her candid honesty, warmth, humour, and deep sense of presence to her writing—inviting audiences into a soulful pause, where reflection, motherhood, and melody meet.

INTERLUDE
AUDIOBOOK

NEWSLETTER

STILLNESS
ALBUM

www.ingramcontent.com/pod-product-compliance
Lightning Source LLC
Chambersburg PA
CBHW020905060726
47591CB00004B/1093